HAVANA
WITHOUT MAKEUP

HAVANA
WITHOUT MAKEUP

INSIDE THE SOUL OF THE CITY

HERMAN PORTOCARERO

PHOTOGRAPHS BY
JOAQUIN PORTOCARERO

TURTLE POINT PRESS   BROOKLYN, NEW YORK

HAVANA WITHOUT MAKEUP

Quote from *Paisaje de Otoño* © 1998 by Leonardo Padura.
First published in the Spanish language by Tusquets Editores, Barcelona,
Spain. First published in the UK by Bitter Lemon Press, London,
United Kingdom, English translation © 2006 by Peter Bush.

Requests for permission to make copies of any part
of the work should be sent to:

info@turtlepointpress.com

Library of Congress Cataloging-in-Publication Data is available
from the publisher upon request

Book design by Wah-Ming Chang
Map by Tracy Porter

ISBN: 978-1-933527-88-8
ebook ISBN: 978-1-885983-54-1

Printed in the United States of America

¿Qué quedaría de aquella ciudad castigada y envejecida que
llevaba en el corazón . . . ?
Posiblemente nada . . . Quedaría, si acaso,
la memoria, sí, la memoria . . .

What would be left of that aged, much castigated city
[he] carried in his heart . . . ?
Possibly nothing at all . . . Memories would perhaps
remain, yes, memories . . .

—**LEONARDO PADURA**, *Paisaje de Otoño / Havana Black*

CONTENTS

Preface   xiii

1. Walls of Illusion   1
2. Exceptional   5
3. Nocturnes (Havana by Night)   7
4. Afro Cuba   12
5. Havana in Black and White   15
6. *Rumba*   17
7. Santería   18
8. Santería and the Racial Divide   21
9. Communist *Orishas?*   23
10. *¡Salsa!*   27
11. Asia de Cuba   29
12. *"Achinado"*   31
13. Sex & Cenesex   33
14. *¡Tremenda mariconada!*   36
15. Havana's Hour Zero   38
16. Proposal for a Controversial Monument   40
17. Good Money, Bad Money   43
18. The Economy as a Book and a Beast   45

19. Looking West – to Asia Again   48

20. *La mula como vaca de leche* (The Mule as Cash Cow)   51

21. *La libreta* (The Ration Booklet)   52

22. *El cañonazo*   55

23. The Last Salvo   59

24. 1762: British Occupation and a Defining Moment   60

25. It Takes (at Least) Two to *Rumba*   62

26. Sitting Down (and More) with Europe   66

27. *Cuba no soy* (I Am Not Cuba)   69

28. Traffic Lights of History   71

29. Ghosts of Revolutions Past   74

30. Much Louder Ghosts   78

31. Napoleon in Cuba   80

32. The Orestes Ferrara Secret   82

33. The Cave at the End of the World   86

34. Conversation in Café del Oriente   90

35. Palacio de la Revolución   94

36. Who's the Terrorist?   96

37. Parque Lenin   99

38. Playas del Este   102

39. Jardines de la Tropical   105

40. Two Shores of Art Deco   107

41. Rum and Cigar Wars   109

42. Waves over the Wall   112

43. *Patria es humanidad es patria* (Homeland Is Humanity Is Homeland)   115

44. Havana's Palestinians   118

45. Next Year in Havana / Jerusalem   122

46. *Cantos de ida y vuelta* (Songs of Coming and Going)   127

47. *Mulatas de rumba & Puellae Gaditanae*   130

48. Alma Mater — 132

49. God's Crocodile — 138

50. *La Fábrica* (The Factory) — 141

51. Mercenaries — 142

52. Bloggers' Breakfast — 145

53. Primero de mayo — 149

54. The Pen & the Sword — 152

55. *Prima Ballerina Assoluta* — 159

56. Le Parisien — 162

57. Hatuey & Huracán — 163

58. *Todo el mundo canta* — 167

59. Who's the Boss? — 171

60. The Holy Spirit on the Plaza de la Revolución — 172

61. Winners and Losers — 173

62. Jacobins & Dinosaurs — 176

63. Other Churches, Other Gods — 177

64. *Misionero de la Misericordia* — 181

65. Mozart in Havana — 184

66. Art & Politics — 186

67. *Pelota* (The Ball Game) — 188

68. The United Mobsters — 193

69. *Una mal criada* — 197

70. Hollywood Havana — 199

71. Pirates of All Kinds — 201

72. Elián — 205

73. New York Connections — 209

74. Music Has No Enemies? — 210

75. *El Paquete* — 213

76. Hemingway — 216

77. Fuster — 220

78. The Last *Cimarrón*   222

79. Fabelo   225

80. KCHO / STAINLESS / CUTY   227

81. Casa Verde   230

82. Río Almendares   235

83. Havana and the Chocolate Factory   236

84. Tallapiedra (Havana High Line)   239

85. Radio Reloj & Radio Bemba   241

86. *La muerte*   244

87. Apotheosis   245

    Postscript   249

Acknowledgments   255

Notes and References   257

Index   265

PREFACE

This is a special evening.

The faithful of Cuba's Santería religion are getting ready to celebrate the Night of San Lázaro. San Lázaro is the patron saint of the sick and those who suffer, the poor and the oppressed. Thousands will converge upon the sanctuary of El Rincón outside the capital, many doing penance by undertaking the long trek on their knees, or carrying a heavy stone on their shoulders. More often vibrant and celebratory, dancing to ecstatic African rhythms kept intact from the era of slavery, for one night Santería moves closer to the sinister and masochistic aspects of Roman Catholicism – seeking redemption through self-punishment, recognizing suffering as an essential aspect of the human condition.

Spiritists and seers, carrying images of the saint and his African equivalent Babalú Aye, roam the streets of the poor barrio of Jesús María in Old Havana. A grandiose puppet on stilts, dressed in the purple associated with the saint, parades through the neighborhood.

Is there something else in the air? At this same moment, in the small Jewish community in Vedado, preparations are underway to celebrate Hanukkah. It is hoped this could be an auspicious date for the release of Cuba's most famous prisoner, U.S. citizen and alleged spy Alan Gross. Gross brought sensitive computer and communications equipment to Cuba as a subcontractor of a project paid for by the U.S. government. He was accused of subversive activities, arrested in Havana in December 2009, and sentenced to fifteen years' imprisonment in March 2011. The Beth Shalom community has been caring for him. For several years his imprisonment has been a constant hurdle to improved relations between Cuba and the United States.

The omens are good. And in spaces as mysterious to mere mortals as the abodes of the saints and the African spirits we are trying to please and to placate, history is being made. Both in the White House and in the Palacio de la Revolución, final versions of groundbreaking speeches by the U.S. and Cuban presidents are being checked. By late morning on the 17th, when the candles for San Lázaro have guttered out, and Hanukah is underway, Alan Gross will be on a homeward bound plane. In a reciprocal gesture, the United States will also liberate three Cubans still serving long-term sentences for alleged espionage, the remaining three of the *Cinco Prisoneros del Imperio* who were at the center of Cuban activism for almost twenty years. By midday, Cuba and the United States will have announced that they are burying half a century of tropical cold war. In the real Havana these announcements were met with tears of deep joy, in a rare, spontaneous outpouring of collective emotion.

In the pages that follow, we will try to explain how the Havana of that morning became who and what she was, is –

and remains. We will do so mostly away from the predictable pitfalls of entrenched political positions, concentrating instead on the deepest roots of the city and her people. A small dose of politics is unavoidable here and there, but we will always remain conscious of the real subject: the complex soul of a unique city. We will explore it gradually. Whenever a term or a fact may seem mysterious at first, we explain it later. This is a rambling walkabout, please enjoy it as such.

Santería throne for Ochún set up on the eve of San Lázaro:
sweetness next to suffering

1. WALLS OF ILLUSION

When Fidel Castro renounced his official functions in 2008, he settled in the outlying Havana neighborhood of Siboney, about ten miles west of the city proper. From there, he entered the last phase of a lifetime of carefully choreographed secrets about his exact movements and whereabouts. He would live in Siboney until the end in November 2016, a few months after his ninetieth birthday. Increasingly frail but lucid and intellectually active, and as opinionated as ever, he continued to see a steady trickle of foreign visitors. El Comandante kept a discreet grip on the power he had supposedly relinquished, and the environment in which he did so naturally came to the attention of the international press. It was often described as "a leafy suburb."

Siboney signpost: rulers retire where native
Cubans once found refuge.

1

This description reflects the frequent inability of the outside world to capture Cuban realities.

If "leafy suburb" evokes images of upper-class wealth and ease, Siboney is a far more complex neighborhood: a mixture of grandiose mansions in good and bad repair, small and medium-sized agricultural plots, patches of no-man's land, social housing units, enclaves of privilege, and sometimes cheerful, sometimes sad anarchy. In fact, Siboney can be seen as a microcosm of Cuba as a whole. But Havana as a city is even more complex.

Built on deep contradictions, the Cuban capital has become a place like no other. In the first half of the twentieth century, it was a center of elegance and political violence, of commercially exploited sensuality and endemic corruption. But at the same time, it was a thriving and multifaceted society, albeit a socially divided one. The Cuban Revolution put this small country on the world map as never before, as a focal point of slogans and fiery speeches enforcing equality and conformism as a price to pay for national unity and independence from the United States. Half a century later, these stages through which it has passed have molded and scarred the city in a unique way, leaving it suspended between dreams and results of extreme utopia and the reality of sometimes extreme neglect. There are peculiar connections between the people of Havana and the walls between which they live.

Havana may be the most sensual ruin on the planet. Much like New Yorkers outdoors in summer, the people of this city wear the buildings like flesh, but in Havana the border between flesh and stone is much more blurred. And yet, at times, the city also exudes an overwhelming melancholy, never better expressed than by the Cuban singer-songwriter Carlos Varela.

In his song "Habáname," he sings about how painful it is to see every wall in the city he loves deeply crumble. This refers not just to physical decay but also to the aging slogans on the walls. This peculiar song, with all the weight of personal experience it carries, never fails to move me to tears; but then, at every street corner of this Havana of the end of illusions, I am seized by the raw and youthful energy of the city, and pulled into its currents and undertows. I will add my voice to Carlos Varela's, to state that everything I say about Havana will be inspired by love and by respect, even when I disagree with her sometimes, as an honest lover should.

It's the mixture of extreme melancholy and energy that best defines Havana.

Large sections of the city are elegant ruins. For the purpose of tourism and the preservation of historical heritage, parts of Habana Vieja − the colonial city − have been and are still being beautifully restored. Much respect is due to city historian Eusebio Leal, who has overseen this restoration since the 1980s, masterfully blending history with the present, and who has skillfully avoided turning the old city into a sterile theme park, maintaining a living city while catering to the demands and expectations of foreign visitors. No place on earth has been more soulfully preserved and brought back to life than Habana Vieja.

But follow me now into some ordinary outlying neighborhoods, cutting through the decidedly un-touristy barrios of Centro Habana, Diez de Octubre, Luyano, La Víbora, Lacret, Lawton, Santos Suárez . . . Everywhere, even in the remote suburbs, you will see the same once-grand buildings with their galleries and sculptured terraces, transformed into improvised multifamily dwellings of often astonishing complexity, lived in by the liveliest and most quick-eyed of inhabitants, ready to seize the moment and the fleeting happiness of music and a bottle of rum, alongside the philosophical beggar and the staunch communist unwilling to concede defeat.

In the run-down neighborhoods you become immersed in a lazy sensuality impossible to recapture elsewhere, since both the setting and the spirit of the inhabitants are so unique. Perhaps there is no future here, but this only adds to its seduction. And the strangest paradox of all is that the overregulated life of communism has resulted in this sensual labyrinth of flesh and stone, a final proof that human beings will not be regimented, and that perseverance and inventiveness will prevail, infusing every ruin touched by bare feet and lazy arms with sweat and soul.

But the paradox runs even deeper, for most Cubans are happily unaware of how unique their world and their city are. As a saying goes: *El pez no sabe del agua* (The fish is unaware of the water).

Next to buildings, cars have become the most obvious Cuban icons. The average Cuban 1959 Chevrolet – called *almendrones* ("big almonds") – now often runs on improvised carburetors and engine blocs partly filled up with lead to close off excessively hungry cylinders. Not to mention the often exuberantly refurbished interiors. Many of these cars, mostly parked around the Capitolio and in front of the Gran Teatro, have now been converted into tourist attractions, but in their original run-down versions most still serve as collective taxis, plying routes at affordable fares for the people of Havana.

As a foreigner your hour-long ride in a shiny convertible *almendrón* will cost you the equivalent of an average monthly salary for a Cuban citizen. Only a few hundred yards away, a woman is getting into a much rougher car of the same make and year in the busy parking lot behind the Parque de la Fraternidad, where improvised dispatchers help her find a 10 peso ride to her remote home in the suburbs of La Lisa, Lawton, Diez de Octubre or Santos Suarez. The cars fill up with passengers packed together in forced intimacy taken mostly with humor and as an occasion to exchange gossip, and set off with a rattling clutch in a cloud of exhaust fumes.

Immersed in Havana, you tend to take her for granted in her frozen time, her langourous sensuality, and the complicated procedures of her daily life. You wish or hope for improvements, not realizing that such changes might subvert much of what makes her so special.

The Walls of Illusion still bear the slogans of defiance: "*¡En Cada Barrio Revolución! Aquí no se rinde nadie*" ("Revolution in every neighborhood! Here nobody surrenders"). This thick layer of revolutionary makeup no longer hides the aging skin underneath.

But the ultimate symbol of its kind is the seaside Malecón wall, the last rampart of the Cold War, a frontier between two worlds. It exerts a magical attraction. You sit on it, watching the ocean, and become part of the history of the world. Over this very stretch of sea passed the gold and silver of the Spanish empire, the slave ships from Calabar and the West African coast on their way to the Mississippi, and the trade between Asia and Europe long before the Panama Canal existed. In the 1960s, when the world risked nuclear annihilation, this wall stood right in the middle.

2. EXCEPTIONAL

It's not easy to define one's loyalties when it comes to Cuba, especially when one has had a long and intricate relationship with the country and its people. One might begin with a simple and abstract idea, such as "I wish the best possible future for Cuba." But the sentiment becomes complicated almost immediately.

Over more than half a century, so much of the country's personality has been built up in sheer opposition to the United States that the main question becomes: How will that personality survive in the long run, once that opposition is removed? How will Cuba define herself once freed from that contradiction?

Many societies throughout history have defined themselves in opposition to an outside enemy. It's one of the oldest political games on the planet.

But Cuba's case is extreme: a small island state has built an iconic image for itself, and had a global impact on the collective imagination, by opposing the superpower next door. For an apt comparison in ancient history, we might imagine a bold Sicily resisting and taunting a Roman Empire unable to subdue it.

Cuban exceptionalism – the belief in the uniqueness of the island – has some justification in history. Cuba developed differently from other Spanish colonies. Its struggle for independence came much later than in the rest of Latin America, and took a different form. Nor did it share much history with the other Caribbean islands. Slavery was different here, and Cuba was more mixed and diverse than the other islands; it was always a global crossroads and an outward-looking society. Though conditions were harsh for many or most, it was also characterized by a pursuit of pleasure. Early on, its beliefs became a mixture of the European and the African. Havana always lived on the quick wits of its inhabitants as much as on the gold of traders and speculators.

The communist dogmatism imposed by Fidel's unyielding personality had nothing in common with Havana's opportunism as a port city, absorbing languages, attitudes, and fashions with the ease of a wild child roaming the quaysides and gladly dancing and sleeping with the enemy, as the city had done during the brief British occupation of 1762. Even today the Castros – second generation immigrants in Cuba – define themselves as stubborn *gallegos*, sons of the hard-working, no-nonsense northern Spanish region of Galicia.

Heroism, subversion and seduction became shared national traits of the new Cuba, however mutually contradictory. Centuries of day-to-day survival skills were honed to a fine art during years of penury, as became obvious in the 1990s when the collapse of the Soviet Union, Cuba's then near-exclusive economic and political partner, plunged the island into a deep economic crisis.

One can't help but wonder how all those contradictions will play out in the future.

3. NOCTURNES (HAVANA BY NIGHT)

By day the city's walls become the very flesh of *habaneras* and *habaneros*. Past midnight, the flesh becomes palpable shadow. Follow me now through Centro Habana, along Belascoaín to Cuatro Caminos, and from there, along Calzada del Cerro and Monte towards the Belle Epoque city center around the Capitolio. The sidewalks look mostly deserted, with a game of dominos in progress here and there. Some furtive passersby on foot or on a squeaky bicycle are carrying modest bundles of contraband.

The dilapidated buildings with their columns and balconies, which by day still display traces of their former elegance,

Reality check: Centro Habana from Calle San Lázaro rooftop

now look more menacing. They transform into a city besieged and half-bombarded, survivors scrambling through secret passages. The buildings in this neighborhood, like in many others, have turned organic. The result of neglect and improvisation, their stately architecture has gradually melted into a maze of mysteriously connected hideouts. Beneath the high ceilings of the former palaces, many rooms have been horizontally subdivided to create extra spaces, lofts known as *barbacoas* often accessible only through gymnastic contortions. The narrow shelters many *habaneros* in poor neighborhoods call home are reflected in the name of the fashionable restaurant La Guarida in Calle Concordia in Centro Habana. The name, taken from the movie *Fresa y chocolate* (1994), means something like "the foxhole."

Another Cuban movie, *Juan de los Muertos* (2012), poked grotesque fun at the psychological consequences of tired revolutions by turning the entire population of Havana into zombies. There was no need to build sets: the city provided the perfect environment for the undead to roam, and for survivors to seek refuge from mutants in their foxholes.

Along Calzada del Cerro, under a full moon, deep shadows carve out contrasts of dramatic detail against fantastic skies, with here and there an incongruous royal palm tree emerging out of a hidden garden, towering over rooftops crisscrossed with generations of improvised plumbing and wiring. These snakelike skeins look just as jungle-like as the roots that hug and penetrate walls and columns in acts of slow motion copulation with the mansions of the "leafy suburbs."

The mysteries deepen in the narrower streets. A lone smoker sitting on his doorstep converses with street cats and dogs, thriving in a miasma of noxious gasoline, burned and spat out as hallucinogenic fumes by 1950s Chevrolets that are packed at night with *chulos* and *chulas*, some of them proudly proclaiming by way of bumper stickers: *Soy el 13 de más 12*, in the code of the *bolita*, or street lottery, *I'm the pimp with the most whores*.

Abandoned nineteenth-century trains slowly rust away in the Cristina station at Cuatro Caminos – industrial dinosaurs without a museum. One wonders when those ghost trains last entered the station, what voyages ended here. The older barrios south of the Avenida del Puerto lie beneath the grandiose *Mad Max* architecture of the ancient Tallapiedra power station. Here, life becomes teeming again, with animated domino games in progress, and quick eyes on the lookout for intruders.

During the hot summer nights, life increasingly spills out onto the streets. Kids run around sidewalk craters displaying sewer systems gone geological with age. Among their elders, sudden, vicious quarrels erupt about sex or territoriality, fueled by too much rum or other less benign substances.

In these parts of Habana Vieja, a world removed from the tourist streets, here and there semi-collapsed buildings have become half-open spaces and floating floors become grottoes, some of them still inhabited. On the ground floors, deep corridors leading to successive mysterious patios have likewise become objects of speleology rather than of architecture. These barrios of Habana Vieja slowly turning organic, resembling a Piranesi engraving, may be fascinating to the poetic imagination, but what effect do they have on their inhabitants? It's almost a *Life After People* setting. And then all of a sudden, an angel appears: a girl with the incredible, sometimes almost painful beauty of all the Cuban races combined, happy in her minimal body armor, smiling at life such as it is and will be.

Legend has it that in his younger years, Fidel roamed the streets at night to stay in touch with *el pueblo*. All such legends go back to the *Thousand-and-One-Nights* example of the khalif Haroun-al-Rashid anonymously exploring the alleys of Baghdad. As a child I heard the same legends about the emperor Charles V in Flanders. It's true that Fidel was genuinely interested in the details of peoples' lives, sometimes to the point of micro-management, but of course he could never disguise himself, even under the cover of darkness and extremely poor street lighting.

But supposing the stories are true, what would the Man have had to say to the people here? Maybe the extreme neglect came from only looking at a bright future and never at the dark past. These neighborhoods were of colonial origin and thus tainted with the original sins of the ages without the blessings of Marxism. Even the grand monuments on the

Plaza de Armas and the Plaza Vieja, the two main squares of the old city, only got official attention once tourism became the new national industry in the 1990s. In the intervening forty years after the Revolution they were treated with contempt for reflecting the wrong history. On the bronze doors of the Capitolio, the face of former president Machado has been chiseled away. Machado was a corrupt politician of the 1920s and '30s. He got the treatment Egyptian pharaohs sometimes inflicted on their predecessors by being erased.

Maybe the Revolution would have preferred to also obliterate the old popular barrios. Luckily, no Cuban Robert Moses ever had the clout or the budget to sanitize the city, as happened to large parts of New York. Marxist theorists often abandoned such neighborhoods to what, in their jargon, was the lumpen proletariat. It has to be said, in fairness, that such terms were never used in Havana, and that the revolution's declared intention was always to be inclusive and

Havana *with* makeup: the beautiful panorama

to leave no one behind. But febrile, teeming life prevails, long after the dogmas and the ideals of orthodox Marxism have disappeared.

Havana is such an organic metropolis, that I know of no city with a richer and more fascinating variety of urban textures, spontaneous recycling of spaces and materials, or more lively interactions between flesh and stone. This covers the entire spectrum from the graceful to the desperate, from the super-kitsch to the intuitive or the resolutely post-modernist, with a good measure of bad taste thrown in by sudden influxes of money, ominously spelling future architectural horrors when real estate speculation starts running wild. Havana may go the way of some parts of Manhattan, where buildings born of the oversized egos of fashionable architects regularly kill the souls of entire neighborhoods.

I may live to regret the disappearance of Havana's sexy ruins. But that, admittedly, is backward thinking.

4. AFRO CUBA

Roaming Havana's streets, you'll encounter a remarkable mixture of races in every neighborhood. According to the latest available census, only about 10 percent of Cubans self-identify as "Afro-Cuban." This figure seems seriously underreported, yet it's a fact that people of African descent are a minority in Cuba, as compared to the overwhelmingly black population of the other Caribbean islands. On the ever-sensitive issue of race, self-identification in a census is notoriously unreliable, due to a range of social and psychological factors. Europeans, without the legacy of slavery at the receiving end, are often unaware how sensitive a topic race still is in the Americas, and especially in the Caribbean. The ongoing claim for reparations for the slave trade, kept on the agenda at the United Nations, illustrates this. Yet Cuba is more relaxed about the issue than most of her neighbors. By U.S. standards, racial attitudes and vocabulary in Havana are often downright politically incorrect. And despite people of African descent being a minority in the country, nowhere in the Caribbean, possibly nowhere in the Americas, are African traditions stronger and more alive than in Cuba. Among possible explanations, a few stand out.

Although slavery in Cuba was abolished late – in the 1880s, half a century later than in the British colonies – the peculiar slavery laws under the Spanish colonial system allowed for a greater number of Africans and people of color in Cuba to be manumitted, or to buy their freedom, than in English or French territories. As we will see, Cuba was still bringing new slaves from Africa almost until the system was abolished, although in theory this had been illegal under international law since 1815, when the Vienna Congress decreed the end of the transatlantic slave trade.

Before and after the abolition of slavery, the "cabildos de nación," which regrouped free Africans according to their ethnic origins, developed into genuine lobbies that defended the interests of their members, and also maintained their traditions. In some cases the *cabildos* survived well into the twentieth century. In fact, some exist even today, albeit no longer as such formal institutions.

This made Havana unique once more: new slaves continued to arrive until the end of the nineteenth century, while at the same time the city saw a thriving social life among free Africans. These two phenomena came to mutually reinforce one another.

Like the Spanish immigrants in Havana who regrouped in

regional clubs, so the Africans came together in their *cabildos*. These institutions had their remote origin in Spain, specifically in Seville, where the first *cabildos* had started to organize an annual carnival on the sixth of January, King's Day in the Catholic calendar. This was always considered a special holiday for Africans, since one of the three kings or wise men, Balthazar, was the only acknowledged black saint.

Soon the Día de Reyes carnival became a Havana custom.

If we take a close look at the representations of these festivities as recorded by the nineteenth-century *costumbrista* painters, a few elements are striking.

The parading Africans were allowed to caricature their white masters or former masters – the age-old function of any carnival as a social safety valve. Those masters looked on suspiciously, half-barricaded in their homes, while their womenfolk on the balconies seemed almost too fascinated by the rhythms of the drums and the exuberant dancing.

But the political establishment around the captain general (as colonial governors were called) considered it their duty to stoically review the parade – one may imagine with what kind of comments behind the white gloves – and ended by throwing handfuls of coins to the crowds, thus creating a stampede which would reinforce white feelings of superiority for yet another year.

By the mid-nineteenth century, the balance between the races had become delicate due to the late flourishing of the sugar industry, which in Cuba only really took off after the British occupation of Havana in 1762–1763, and occasioned the enormous late influx of Africans brought to work on the plantations. On top of that came the independence struggle in Haiti, which resulted in the creation of the first black state in the Americas in 1804. From then on, the fear of a black republic would always be present in Cuba.

5. HAVANA IN BLACK AND WHITE

From its very beginnings, Cuba's own independence struggle was closely linked to the racial question. When Carlos Manuel de Céspedes launched the first call for liberation from Spain in 1868, he simultaneously freed the slaves from his own plantation, because there was no room for slavery in a free Cuba. This was the Grito de Yara, named after the plantation where it occurred. The date, October tenth, is still a national holiday, and also explains the name of the Diez de Octubre municipality, next to Old Havana. Céspedes was from Bayamo, a provincial city in Oriente between Las Tunas and Santiago. Bayamo would become a symbol of the independence struggle. The present day Cuban national anthem still reflects it: "*Al combate corred Bayameses,*" or "Onward to battle, people of Bayamo!"

Among the later leaders of the struggle, the black general Maceo – known as "El Titán de Bronce" – stood out for his leadership and bravery. His part in the struggle turned him into a symbol of a united, multiracial Cuba. Moreover, the independence war was in essence a rural *guerrilla*, and could not have been waged without the experience black Cubans had accumulated from survival in the wilds as *cimarrones* (runaways).

But Cuba's hard-won independence was immediately hijacked by the United States, which turned the island into a de facto protectorate as of 1900. The United States imported its own racial attitudes – mostly the post–Civil War Jim Crow mentality from the South. This was a sad irony, because many of the Cuban freedom fighters had formed their political convictions in the United States, most notably the national hero José Martí in New York. Under U.S. influence, Céspedes' dream of a post-racial Cuban society became an impossible utopia almost overnight.

The African *cabildos* gradually became the object of disapproval by white Cuban intellectuals, who saw them as remnants of the backwardness that should be eliminated now that Africans could become "civilized." But African traditions survived both on the vast sugar estates of the interior and even in Havana. Cuba's greatest twentieth-century writer, Alejo Carpentier, explored these situations in his writings as late as the 1930s. The yearly influx of workers from other Caribbean islands for the sugarcane harvest – mostly Haitians and Jamaicans – even shaped new blends of beliefs, rhythms, and traditions.

The changing attitudes between white and black Cuba are best illustrated by the career of Fernando Ortiz, the greatest of early Cuban anthropologists. Like his contemporaries, he originally saw the African traditions in Havana and Matanzas as examples of backwardness to be eliminated through enlightened education. His first studies of those traditions connected them almost exclusively to the Havana *hampa*, or underworld. Ortiz's early writings explored Havana's black culture as a criminal milieu, maintaining louche traditions and attitudes imported in colonial times from Seville and Cádiz. Yet precisely because they record that entire culture in great detail, these works – *Los negros curros, Los negros brujos* – are priceless uncensored testimonials of early African culture in Havana. His later trajectory illustrated the ambiguity of his early disapproval of black Cuba: like the upper-class ladies observing the Día de Reyes, he became fascinated by his own fears. He evolved in his own lifetime to publicly display respect and admiration for Afro-Cuban culture, passing on his later attitude to his main disciple Miguel Barnet, who became an active chronicler of *Afrocubanismo*, including in his recording of the last direct testimonials of runaway, or *cimarrón*, life in Cuba.

6. *RUMBA*

On Sunday afternoons, the neighborhood of Calle Aramburu – a side street of San Lázaro near the University – organizes a *rumba*. Over the years it has become a tourist attraction, but it has kept some of its original raw energy.

The neighbors gather in an extended patio along the workshop of the painter Salvador. This is an expanded version of a *solar*, an urban "yard" around which *habaneros* in poor neighborhoods organize their daily lives. These *solares* are not only like village squares used for communal activities, they also serve as spontaneous temples for the discreet practice of ancestral rites. Salvador has decorated his space with exuberant Santería themes.

The *rumba* performed here has been watered down to a concert, but remains close to what in Santería is called a *tambor* or *toquesanto*, a drum-session intended to invoke the spirits to allow the initiated to identify with them in a state of trance. The *rumberos*, whether commercialized or not, play both the vertical congas and the horizontal *tambores batá*, a set of three drums placed on the knees and played at both ends. These were originally sacred instruments, meant to invoke the ancestors, and are always handled with special care and ritual. The conga is also a popular instrument in pop and jazz, but here it's played with such virtuosity that a mediocre Cuban *congero* is likely to give even the experienced American or European player an inferiority complex.

In the 1920s, Fernando Ortiz started to participate in such *rumbas* when they were still completely authentic, and when few, if any, white Cubans of his social class did so. He later commented with self-deprecating humor on the reactions of the participants when he roamed the often still semi-rural neighborhoods around Havana in search of active *solares*: What's this white boy up to? Is he after the girls? (*"Qué se traerá ese blanquito . . . atraído por las hijas de la Virgen de Regla más que por los cultos . . . ?"*)

Let's see what he saw, and where it came from.

7. SANTERÍA

The slaves brought to Havana and Matanzas in the nineteenth century came predominantly from territories that are now part of Nigeria, the Congo, and Angola.

Nigeria and Congo are the principal roots of all African traditions in Cuba. The most visible and lively African culture in Havana is that of the Nigerian *Yoruba*, while the more hidden and secretive rites fall under the general heading of *Congo*. A Cuban proverb sums it up: *"quien no tiene de Congo tiene de Carabalí,"* meaning: every Cuban has some African blood, be it from Congo or Calabar (southern Nigeria).

The predominance of the Yoruba may be due to the fact that back home they had an ancient and sophisticated culture, with a rich pantheon of ancestors transformed into worshipped archetypes. Those could easily be identified with Catholic saints when the slaves were baptized en masse upon arrival in Cuba.

The Spanish slavery system, as practiced in Cuba, was far

more calculated than the British and the French. The Cuban slave masters realized that the growing numbers of slaves could only be kept in check if they were allowed to preserve some of their own social structures. The British system intended to break those up completely and, by and large, did so elsewhere in the Caribbean, killing the ancestral traditions or driving them so deep underground that they only surfaced during slave revolts. Together with the easier manumissions and the gradual creation of a free black and colored class in Havana, the African *cabildos* not only maintained but even codified and refined those traditions and soon did so, as we will see, even beyond color lines. This became a very important development for the post-colonial history of the Spanish territories. Whereas in North America the colonial system was basically a fully-fledged apartheid, in the Spanish colonies there was far more mixing of blood and culture. And nowhere more than in Havana. This explains a paradox I've often observed: while Jamaica is 90 percent black, it has not preserved even a tiny fraction of the African traditions existing in daily life in Cuba, which is predominantly white.

The worship of African spirits under the guise of Catholic saints (which is the very definition of *Santería*) was gradually codified during the nineteenth century, first to identify a specific African *orisha* with a specific Catholic saint. This identification could be based on various criteria, mostly on how a saint looked or dressed or what symbols or tools she or he carried in traditional imagery. Some of the associations are easier to understand than others. The motherly, black Virgen de Regla became the ocean spirit Yemaya. The Caridad del Cobre in her bright yellow and gold outfit became the seductive mulatta Ochún. The mischievous Niño de Atocha, the unpredictable lord of the crossroads, Eleggua. San Lázaro, the patron saint of lepers, turned into the equally suffering Babalú Ayé. And so on.

More mysteriously, Santa Bárbara underwent a sex-change and became the super-macho Chango, probably because the saint, unexpectedly for a female, carries a sword. This was the symbol of her martyrdom, but Santa Bárbara was also associated with the lightning that was supposed to have struck her torturers. As such, she became the patron saint of the Spanish artillerymen and of anyone working with explosives. Chango was also the spirit of thunder and lightning. In this way, in Havana a virgin saint became a virile African.

By identifying an *orisha* with a saint, the corresponding Catholic holiday could be observed by the Africans in their own ways. The Día de Reyes carnival was the yearly culmination of that system.

Apart from these identifications, oral legends regarding the deeds of the *orishas* were recorded in so-called *patakis*, the equivalent of the Catholics' equally fanciful saints' lives. The difference, though, is that the *orishas'* adventures are anything but exemplary or edifying: they're much closer to the endless quarrels, conflicts, and affairs of the Olympian gods of Greek mythology.

The *orishas* are often wrongly described as "African gods," but Santería is strictly monotheistic. The *orishas* are mostly accessible intermediaries to plug into the vital force permeating the cosmos, a force known as *aché*, to bring the worshipper personal energy and luck called *iré*. This is best obtained through the trances brought about by the African drums, when for a short time the worshipper identifies with the *orisha* ruling his or her destiny.

8. SANTERÍA AND THE RACIAL DIVIDE

As late as the early twentieth century, Fernando Ortiz saw a deep cultural divide between black and white Cuba. In fact, he was wrong. Already in the middle of the 1800s a remarkable figure, Andrés Facundo Cristo de Dolores Petit (1830–1878), a Cuban *criollo* of partly Haitian ancestry, not only integrated elements of Yoruba and Congo traditions in his *Regla Kimbisa*, but also promoted the rites as a culture unifying Cubans of all races in the struggle against Spain. He was the first to think of a Cuban national identity, or *cubanía*, in post-racial terms.

Through a bit of *orisha*-inspired detective work, we even know where the very first initiation of white Cubans into the African rites took place: in 1863 at number 115 of the street then called Calle Ancha del Norte, now Calle San Lázaro, between Galiano and San Nicolás. Petit was a visionary well ahead of his time. Black Cubans accused him of seeking to initiate whites for financial gain only, but that was slander. It's known that the first white *santeros* were indeed from prominent

Santería trade in Cuatro Caminos

families, but also that Petit responded to their own request motivated by their anti-Spanish patriotism.

Today, when it comes to Santería, the color barrier has completely disappeared. This is immediately obvious in Havana, where recent initiates wear their white clothes and the *collares* (necklaces) of their master-*orishas* for a full year. You'll spot those *iyabo*, as they are known in Cuban Yoruba, of any skin color.

Besides being a racial unifier, *la religión* has also become a strong link between the island and Miami Cubans, bypassing divisive politics.

When you see elderly people *de iyabo* in Havana, it means that they have been saving their entire lives to pay for the initiation and its requirements. It's a costly procedure because of all the implements you have to buy. But you'll also see initiated young children, and in some cases a baby is dedicated to

A recently initiated Santería *iyabo* on lively
Calle Monte in Centro Habana

the *orishas* while still in the womb, or when born *en zurrón*, still wrapped in the amniotic sac, which in Cuba is considered an omen of good fortune.

The white clothes of the year of noviciate add a special touch to Havana's elegance. Girls and women have to cover their head and shoulders and wear white stockings. Together with the long skirts and the white umbrellas they favor, the embroidered shawls give many female *iyabos* a traditional eighteenth-century look, and form beautiful and spontaneous passing vignettes against the backdrop of the buildings in Old Havana. As part of the tourist attractions in the old town, women in colorful traditional dress and smoking big cigars are sent about to have their picture taken with visitors, but the dignified *iyabos* dressed in white are real.

The white clothes and the colorful *collares* disappear after one year. The initiate will have a yearly celebration on the anniversary of her *hacerse santo* and has assumed life-long obligations and interdictions in exchange for the spiritual ease drawn from knowing one's path in life, as being determined by this or that *orisha* as an archetype of behavior. In that sense, there is a strong psychological factor in the traditions.

Long after the initiate can no longer be so easily identified, discreet bracelets with the colors of the *orisha* will be peeping out of sleeves or cuffs, where one least expects it, including from members of the communist party. That was unthinkable only a few years ago. Let's take a look at how *that* came about.

9. COMMUNIST *ORISHAS?*

The Cuban Revolution had its own specific impact on that culture. First, the egalitarian utopia did away with many – though certainly not all – aspects of racism in Cuban society.

Yet at the same time, the Afro-Cuban religions were once again seen as backward superstitions. This drove them back underground, where they had been to a large extent under slavery. In the 1970s, newsreels in Cuban cinemas routinely attacked *santeros*, along with evangelical Christians, as counterrevolutionary reactionaries. But since the Santería traditions were too strong to be eliminated, at the same time the government attempted to co-opt them as purely cultural manifestations, especially via music and dance. In fact, under Communist rule, the religious aspects became stronger and stronger, and one may safely say that Santería, next to the stubborn Catholic Church, became one of the few powers in Cuba outside the Communist party to exist in their own right and maintain their own networks while having a real impact on the society. This also resulted in a very peculiar relationship between Santería and Freemasonry, which was widespread before the Revolution, and was also driven underground.

As of 1992, when the Cuban constitution was amended to change Cuba from an "atheist" state into an agnostic one, and to counterbalance attempts by the Catholic Church to monopolize the new religious freedoms, the Cuban state began to openly court those involved in Santería as part of its balancing act. This was especially obvious at the time of the Pope's visit in 1998. The national patron saint La Virgen de la Caridad del Cobre was paraded around the island to warm people up for the visit, but one may safely assume that half of the worshippers turning out came to greet the *orisha* Ochún.

The new religious freedoms also resulted in other ambiguous situations. Local officials, aware of the influence of the *santeros* in their communities, sometimes maintained discreet contact with them, and at times openly joined their activities.

Stubborn beliefs: on one intersection, the impressive but rundown Masonic headquarters faces Pope Francis and a well-kept Catholic church amid the *inventos* of the Havana habitat

The Communist government contributed to the strengthening of traditions in another way. In the mid-1990s, when Cuba opened up for tourism, Cuban music became very popular worldwide. Given the importance of percussion in all of Cuban music and the close links between popular music and the sacred drum, this gave Santería a new boost.

The recognition of religion and religious pluralism changed the official discourse on African traditions. African tradition is now more recognized as an integral, even essential, part of the Cuban soul and of *cubanía*. But this has been given some peculiar twists. The revival of the traditions as of the 1980s is sometimes presented, in part, as a result of the massive Cuban presence in Africa in military operations and development co-operation. In this view, the families of the 50,000 or more

Cuban soldiers fighting in Angola and Ethiopia reportedly turned to the *orishas* for spiritual solace.

It may be true that individual Cuban soldiers in Angola, during a long and often difficult struggle, became aware that they were fighting on ancestral ground, but truth be told, this was not recognized until much later. In fact, the harsher truth may be that Angola veterans, disappointed by their return to the island after being called heroes during the conflict, turned inward. In extreme conditions, it is common to turn to religion, particularly for younger people.

In another typical attempt to recuperate souls for political purposes, the popularity of Santería is now sometimes presented as part of a worldwide search for values against the evils of Darwinist capitalism. Nevertheless, many Cubans of African descent continue to feel that their culture is at best partially recognized and appreciated by the State. The resurgence of African cultural identity has been fueled, in part, by academics and their publications. There is now a critical mass of scholars studying Afro-Cuban culture, and the Fundación Fernando Ortiz actively links the works of the master to current social themes.

Santería traditions, especially the practices of initiation, are more widespread and more visible in Cuba than ever before. Santería has also gone global, not without becoming increasingly commercialized. There is a tendency in the United States, especially in New Orleans, to consider and even to practice Santería as part of a vague New Age mysticism. In Cuba, on the contrary, believers are held to very strict rules and rites. Santería has been open to many influences, including some from Islam and early twentieth-century spiritism, but in Cuba at any rate the practice is codified, and new syncretism or transculturation is warded off.

The impact and influence of Santería on Cuban society are deep, both in terms of outlook on life and social connections among initiates. In its varied manifestations – popular beliefs and rites, music, visual arts – it's simply part of daily life in Cuba. *Santeros* take a much longer view than the politics of the moment: if we could survive four centuries of slavery, we'll outlive a few more years of communism as well. Time is on our side.

All of the above is serious stuff. But then there is the fun part, too. Especially when it comes to the soundtrack.

10. *¡SALSA!*

At the Teatro de las Américas on Calle Galeano, a well-preserved district of Centro Habana, Havana's best salsa orchestra, Los Van Van, is in concert. The orchestra was started in the 1960s, when Cuban musicians got tired of traditional music, but wanted to keep its essential rhythmic structures, which they blended with modern soul and pop. Until his passing in May 2014, the band was led by its founder, the legendary Juan Formell, whose songwriting over the years had become a true chronicle of life in Havana with all its ups and downs, wrapped in some of the most rousing music ever performed.

In remembrance of Formell, the song "Te pone la cabeza mala" is now played with an extra long introduction by Los Van Van's signature horns section, sustained by diabolically virtuoso conga rhythms. Members rise from their seats, and bodies come whirlingly alive in a physical adoration of the rhythm dedicated to the late Formell and all the good times he brought his people. The *orishas* immediately come into play with the lyrics of the song. They speak of the Nigerian and Congolese roots of the music, inherited by all Cubans as children and grandchildren of Africa.

The collective musical ecstasy goes back to the *toquesantos* – the use of the congas to invoke the spirits – but the fun part can also be traced at least to the eighteenth century, when chroniclers of the scandalous life in the port of Havana – just like Ortiz, who was already fascinated by what they wished to censor – described the early Cuban music such as the *guaracha*, as "the most viscerally enticing rhythms of three worlds" – inducing all kinds of mischief, of course.

While Los Van Van have Havana in a trance, at the same moment in New York, salsa diva La India may well be singing her odes to Yemaya and Ochún, the most revered female *orishas*.

Visitors and tourists may simply dance to salsa and the more pop-related *timba*, but to understand what the music is about, one needs to explore its religious roots. The music crosses over and again the thin line between sensual dancing as a mating ritual and being possessed by the *orishas*.

Another salsa superstar, José Luis "El Tosco" Cortés and his NG La Banda, illustrates the mysterious sex change transforming Saint Barbara into the highly virile Changó. El Tosco himself, onstage, almost incarnates the lyrics. A very macho presence, when switching from Changó to Santa Bárbara, he becomes the very talented classical musician that he is, and serenades the virgin saint not on the proverbial lyre but with sophisticated flute solos.

The camouflage of Santería themes in popular music probably helped *la religión* to survive times of official disapproval. It also maintained the festive and colorful aspects of the Yoruba beliefs and rites. Each good salsa concert gives a remote idea of what the Día de Reyes carnival was like in slavery days.

11. ASIA DE CUBA

Before I came to live in Havana for the first time in 1995, in New York I had often wondered about the origin of such restaurants as Asia de Cuba and Caribbean greasy spoons advertising *comidas chinas y criollas*. These questions led me to decipher an almost forgotten chapter of world history.

In Havana, when you pass the Capitolio, you reach the Parque de la Fraternidad with its white marble statue of a supposedly native Cuban girl symbolizing the city and its remote origins. Incidentally, this is also a nightly hangout for transvestites, as tragicomically illustrated in the 2014 film *Fátima o El Parque de la Fraternidad*. To the right you now face the monumental gate to the Barrio Chino, Havana's Chinatown. The gate is a late addition, a gift from the People's Republic

Barrio Chino: gate to forgotten history –
and awful food

to what is officially a brotherly communist nation. We'll explore later to what extent that is still the case.

The Chinese presence in Cuba began after the Spanish conquistadors reached the Pacific via Cuba and Mexico. The Spanish extended their colonial empire all the way to the Philippines in the 1540s. Mainland China was mostly forbidden territory, but the Chinese state had a great desire for the silver from Peru and Mexico. This expanded trade over new routes and vast distances, of which Havana became the focal point.

Goods traded for Spanish silver reached Mexico in the so-called *galeones de Acapulco* from Manila to Mexico's west coast, and were then transported overland to Veracruz, and from there on to Havana, to become part of the cargoes sailing to Cádiz.

In colonial times, the term *pacotilla china* became a saying in Havana, referring to the cheap or not-so-cheap chinaware and other exotica and *bibelots* left behind or "fallen off the ship" (as port thievery was also known in the Antwerp of my childhood). These remnants of early trans-Pacific trade are still to be found in great quantities among the inventories of the Havana mansions frozen in time since the Revolution. They may also be discreetly on sale from unlicensed antique dealers, although the best pieces, as part of a jealously monitored *patrimonio nacional*, are not supposed to leave the country.

The Chinese presence in Havana also grew with trade. This Asian population further expanded after the abolition of slavery, when Asian indentured laborers arrived in considerable numbers. At the outset, those workers were hardly better off than slaves had been, but many worked themselves up as traders and merchants, and the Barrio Chino grew and prospered.

There may have been a new influx of Chinese migrants after Mao's triumph in China in 1949. Despite earlier restrictions on immigration in Cuba, as elsewhere, by then official Cuba welcomed any immigration as long as it counterbalanced the fear of a black republic. When those recent Chinese immigrants, who had fled communism, saw themselves faced only ten years later with the Cuban Revolution, many emigrated yet again to New Orleans, San Francisco, or New York. Deprived of commerce and the upward social mobility it had brought, Havana's Barrio Chino began to fossilize.

The present-day *barrio* is often criticized for being an artificially maintained tourist trap, with the obvious tricks of some calligraphy, dragons, and red lanterns. That's partly true, yet as late as the 1990s there was a Chinese-language newspaper and at least one authentic Chinese herbal pharmacy still operating. Now the barrio is mostly a concentration of Chinese restaurants of doubtful cuisine and even more questionable hygiene. But lurking under the artificially maintained chinoiserie there are a few clubs and traditional cantinas where the last authentic inhabitants, stubborn men at least in their eighties, maintain relics and traditions.

12. "ACHINADO"

Havana's semi-clandestine vendors of antiques offer countless porcelain Buddhas for sale – of the Chinese variety, looking like fat Cantonese businessmen in their underwear, rather than stylish Indian ascetics. But the most authentic traces of the Chinese presence come from much deeper: they are in the Cuban blood. The racial mix of the first encounters was never undone. With the typical Cuban nonchalance about race, *habaneros* will argue that *la mulata china* – brown skinned with slanted eyes – is their most attractive woman. *Mi chino* is an affectionate nickname for a lover of any race. And every *habanero* even with slightly Asian features will be described as *achinado*, "Oriental-looking or 'Chinesed.'"

A close friend of mine, happily equipped with such eyes, maintains that Havana is a chakra of the planet, where blood from all over had to converge. That's a beautiful idea and I'm grateful for it. Nevertheless, after the Revolution, the Barrio Chino degenerated into a truly marginal ghetto, and the dream of joining the middle class, after all the misery the Cantonese immigrants had known back home, evaporated, together with the solace of opium and discreet brothels.

Here, as elsewhere in Havana under growing social controls, the ever stubborn life of the traditional city went underground, and the barrio became the focal point of clandestine gambling and lotteries, while those inhabitants too poor or too old to reach the United States – or scared off by horror stories of what the new emigrants underwent at the hands of people smugglers – waited for death in increasingly miserable hovels under the wise or cynical smiles of ancestral spirits. Many Chinese never fully learned Spanish, adding to their isolation.

Those who had reached prosperity were long since buried in the Chinese cemetery in Nuevo Vedado, where their opulent tombs can still be visited. The cemetery was closed for many years out of security concerns because Raúl Castro lived in an apartment just across the street. When he became president and moved in his turn to the western suburbs, the gates were unlocked. Many of the graves had been robbed in the meantime, because in the darker Congo-rites of Santería, Chinese skulls and bones are highly valued, apparently because the Chinese were thought to hide deep secrets. Was it because they were so discreet, spoke so little Spanish, and smiled against all adversity? The same phenomenon happened on an even wider scale at the Jewish cemeteries in Guanabacoa.

Even with the attempts at recuperation for the tourist trade, the barrio still contains some of Centro Havana's dirtiest blocks, often to the dismay of the well-to-do Chinese visitors, who find little reason for ancestral pride here. But there is a culture of stubborn survival: among some of the worst Chinese restaurants of the world, sellers of little songbirds maintain an authentically Chinese tradition I remember from Sundays in Manhattan's Chinatown. The delicate singing and chirping bring a little cheer to an otherwise depressing environment.

13. SEX & CENESEX

Bluntly put: if everyone had not slept with everyone else, Havana today would not be so racially diverse. As essentially a port city, Havana was notoriously sexually riotous and libertine from its very foundation, and even the Catholic Church was quite powerless to counter this.

Large-scale sexual abuse was a characteristic of early colonization, but the resulting mixed-race population became a national trait.

Traditional Catholic marriage had been laboriously upheld for centuries over the uninhibited life of the port and the popular neighborhoods, but the Revolution was all too happy to do away with what it saw as a stifling bourgeois institution. Marriage and divorce were reduced to minimal procedures, in a move seen as liberating women from repressive bonds. Unconsciously, by scraping away the upper-class veneer, revolutionary idealism or dogma favored a return to the sexual freedoms of a much older and rougher Havana.

A Cuban colleague of mine, a high-ranking official, provoked first admiration and next utter dismay on the part of a prominent UN official, when he told her during a ceremonial dinner that he had been married for forty-three years . . . to six different spouses. His case is not uncommon. But there are other unexpected side effects. In spite of loose marriage vows and cost-free 48-hour divorces, extended families of half-siblings from various unions tend to be very close, and there is a true and caring veneration for grandparents, in sharp contrast with the growing "park-Granny-in-a-home" culture elsewhere.

There was a more comical side effect during the deep economic crisis of the 1990s. Friends would marry for the cake, the crate of beer, and the free honeymoon weekend in a hotel which the State still provided to newlyweds, would divorce on Monday, and start over.

The liberation of the Cuban woman from oppressive bourgeois marriage went hand in hand with authentic attempts to emancipate the female half of Cuba from traditional macho culture. The Federación de Mujeres Cubanas (Cuban Women's Federation) was founded as a close corollary of the Communist Party by Raúl Castro's passionate and charismatically handsome wife Vilma Espín. Thanks to her, Cuban women are certainly more emancipated that many of their sisters elsewhere in Latin America. Yet the macho culture is difficult to uproot. Domestic violence remains a problem here, but is constantly challenged by social campaigns.

Sexual freedom under the Revolution still only meant heterosexual liberation. But opposition to this came from the most unexpected quarter: from Raúl Castro and Vilma Espín's daughter, Mariela Castro. Following in the footsteps of her mother's social activism via the FMC, Mariela in turn founded CENESEX, the national center for sexual education, and became an internationally recognized lobbyist for LGBT rights. Mariela holds her mother – who certainly did not share her convictions – in awe, and sees her own work as a natural progression from Vilma Espín's work for women's emancipation. Mariela's forthright explanation of her ideal is extremely refreshing in the Cuban context. It goes like this: a person can only be a good citizen if they can fully and publicly assume and express their sexual persona. Repression thereof breeds frustration and discontent and unhappy citizens. The society as a whole should accept this. In her own convincing way, and with the charm she inherited from her mother, she has quietly reversed one of the basic tenets of revolutionary morality: that personal happiness is secondary to good citizenship, and flows from obedience to the rules of society. She has understood much more about human nature than her parents' generation.

Anti-gay prejudice was, of course, deeply rooted in Cuba. I overheard a woman in Santiago sighing about her toddler son, who showed too much fondness for dolls and frills: "*Más bien sea asesino que pájarito ...*" ("Let him be a murderer rather than a 'little bird' [slang for *gay*]"). In 1994, my friend, the Cuban movie star and director Jorge "Pichi" Perrugoria, played the part of a homosexual in Cuba's first international hit film, the Oscar-nominated *Fresa y chocolate*. He's not gay and he's happily married to a remarkable woman, mother of his four grown sons (collectively known in Havana as the rock band Nube Roja). But back in the 1990s, he was regularly insulted on the streets for being a *maricón*. This faces any sexual free thinker with a difficult dilemma: to deny – "but I'm not a 'faggot,' *compadre*" – can be read as rejecting a stigma; but at the same time, to see one's own sexuality denied in public is also demeaning. Pichi must have found the right dose of humor and diplomacy because today he's popular with all persuasions.

The LGBT movement in Cuba is all the more remarkable given the extreme homophobia elsewhere in the Caribbean, often still descending into lynchings. Mariela Castro's groundbreaking work illustrates how one person can affect long-standing discrimination. She has breached a thick wall of silence, and as one of the Castro clan, in this regard she has gone bravely against the early attitudes of the Revolution. Her sexual liberalism is so refreshing that one often wonders why so many other walls in this society remain so difficult to overcome.

14. *¡TREMENDA MARICONADA!*

On weekends, people flock to the Malecón wall for the weekly *botellón*. *Botellón*, or "big bottle," became a popular tradition in Spain because of the economic crisis that began in 2008. Young people gather in public spaces to share drinks straight from the bottle, since it's much cheaper than going to bars and clubs. No traces of prohibition there or here to inhibit this.

Now everyone sitting on the Malecón wall turns to the city. The sea has nothing to offer at night, except for *santeras* discreetly doing their devotions to the ocean spirit Yemaya on the sharp-edged coral rock – *diente de perro*, dog's tooth – below the wall. Maybe a rusty freighter or container ship will be passing, but without messages for or against a great escape. Back in 1994, thousands of *balseros* (boat people) threw themselves upon the mercy of the sea and the U.S. Coast Guard from beneath this wall. Legend has it that for every Cuban who made it to Florida, three perished at sea.

The symbol of this wall as the last stand against the other side, or the ultimate frontier, is always present, but frankly, on Saturday nights we choose to ignore it. So we turn to the city and just have a good time. Modest street vendors push improvised carts peddling snacks, balloons, plastic flowers, toys, and cuddly stuffed animals. In all their modesty, in their clean clothes and worn shoes, but already with a sense of initiative and competition, they are pioneers and prominent operators of the new economy, the tolerated private sector, or rather, as the jargon still has it, *el sector no estatal* (the non-state sector).

The section of the wall in front of the Hotel Nacional belongs to an exuberant gay, lesbian, transgender, and transvestite gathering that gets more and more Felliniesque as the night progresses. Tall and exquisitely feminine cross-dressers flaunt their charms and desires. This rough street version of the famous Tropicana show has its own stars draped in improvised glitter, presenting their sidewalk catwalk routines with swaying hips on impossibly high heels to an appreciative audience sitting on the wall. The main star for a number of nights some years ago was known as La Hurona, after a large, weasel-like rodent. But the turnover of such stars was fast, as I often noticed a suicidal streak in their exuberance, a forward flight putting them way out of the reach of social activism, even when sex-change operations became available.

Young policemen, mostly from Oriente, visibly embarrassed in their provincial innocence by such scenes from a perverse Havana purgatory, neutrally keep the peace but have clearly been instructed to tolerate these extravagances that fall well beyond their personal comprehension.

The stars of the show appear tireless. One feels their pent-up energies from an entire week of posing as what they are not, liberating themselves in these few hours of baroque extravaganza. But too-wide feet are swelling in the sequined shoes, make-up melts under the humid heat, and stubble penetrates the rouge. The defiance in their eyes now also contains despair.

When finally at around three a.m. the jealousies and competition degenerate into drunken rows, the battered gray police van quickly turns up, and an entire improvised open-air ballroom of glitter and revealing half-torn gowns is arrested under loud protests and giggling by the hugely relieved cops, who are finally allowed to restore morality, while the arrested birds of paradise throw kisses through the bars of the jail van. They will be released a few hours later with a warning about drunkenness in public, not about the improvised burlesque show.

15. HAVANA'S HOUR ZERO

It may seem preposterous that the modest nighttime street vendors along the Malecón wall were until very recently seen as subversives and counterrevolutionaries by official Havana, as they undermined the state monopoly on *any* commercial activity since the 1970s. When I was present at a long private monologue by President Raúl Castro in March of 2015, he spontaneously admitted that "when we were young we didn't know too much about the economy, or else we would have handled things differently."

But my view on this was also shaped by my experience in New York in late 1988. On the seventh of December, Mikael Gorbachev in the General Assembly of the United Nations purely and simply buried the global Cold War, unwittingly signing his own political death warrant, the failure of his *pere-*

stoika reforms and the implosion of the Soviet Union in its unavoidable aftermath.

When Gorbachev visited Havana shortly after his UN speech, in early 1989, he basically told his Cuban allies that the years of massive economic support were over. Authentic dismay was written on Fidel Castro's face for the first time in thirty years. Cuba had become almost entirely dependent on Soviet-bloc aid and trade. The end of the support system was a first blow. Worse would follow soon.

Moscow's rule and empire imploded in 1991. The end of communism in Europe was not just an unimaginable catastrophe to the Cuban revolutionaries. It was also the final proof that Leninism/Stalinism was impossible to reform – a lesson not forgotten in Havana even today. But back then, there were more immediate concerns. The country had thrown in its lot and the conditions for its very survival with a supposedly eternal Soviet Union. The Cuban economy collapsed overnight. Havana was gripped by despair that soon turned to acute panic.

Still clinging to a tradition of euphemisms, this deep economic and social crisis was officially labeled *El Período Especial* (the Special Period). Havana had long been used to lining up for food and other necessities, but for all its shortcomings and unavoidable black-market correctives, the system had nevertheless worked.

The economic relationship with the Soviet Union was in essence based on bartering overpriced Cuban sugar against underpriced Russian oil. As a consequence, the country had long given up growing anything but sugar cane, which was now suddenly without a market, and electricity and transport in Cuba depended on the cheap oil, which was now drying up. Food was mostly imported from within the communist common trade system, the Comecon, and mostly from Soviet allies in Eastern Europe. That network was now also dead.

On top of the food shortages, and the black market taking over what little was still available, the energy shortages resulted in such frequent and extended power cuts that the joke became to replace the complaints about *apagones* (power outages) with short rejoicings over *alumbrones* (light-ups) at the rare moments of continued electricity.

During Havana's annus horribilis, 1994, thousands of boat people setting off from the Malecón under the eyes of overwhelmed policemen threw themselves on the mercy of the waves in improvised and unseaworthy rafts, hoping to reach Florida. Many would perish. In kindergartens in poor neighborhoods, toddlers scraped plaster from the walls to eat it, spontaneously trying to make up for vitamin deficiencies. I knew the habit from poor gypsy kids doing likewise in Andalucía.

Elegance and strong character had always represented the city's self image, as illustrated by her allegorical statues and by trademarks on cigar bands: a multiracial *india fina*, like the monument in the Parque de la Fraternidad. Now she was suddenly dressed in rags of despair.

It was Havana's Hour Zero.

16. PROPOSAL FOR A CONTROVERSIAL MONUMENT

Precisely then, I was preparing for my first years of work in Havana. In the spectacle of dismay witnessed all over the world, I heard from pundits and colleagues: "You'll live the Great Change." I was still unaware at the time that various generations of diplomats posted to Havana had believed and predicted this, and had had to pack up at the end of their four-year terms with their prophecies unfulfilled, useless as chapters for their memoirs.

But I was more guarded in my expectations, in part because my own background and childhood experiences had made me aware of resilience and capacities for survival. Unbeknownst to myself, I had captured Havana's soul even before knowing her.

After her Hour Zero, the clock started to tick again as of 1995. The army began to produce food to sell to the public. The black market was undercut by legalizing the possession and use of the U.S. dollar as legal tender. *Habaneros* were allowed to rent rooms to tourists.

Responding to these and similar measures, almost immediately a wave of foreign tourists flocked to Havana: a mixture of young backpackers and middle-aged men seduced in equal proportions by cigars, rum, music, political mythology, and easy sex, if not straightforward prostitution. Havana, reawakening the untamed spirit full of contradictions that she alone knows how to live with, catered to all. It turned the capital into a more vibrant, adventurous, and edgy place than it had been at any time since 1960. Nightlife of all descriptions and for all persuasions flourished as colorful anarchy, and was oddly tolerated by the establishment as long as it brought in the hard and convertible currency needed for the island's economic survival.

Forget Gorbachev: Fidel had his own plan, and Cuba would save herself her own way, taking the side effects and the excesses in stride.

Look the other way for a few years and tolerate all that has been forbidden but now brings you *fula*: dollars. Speed up the building of twenty-five thousand four-star hotel rooms on the beach of Varadero and on the *cayos*, with the help of Spain,

France, and Holland. Allow *habaneros* to produce some hand crafted souvenirs and open small restaurants for tourists. Send every unemployed musician to the Plaza de Armas to sing endless "Guantanameras" at a buck a pop. Keep the foreign youngsters amused in Havana while you negotiate with Canada and Europe to receive charter flights to bring the average tourist for a week to a Cuba that doesn't really exist. And of course, have every *habanero* who wants to take advantage of the new possibilities pay for a license and charge them a flat tax.

It worked remarkably well. And once the new system was up and running, there followed a thorough spring cleaning of the city, carried out by a special new police brigade to arrest every *jinetera* (prostitute) and to pull her off the arm of the *yuma*, or foreigner, by her side. This operation, too, was successful, on the surface. It's not that the naughty and rough Havana was wiped out; it simply went underground again, where it had been hiding for centuries.

In fact, the city should have built a monument to the Unknown *Jinetera*. Every city has moments as a muse and as a whore. In Havana's most miserable years, prostitution was a sizeable part of the new dollar economy, saving many families. It was in the statistics – or rather, in what the official statistics never showed. There was no longer any "black money," but the dollar expenses of the national budget widely exceeded the legitimate hard currency income. So where did all the other dollars come from? The *yanqui* currency no longer had a bad taste.

A close friend, a prominent salsa band leader, jokes that the *jineteras*, "social workers of the night," saved the Havana music scene by bringing their escorts to concerts, which would otherwise have played to empty theaters and *casas de la música*.

Abandoned by the hugging Soviet Bear, Havana was rescued by a dancing girl. She should be immortalized.

17. GOOD MONEY, BAD MONEY

It became a classic case of good money, bad money. Only in late 2004 was the dollar fully replaced by the so-called *peso convertible* of equal value. But the non-convertible peso or *moneda nacional* remained in circulation. The convertible peso is in fact not all that convertible, except one-way, from dollar or Euro, or any other real-world currency, to the CUC as it's known for short, but never the other way around. The main purpose of its introduction was to make retail and services twenty-five times more expensive than any price in the national peso, both for tourists and for Cubans lucky enough to own dollars.

It was unavoidable that more and more products would slide to the CUC-denominated commerce. But at the same time, all Cuban salaries were paid in *moneda nacional*, in a country where literally all employment depended on the State. This created a growing gap between the CUC market and the purchasing power of the average Cuban citizen. People with access to dollars and CUC could make do, whether the good money came from steadily growing remittances from family members in Miami, from tips in the expanding tourist industry, from the few tolerated private sector activities, or from shady dealings in Havana's night life.

For the others, the rationing booklet or *libreta*, providing basic foodstuffs at highly subsidized prices in state *bodegas*, was the only rescue. In better times, the State had provided all staple foods – rice, beans, chicken, eggs, cooking oil, bread, sugar, coffee, powdered milk – in sufficient quantities to maintain a balanced diet. There were also allowances for clothing, personal hygiene, and special packages for pregnant women. But as a consequence of the double money standard, more and more products disappeared from the subsidized network and ended up being available only in CUC. Those without access to it saw their diet and their basic comforts slip away.

Because Cuban agriculture is dramatically deficient – most of the cultivated land having been devoted to sugar cane, and a lot lying fallow – between 65 and 80 percent of all foodstuffs have to be imported, paid for in hard currency, and sold to poorer people at prices way below their cost. The weight of all this on the national budget is huge, made worse by the fact that the country now also has to feed more than three million tourists each year.

The government was and is well aware of all the social consequences this entails, especially the growing inequality between Cubans with and without CUC access. Economic reforms to remedy these ills went ahead in the second half of the 1990s. These included allowing more private activity and closing down sections of a largely unproductive public sector, attracting foreign investment to create better paying jobs, and attempts to improve the country's own food production.

These reforms were carried forward with support from Europe and Canada, but that support was never entirely unconditional. It was always somehow linked to a political discourse insisting on greater citizens' freedoms. Cuba swallowed this out of sheer necessity, and even Fidel Castro lent a diplomatic half-ear to this discourse during the frequent nighttime meetings with ambassadors that became part of his routine.

But then there was a spectacular new development.

In early 1999, Hugo Chávez came to power in Venezuela. He saw himself as Fidel's spiritual heir and started to provide support that was not just unconditional, but based on a strong political sense of brotherhood. Cuba's leadership now believed that their original dream, rescued from economic tatters, could be resuscitated and maintained forever.

The effects in Havana were immediate and tangible. Simply put: Chávez's generous supply of cheap oil brought back the electricity, and turned on the lights and the fans (or ACs for the happy few) for the long hot summer nights in Havana's crowded rooms and buildings. There is no denying that the people were grateful.

Chávez's support allowed Cuba's ruling elders to delay fundamental economic reform for another ten years, and the incipient reforms undertaken from sheer necessity since 1995 were either frozen or implemented with dragging feet.

18. THE ECONOMY AS A BOOK AND A BEAST

It took until 2011–2012 for the government to realize that President Chávez was mortal, and that Venezuela was now so deep into her own economic difficulties that the reform process in Cuba had to be taken up where it had ended in 1999.

In the meantime, Fidel had resigned from power in 2006 due to ill health, and his brother Raúl had taken over as leader of the Communist Party, the Government, the State, and the Armed Forces, all in one. Not only had economic reform come to a standstill, but the main architects of the 1990s changes – the dollar, limited private entrepreneurship, conditional foreign investment – had disappeared from the political scene.

By the time the Venezuelan aid was running out of steam due to President Chávez's declining health and Caracas's own troubles in 2012, the entire situation had created yet another time warp, like the 1950s Chevrolets still dominating the cityscape.

It was the debate about reforming a communist economy – a debate that had occurred between 1985 and 1989 in the Soviet Union, and was of course fatally lost by orthodox communists clinging to their dogmas while their society was waking up to entirely different realities. But Havana ignored this and tried to do it over.

To go again through all the false starts, absurd speculation, and pussyfooting around the crucial issues, as official Havana started doing in 2012 as part of the "updating" of the economy, was frustrating at best.

The very phrase *actualización del modelo económico* became coded language to avoid speaking outright of *reforms*.

Also, having to revert to the "Kremlinology" of the 1970s and early 1980s to gauge the daily reformist or conservative moods of leaders who were well into their eighties, was not exactly forward looking.

It became a long narrative of the past of the future: the sliding of an enforced utopia into the harsh realities of a freer but unforgiving world. On top of that, the world financial crisis of 2008 raised legitimate questions even for committed Cuban reformers: what did the outside world really have to offer? Weren't many Western politicians themselves now at a loss about the future?

A passionate onlooker would want to say, or sometimes scream: Friends, you haven't understood a thing. You treat the economy as if it were an intellectual exercise. But you know what? The economy is an animal. If you feed it, it will feed you.

Being an organism, the economy can be wild, it can be tamed, it can be controlled, and it can be manipulated. Freed up, it will drag you into a rollercoaster of wealth and misery; you don't want it to run wild, but you can't keep it caged forever either. Enormously complicated decisions face you, for which you have no training. You'll learn, like all of us, with black eyes and bloody noses, and there will be winners and losers. That, my friends, is the economy – because that's the human condition, too, for better or for worse.

But you have to let it live first, not suffocate it with rhetoric and academic overthink. Your theories cannot replace decisions. And sooner or later you – and the poorest of your people – will pay the price for the delays and for the hesitations: for if you don't make your moves, the good things will sink with the bad. The real-world economy will not obey linear decisions. Everything you decide will have side effects and ramifications you'll have to deal with. The economy is a very complicated animal indeed, and you will never be entirely on top. Even the BRIC countries are going through learning curves, realizing that you can't adopt capitalism as a pet; it will bite back, and you'll have to go through its cycles of boom and bust and all the unintended ills of rapid growth. But in Cuba, that process hasn't even really started yet.

Official Cuba still rejects the label of "an economy in transition." Cuba is supposedly just adapting and perfecting the system. The Chinese model goes too far. The Vietnam one feels better. We'll keep what we have, only make it better.

This may be a noble intention, but how feasible is it, with Cuba being where and what it is, in size, resource base, infrastructure, and outlook? Young people are not immune to the worst materialism, which has been exacerbated by the denial of its aspirations. Will not a massive brain drain soon bleed the island of her brightest?

19. LOOKING WEST — TO ASIA AGAIN

During the economic crisis of the 1990s, coinciding with the economic reforms in China, Fidel himself investigated the Chinese model. But given differences in scale, the proximity of the United States, and a very different labor situation, the conclusion was that it was not applicable in Cuba. It's not on record what Fidel thought about the side effects of accelerated industrialization in China, but he must have had an eye for the social consequences of cheap labor on a near cosmic scale. So there was to be no imitation of the Chinese model.

But what did happen was a resumption of trans-Pacific patterns. The new *pacotilla china* (Chinese merchandise rather seen as tacky "bling") which started flooding Cuba in the 2000s, included cheap consumer products for the new middle class that was emerging thanks in part to Miami remittances and family visits.

China was doing in Cuba what it did elsewhere in the region: getting a foot in the door and eyeing a future when Cuba would be the ideal springboard to reach the United States, with a widened Panama Canal around the corner. Significantly, the expanded port of Mariel would be managed by a company from Singapore. But Chinese suggestions, even between the Communist Parties on both sides, to allow for faster privatization or to open an internal capital market, fell mostly on deaf Cuban ears.

Looking for a more suitable Asian model, Cuba turned to Vietnam, a country with which it had had friendly relations going back to the Vietnam War. Many schools and other public institutions in Havana still bear heroic names from the war years. There is a large monument to Ho Chi Min in a park in Nuevo Vedado, and the Vietnamese General Giap, who beat the French at Dien Bien Phu, was always seen as a model for the Cuban armed forces.

Vietnam was thus an attractive example, but again, copying it was not possible. Cuba is an 80 percent urban society and Vietnam is rural in the same proportion. The work ethic is different and the acknowledged side effects of fast economic growth in Vietnam also frightened the Cuban establishment.

But could the Cuban economy achieve a blend like the one of the much loved *mulata china* to find its own best formula? It had worked for the mingling of the blood, but how could such a mixture of forces create prosperity and run the country?

That Cuba has just as much entrepreneurial spirit as China could easily be illustrated by the success of the Miami diaspora, and in Havana itself by the fast rise of trendy restaurants and bars when private initiative in selected sectors became further liberalized as of 2012.

But there are still huge differences with China.

The size of the economy, to begin with. The complications of the lingering U.S. embargo interfering with easy access to supplies and equipment and impeding access to the most natural nearby market. Access to credit. The rudimentary internal financial networks. A still rather restricted, or at any rate overregulated, environment for foreign investment. And, as a colleague of mine bluntly puts it, Cuba lacks a few thousand years of Confucianism.

So far, therefore, there has been no groundswell of private initiative or a massive move toward profitable manufacturing. Cuba's labor might be cheap — a fact that may become cynically exploited — but it is also over-qualified and mis-qualified. Few people are willing to till the land, and my guess is that even fewer are willing or would opt to participate in, and survive, industrial labor under hugely competitive circumstances. Entering the textile, sporting goods, and cosmetics industries as a late-comer, how can the country offer employment that is both remunerative and dignified? Should Cuba skip the industrial development phase, and enter the high-tech sectors immediately? Should it concentrate on biotech and pharmaceuticals and become a hub for immaterial trade and services? It's an attractive proposition. The geographical location and the brains are there, but how feasible will it be unless the old guard lets go of its controls and its illusions?

Cuba does not lack entrepreneurial spirit, but for the large majority of people coming from half a century of heroic slogans and quiet survival, it will be a very rude wake up call to discover what industrial capitalism is really like. Even in a mostly welcoming environment like Miami, waves of Cuban immigrants from the 1990s to the present have had difficulty adjusting to the competitive labor market, the eight-hour day, and the expected levels of productivity.

Already now in Havana, old-guard citizens stuck in the ideas of fifty years ago, clinging to the pride of their *cubanía* but with holes in their shoes, have to coexist with super-wired young hipsters and with a well-fed new middle-aged bourgeoisie flaunting their cars and their gold. How would I feel to be one of these elders standing on a grimy corner in Centro Habana, waiting for a squeaky *bicitaxi* to take me home, while the newly rich speed by in Miami-financed SUVs with extra chrome? In China, the newfound belief in upward mobility has so far made possible the coexistence of rich entrepreneurs and a poor workforce. But in Cuba, a generalized social intimacy developed over fifty years in an infinitely smaller territory makes that coexistence far more problematic.

But keep despair at bay. If anything is alive and kicking here, it's an enormous capacity for survival.

20. *LA MULA COMO VACA DE LECHE* (THE MULE AS CASH COW)

Even before the announcements of December 17, 2014, there were a number of weekly charter flights between Havana, Miami, and Tampa. A flight to and from New York existed on and off. These were used mainly by Cuban-Americans to maintain family ties. Since the December 17 breakthrough, the flights have multiplied quickly, and the trade they are used for has increased exponentially.

Summing up: an aunt or uncle visiting from Miami is now supposed to bring along a kind of standard package to fulfill the expectations resting on the successful emigrant. Judging from the enormous amounts of luggage coming off the flights, the average package contains a flat-screen TV, a computer, a Playstation, a mountain bike, and a microwave. The more demanding families will have asked for a Nespresso machine – cleverly creating the need for further visits to continue supplying the pods. The unavoidable next generation iPhones are probably carried as hand luggage, and you may safely bet that a few of the wheelchair passengers are faking a medical condition or a handicap in order to get the chair into the country duty-free.

Yet all this visible trade is still only the tip of the tropical iceberg. What's mostly needed from Miami is cash, and lots of it is coming – anywhere from three to five billion dollars a year. This enters in part as remittances handled by Western Union, whose offices in Cuba can receive but not send money. Those official remittances were subject to quite narrow restrictions from the U.S. side until recently. You could send only a limited amount in any three-month period, only to proven family members, and only by doing extra paperwork at the U.S. Western Union pay windows – often to the annoyance of the employee and of those waiting in line behind you. Although those restrictions were next to impossible to really enforce, they created a thriving network of *mulas* bringing large wads of cash dollars, tens of thousands at a time.

With a cheap metaphor about an expensive habit, I would say that Havana has replaced the *jinetera* with the *mula* as her cash cow.

21. *LA LIBRETA* (THE RATION BOOKLET)

The good money, bad money situation attacked the utopia where it hurt most: by recreating social class through cash, and by slowly undermining the protection of the weakest and most vulnerable members of society – often the ones who had blindly thrown in their lot with the ideals of the Revolution.

The U.S. dollar – the actual greenback – became legal tender in Cuba in the mid-1990s. As we have seen, this was a clever move to undercut the black market. Many essential products were scarce in the 1990s, and a thriving black market threatened to shift such products as were available more and more to the clandestine dollar economy.

For a while, the U.S. dollar coexisted with the same-value *peso convertible* and the *moneda nacional*. The triple monetary standard was managed very competently, and the short-term effects were good.

The exchange rate of the *moneda nacional* to the dollar improved dramatically (from about 150 to one to about twenty five to one), and inflation was brought under control. The free access of Cubans with dollars (from remittances or the margins of the nascent tourist industry) to dollar retail stores helped make sure that the new sources of income were spent in such a way as to ultimately flow into government coffers, as retail commerce in new stores and supermarkets remained state-controlled.

Thus, the dollar economy could subsidize the peso economy. Newly introduced *mercados agropecuarios* (produce and livestock markets) allowed state-controlled agriculture and especially the Armed Forces to sell excess produce directly to the public after filling centrally imposed quotas, likewise in non-convertible currency.

These measures saved the island from malnourishment with some help from NGOs like the Catholic charity Caritas, OXFAM, and even the B'nai B'rith community. But malnutrition among the elderly and in some rural pockets may become a growing risk.

The dollar was taken out of circulation and fully replaced with the convertible peso in 2004. This again was done competently and seamlessly, and the country never saw hoarding of good cash or hyperinflation. But the long-term effects of a double monetary standard could not be avoided.

By 2010, the slow erosion of the *moneda nacional* economy became tangible. The sliding of more and more essential products into the convertible currency market proved ultimately unavoidable. Salaries in the state sector – still the largest employer – remained and still remain denominated in non-convertible pesos.

The overall effect of these two sets of facts was growing social inequality.

The purchasing power of an average state salary in the convertible peso market became painfully low. State-employed citizens had to work several extra jobs, often way below their level of qualification, to make ends meet. Worst off were state pensioners relying exclusively on the *libreta* for their meager livelihood.

There was public debate about this situation, but it tended once more to be couched in highbrow macroeconomic jargon. No one dared to remind themselves or the government of the simple truth: that the double money situation had been introduced to recuperate the black market, that it had worked up to a point, but that it could not be upheld forever. It would require more fundamental changes: in the labor market, by introducing salaries with real purchasing power, and in book-keeping and national statistics, where the use of the double standard created artificial economic results.

The double monetary standard makes it indeed very difficult to gauge the real economic performance of the country. In state-controlled enterprises (the vast majority), both currencies are used for statistics in a one-to-one exchange rate, thus hiding the enormous discrepancies between the cost of imported inputs and the low real prices of the end products, in other words, hiding enormous and continuous losses. There is, therefore, no reliable system of national accounts, making it also very problematic for Cuba's foreign partners and friends to help where it's most needed.

But in spite of all this, the *libreta* and the *bodega* created a culture of entitlement and the expectation that the State will always care for you, which will be very difficult to erase after two generations. Lining up at the neighborhood *bodega* (there are 30,000 of them island-wide) is simply part of being Cuban, no matter how disappointing the rations are that you'll get when your turn comes up, *cuando te toca*. What you'll get is now often down to some rice and beans, bread and eggs. Eggs are always in good supply, even though a recently exposed scandal supposedly caused eight million of them to disappear on the black market. Officially, the *libreta* still provides 30 percent of a balanced diet, but anyone who knows the country well will dispute that. Church workers, familiar with situations in the provinces, put the figure as low as 10 percent.

Yet the *bodega* culture remains a part of *cubanía*. It's a common courtesy in Havana, even when approaching an ATM, to enquire *quién es el último*, who is the last in the line, so as to take your rightful place. This now begins to coexist with the opposite culture of elbowing your way to the top, even to keep your belly full.

22. EL CAÑONAZO

After a long day of standing in line, it's with a sigh of relief that Havana hears the daily *cañonazo*.

At nine p.m. sharp, every day, after an elaborate ceremony carried out by soldiers in eighteenth-century uniforms, the cannon called El Capitalino fires a loud blank over the port channel, from the ramparts of the Cabaña fortress, to signify the closing of the city gates. It's a loud *boom!* heard all over, sometimes even as far as the western suburbs, depending on how the wind blows.

These days the announcement is purely symbolic, of course. Havana was a walled city until the mid-nineteenth century. The tumbling of the walls in 1863 was a symbol of progress and the city breaking out of its colonial straightjacket. It was celebrated as a major public event. The independence struggle against Spain was slowly building up, and many in the crowds who heard the speeches and witnessed the music and patriotic flag-waving must have hoped in silence that the end of all the colonial shackles would soon follow.

The present trajectory of Prado is where the wall stood on the west side of town. All of what is now Centro Habana was *extra-muros*, and the elegant Vedado ("Forbidden") neighborhood was once, as its name indicates, a dangerous no-go area. To the east, a remnant of the wall and a bronze map of its outline are preserved just next to the railway station – another beautiful relic of former elegance, waiting for Cuba's extensive railway history and network to be restored. In the meantime, this is a zone with rather rough vibes, even by Old Havana standards, although the train station itself is now being restored.

The port area begins just east of that section of the wall. Up to the nineteenth century, this was a zone of stinking mangroves and badlands, the original turf of *los negros curros* (the black gangs), and another no-go area for the upright citizen. The gradual disaffection of the old port has again given it a somewhat forbidden atmosphere. The gangs roaming here in the old days had their distinctive flamboyant garb, preserved for us in paintings of the so-called *costumbrista* ("traditionalist") artists such as Federico Mialhe and Patrizio Landaluze. Like the bandits in Andalucía, the black gangs of Havana signified a kind of social revolt and resistance, including against slavery. The distinctive dress code of the men and their girlfriends alike, as captured in paintings to be seen today at the Museo de Bellas Artes, illustrated their fearlessness. Their clothing looks surprisingly like sixties hippy outfits, with bell-bottoms, colorful bandanas, loud polka-dot blouses, and long embroidered skirts. They also had peculiar hairstyles, their own slang (unintelligible to outsiders), their own signature swagger, and many filed their teeth to look more menacing. The way Fernando Ortiz described them, based on his older sources, they were a perfect mixture of the Andalusian gypsy underworld (the bell-bottoms were known as a flamenco style) and African traditions (especially the filing of the teeth).

The neighborhoods forming the forbidding *Manglar* and the other ganglands back then have kept their original names: Barrio Jesús María, Los Sitios. The port area remained very much the domain of Afro-Cubans up to the Revolution. Santería practices were concentrated there, and the powerful communist longshoremen's union ruled the neighborhood, led by the charismatic Aracelio Iglesias, who was murdered in 1948 and was later sanctified as an early precursor of the Revolution. But the Havana bourgeoisie defamed the union and the area by describing them as the hideouts for dark sorcery and male prostitution. The fabled *negros curros del Manglar* now became the despised *negros bugarrones del muelle* (the vulgar reference to "buggery" is intentional).

The curfew shot and the closing of the gates meant, among other things, that slaves had to be in their quarters. Immediately after the *cañonazo*, night watchmen or *serenos* began patrolling the streets of the city, chanting reassuring ditties on their rounds, to induce the honest citizen to sleep undisturbed.

But knowing Havana, one must think of what really happened while the innocent enjoyed their rest. The *serenos* chanted while all the forbidden night-life came crawling out from the deep shadows of the streets and from under the porticos of the palaces and the mansions: the fast-whispered passing of contraband by the side of a ship along the Muelle San Franciso; the deserter and the stowaway coming out of the hold of another ship at anchor, and disappearing to an uncertain fate in the muddy streets; sons of the well-to-do escaping from the back door of the family house to meet a forbidden brown or black lover; the flashing smile of the young prostitute; the deadly glint of long *navaja sevillana* knives for the settling of accounts in a passing beam of moonlight.

Sometimes it feels as if these two Havanas – the one constantly watched by *serenos* with reassuring words, and the other one crawling underneath – have never disappeared.

Havana by night was always untamable. The decrees of the Captains-General between 1770 and 1820 are an endless illustration of colorful anarchy, dancing criminality, interracial sex gone wild, and gambling all over, including in the convents. The law categorized all the vices it pretended in vain to eradicate. In fact, the city council itself was so corrupt that it lived mostly off the kickbacks of forbidden activities such as cockfights and the clandestine street lottery (which is still in existence in Havana today). Gambling, especially the card game *monte*, was strictly prohibited, and in fact the aldermen of the city charged a tax of an ounce of gold per day for each *monte* table. Slaves benefitted hugely from these situations because the gambling money helped them to buy their freedom faster. Unable to resist, the authorities finally created an official lottery in 1812.

When I think of this past of Havana by night, it often strikes me that we live yet again in similar ambiguities between taboo and tolerance; and it becomes ever clearer to me that Fernando Ortiz, who did his painstaking research on these themes, became ever more intrigued by the naughtiness he was supposedly criticizing.

During the first half of the twentieth century, Havana tried very hard to reform herself, with clean new neighborhoods full of impeccably designed and maintained architecture. We can still see them in luminous black and white pictures, on streets so empty that they seemed to exist in a permanent Sunday morning. It was as if Havana wanted to deny all of the dirt and stickiness of the past two hundred years.

But the exodus of the middle class after 1960 and the ensuing neglect sent Havana back to her original roughness, and not just in the port area or the former *Manglar*, but now all over the city. It was as if she developed in reverse. From seemingly well behaved and disciplined, she went back to being the wild quayside child she had always wanted to be, deep down.

The Revolution, too, tried very hard to chant reality into reassuring ideas with its endlessly repeated edifying slogans. Maybe this worked sometimes and for some. But in real life, night and the city will continue to follow their own rules and rhymes.

23. THE LAST SALVO

There is also an urban legend about the *cañonazo*.

In stark contrast with the United States, Cuba no longer practices the death penalty. The last executions by firing squad, in April of 2003, were sometimes said to have been carried out at the same fortress from where the cannon announces nightfall every evening. It was whispered that the timing of the executions was set so that the firing of the guns would coincide exactly with the cannon blast, by way of camouflage.

The three executed men were condemned for an act of piracy: they had hijacked the modest ferry boat going back and forth between Havana and Regla, full of subdued commuters, in an attempt to reach Florida. They ran out of fuel thirty miles from the coast and were brought back to Mariel. Their sentence might have been more lenient, had Cuba not wanted to make a point, both to her own people and to the world, that it would not tolerate terrorism in the aftermath of 9/11. Who, especially in the United States, could criticize harsh treatment of terrorists? No one was hurt during the episode, but Cuba's very last homegrown pirates lost their lives to politics.

In 2005, Cuba decreed an indefinite moratorium on the death penalty, in a decision much more in line with the country's declared humanism than with its often bloody past. The cannon blast on that April night had covered a last sinister salvo . . .

This urban legend, though, turned out to be just that. The executions were apparently carried out in a military barracks to the west of the city, far beyond the camouflage of the *cañonazo*.

24. 1762: BRITISH OCCUPATION AND A DEFINING MOMENT

The uniforms used during the daily *cañonazo*, as well as the cannon itself, date back to the period just after the short British occupation of Havana in 1762. It may seem farfetched to call this event and the eleven months of British rule a defining moment of Cuba's entire history, but this is indeed the case.

The reasons for the British invasion matter less that its effects. The invasion was one of the many tortuous side events of the endless wars between European powers that unavoidably spilled over into their Caribbean possessions. In this case, the Seven Years War (1756–1763) involved Britain, Spain, and France. But at least four essential events occurred in Havana.

First, the inadequate defense of the city by the Spanish upset the local aristocracy. The Marquesa de Santa Ana wrote to the king in Madrid, complaining that the city had not been conquered, but simply surrendered ("*dieron por conquista lo que fue rendición*"). The Cuban elite lost confidence in the colonial government. Ideas of political independence were next. The genie was out of the bottle. While loyalty to Madrid was still mandatory, Cuba's patriots now started to call the island *la patria chica*, the little motherland, and cultivated their own expectations for it, no longer coinciding with those of *la madre patria*.

Secondly, the short British occupation opened the port of Havana, normally restricted to trade with the motherland and other Spanish colonies, to a wave of free trade, and shipping began to flourish overnight. From an economic point of view, Spain was revealed as a dead weight on Cuba's shoulders, and for the first time a close relationship with continental North America began to look like a natural step for Havana.

In third place, Havana's spirit revealed itself as indomitable and uncontrollable, if also deeply opportunistic: it was essentially a port city, equipped for survival under any circumstances. The army and the government had surrendered in shame, but the people gladly danced and slept with the enemy. A famous satire from those days about casual sex in the warehouses reports:

Las muchachas de La Habana	The girls of Havana
No tienen temor a Dios	Have no fear of God
Y van con los Ingleses	And go with the English
Entre bocoyos de arroz	Between bales of rice

Fourth, the Spanish colonial system had developed Cuba as a commercial and administrative hub. But once the advantages of free trade had been sampled, Cuban landowners realized that they would be far better off if the country also became more productive. Sugar cane cultivation expanded, and with it the need for slaves. The great surge of slave imports during the late eighteenth and early nineteenth centuries greatly strengthened the African part of *cubanía*.

It was in the days of the British occupation that the first crude forms of Spanglish invaded the port, the taverns, and the warehouses (where, according to the poem, easy sex was on offer). Not surprisingly, the first expressions were the most vulgar ones, as reported by the chroniclers: *Sanavabiche! Guanti foqui?*

The governor who surrendered the city to the British, Juan de Prado Portocarrero, was sent back to Spain in disgrace. He is said by historians "to have lacked the experience for irregular warfare in the Americas and the Caribbean." He had also refused to side with Morel, the bishop of Santiago, who wanted to incite a people's *guerrilla* against the occupation. Morel's ideas would apparently not have worked anyway, but he was nevertheless shipped off to Florida by the British.

Many of the situations seen during that fateful year would return, almost identically, during the *Período Especial* that began in 1989, when the country was politically and economically adrift, and when Havana had to fall back on the same survival mode, with all its ingredients.

A new and vast wave of Spanglish is certainly hanging over Havana now; the Cuban street slang known as chabacano is already peppered with it. Havana remembers 1762 as if it were yesterday.

25. IT TAKES (AT LEAST) TWO TO *RUMBA*

Even the short British occupation shows how Cuba was always someone's treasured possession or partner. She was the proudest Spanish colony, and one of the last to be lost, in 1898, plunging Spain herself into a collective depression and into chaotic politics for three-quarters of a century, until Franco's demise in 1975.

The United States took over in 1900, treating Cuba as a business venture, and Havana partly as a colorful mistress and partly as an always-available prostitute. She became the nearest and most convenient playground to escape puritanism back home in matters of sex and alcohol. Then in 1960 came the Soviets with a new agenda and different interests, making her a pawn in global politics. After a short interregnum, there was Hugo Chávez of Venezuela, more generous and brotherly than any other suitor had been, but more mortal, too. All of them, taking turns, wanted Cuba for themselves.

So Cuba was never short of political dancing partners. But who would become the true love? As of 2012, and certainly after President Chávez's death in 2013, she was very much on her own for the first time in her history.

Didn't this come with deep anxieties? Could she afford to play hard to get? It takes two to tango, but acrobatic Cuban *rumba* can be danced with several partners simultaneously.

Even while Venezuela was still the favorite, Brazil entered the scene in an impressive way, financing the expansion and modernization of the port of Mariel, a project essential to Cuba's economic future.

Brazil under president Lula also brought its experience of combining a fast-growing economy with a social agenda, and it was becoming a regional powerhouse, a relatively short distance from Havana. Due to its desire to be a regional player, Brazil decided to stay engaged even after being hit by its economic downturn in 2015. The Brazilian discourse toward Cuba was also that Brazil stood for an intelligent twenty-first-century socialism, as opposed to the outdated dogma-ridden variant.

Canada always kept its low-key presence and also stayed politically engaged.

With the United States, the Bush years were mostly a lost era. The relationship was often a rollercoaster. U.S. diplomats frequently pointed out that the United States had made repeated attempts to engage Cuba in a positive way: under President Carter, under President Clinton, and even under the second President Bush, when large-scale trade in food-stuffs was legalized in spite of the embargo. But someone on the Cuban side had always thrown a spanner into the works. President Obama, in his first term, had not fared differently. During those years the United States had greatly relaxed certain aspects of the embargo – family, academic, and religious visits, remittances, commerce – but the arrest and sentencing of U.S. Jewish activist and alleged spy Alan Gross in 2009 blocked rapprochement. This created a new stalemate for official contacts and improvements, although the coast guards of both sides and the DEA maintained a professional relationship.

U.S. universities and think tanks visited Havana regularly, as did individual members of Congress. On the Cuban side, official attitudes towards the United States constantly switched between apocalyptic rhetoric and businesslike co-operation, most notably in consular matters. Most Cubans, on the other hand, simply love the U.S. Many if not most of them have family living there. The United States is the only society many Cubans know, or at least think they know, other than their own. And the older generation is still fanatically addicted to *pelota*, baseball.

But the essential question, how to deal in the long run with the neighbor next door, remained unanswered till the morning of December 17, 2014.

Or was it answered even then?

By the summer of 2015, both sides were opening embassies and had normalized their formal relations. President Obama did something essential: he showed respect. Nothing is more important in this part of the world, and no other condition is as crucial to living side by side. Maybe it took the *person* of Mr. Barack Obama, before the president, to understand and acknowledge that. Confidence building starts with people before it can move to institutions. Respect was the first step. How will both societies interact in the future? That's a much more complicated question. The U.S. and Cuban societies continue to live very much on different planets. It will be very challenging for Cuba to make any new relationship with her former master and longtime enemy a win-win situation.

The urgency of a new relationship with the United States, especially for the Cuban economy, was further illustrated in late 2015, when the victory of the anti-Chávez parties in the parliamentary elections in Venezuela cast even more doubts on the future of the extensive help Cuba received from Caracas. A new wave of uncontrolled migration to the United States – the largest since the *balsero* crisis in 1994 – was revealed when the dismantling of a network of *coyotes* left thousands of Cuban migrants stranded in Central America. Around 50,000 Cubans are now emigrating every year, about 1 percent of the active population. To stem this flow hemorrhaging from the society and the economy, new partnerships are urgently needed.

26. SITTING DOWN (AND MORE) WITH EUROPE

And then there was Europe, the oldest suitor of all.

In April of 2014, the European Union and Cuba started negotiations on an overall political and economic agreement. In the meantime, secret negotiations between Cuba and the United States were underway. Havana was cleverly two-timing her oldest suitor. Well, as Napoleon said, in sex and war everything is legitimate. The European initiative had been in preparation since 2008 when the EU rebooted its political dialogue with Havana. Between 2003 and 2008, relations had been at a low point following a series of strong measures against the island's dissidents.

It took years of internal diplomacy within the EU and its institutions to reach a consensus about negotiating with Havana. The EU's relations with Cuba were ruled by a Common Position adopted in 1996. This was a unilateral document with strong emphasis on political demands from the European side.

The Common Position was a product of its times in more than one way. In the mid-1990s, Cuba was passing through its worst economic and social crisis ever. Some predicted imminent collapse. The EU set out its expectations. In Europe the post-communist wave of optimism was strong, and the former satellite states of the USSR were all candidates for EU membership on short notice.

But the Common Position also came into being at the very moment when individual EU Member States, filling the gaps left by the disintegration of the Communist bloc, became very active in Cuba as investors, trading partners, suppliers of new credit, and as the source of hundreds of thousands of tourists.

These new links created the need for specific agreements

in the economic and legal fields, whereas the Common Position was aimed at achieving certain political principles. Of course the Cuban side always saw this as promoting regime change and as an unacceptable interference.

The Common Position was by and large a victory for the conservative Aznar government in Madrid. In Spain, as in the United States, Cuba tends to be a theme of domestic politics. When the socialists are in power, they want a comfortable relationship with Havana, and when the conservatives win an election, they accuse the left of catering in Cuba to the kind of dictatorship they despised at home under Franco.

Ever since 1996, the EU has had this two-track relationship with Cuba: adhering to a very principled policy as a whole, and evolving towards pragmatic state-to-state relations at the level of individual members.

Sixteen years have passed in this position. More than twenty of the present twenty-eight EU Member States now have individual agreements with Cuba. In part thanks to these agreements, the EU has become the island's second most important economic partner. But in some instances, those agreements – especially the more recent ones – have also included political elements. Remember the multiple *rumba* metaphor: Havana sat at the negotiating table with the EU as a whole, and meanwhile was flirting expertly with each individual member state.

The political demands enshrined in the Common Position may not have lost their relevance in the eyes of its defenders, but at the same time the EU is seeking to harmonize its values with the interests of all Member States, and to engage Cuba on the same terms the EU applies to all its other partners.

This is a forward-thinking strategy. Cuba has increasingly involved itself in the Caribbean and the wider Latin American region. In the Caribbean, Cuba's weight is considerable in terms of geography, land mass, proximity to shipping lanes and markets, quality of the workforce, and more. It punches above its weight in multilateral institutions, and in many places and with many people Cuba still enjoys a reserve of sympathy well beyond the true political appeal and resonance the island may have had during the Cold War. Also, the resilience of the Cuban government, the expectations of Cuban society, and the need to support ongoing economic reform, make it more necessary now to talk *to* Cuba rather than *about* it.

Cuba is a unique crossroads, where a blend of American, African, European, and even Asian cultures has been forged over the centuries. This peculiar blend is still being enriched and expanded every day — suffice it to observe the vitality of Cuba in the fields of music, the visual arts, and film. Cuba is a country with a strong sense of history, identity, and destiny. The EU, as a global player, felt it should be part of the ongoing chapters of this history.

In the meantime, beginning in 2008, the Cuban state media had lots of fun describing the "collapse" of the European Union under budgetary austerity measures and their social consequences. Then, from 2015, the refugee crisis and the EU's at times chaotic response, didn't help either. During the worst of the economic difficulties in Greece and Spain, the EU was accused of responding with "neoliberal authoritarianism," and doing away with social gains. To which a possible answer was: don't make fun of the end of the European social model, for it may well be the future of the Cuban system, and our struggle to keep it sustainable will also be yours. But such quiet wisdom didn't stand much of a chance of being heard, even less of being taken to heart. For official Cuba had long adopted the habit of seeing Europe through its U.S.-inspired experiences and prejudices.

Europe's message to Cuba is in fact a simple and very straightforward one: first, Europe has vast experience in turning around centrally planned communist economies to make them prosperous and market-based; and second, Europe – for all the turmoil the EU may be going through – stands for a third option between unfettered capitalism and unsustainable communism. Isn't that a possible model for Cuba's future?

But Cuba must choose her partners now, based on what each has to offer. In December 2016, Cuba and the EU finally signed their comprehensive agreement, after the EU had withdrawn the Common Position loathed by Havana. It was like old lovers finally marrying after years of quarrels. But we take nothing for granted: Havana will always know how to surprise us.

27. *CUBA NO SOY* (I AM NOT CUBA)

Now that we have begun to get to know Havana, it becomes clear how she was abused even by those pretending to be her friends.

Take the movie *Soy Cuba*. This Cuba-Soviet coproduction from 1964 is still seen as a classic by many cinephiles. I disagree.

The screenplay by Evgeniy Evtushenko is sustained by a heavy-handed Slavic melancholy. Director Mikhael Kalatozov admittedly pulls off remarkable feats of cinematography, especially an endless travelling shot through the city. But as for content, to me the movie just has too many things wrong. It perpetuates the lie that in Cuba before the Revolution there were only plutocrats and paupers. In a typically propagandistic distortion, it ignores the existence of the large urban middle class. Of course there was dire poverty in the countryside, and the social contrasts were huge. But much of the middle class had supported the Revolution until it became communist and imposed full social controls. Not to mention that the working class had strong and fiercely independent unions.

To ignore all of that, and moreover to see a Soviet team declare that they "are Cuba," is simply an insult to the real country.

The tearful voice-overs about pure misery only illustrate that the Soviets never had a clue about the real Cuba: the inextricable mixture of harshness and *alegría*, of living hard or surviving on the edge, of exuberant music and the deadly whip, of opportunism coexisting with fierce self-respect. For that very reason the Russians could never belong here, and could only become a footnote to Cuba's history.

The contrasting of rich and poor in a decadent pre-revolutionary Havana and in the countryside has little to do with the real Cuba. Those contrasts, excessively propagandized in Soviet-style, now look ridiculously misstated.

I got my last cynical laugh about the movie when Sloppy Joe's bar reopened in Old Havana in 2013. The scenes intended to be disgustingly decadent were put on a loop on the bar's TV screens to illustrate pre-revolutionary elegance.

Someone in the spheres of power must have intervened, because after a few weeks the loop was replaced with Eroll Flynn's *The Big Boodle* – a much safer choice for showing pre-1959 Havana. Such things never happen by coincidence here. We'll follow Flynn's real footsteps in Havana in a later chapter, because they are better than a movie script.

Other than that, the only good thing about *Soy Cuba* is the exuberant poster designed by René Portocarrero, then at the height of his talent as a graphic artist. Now that's a classic movie poster. Luckily, it has nothing to do with the content of the movie. It shows the strong profile of a woman's face, with the weight of Cuba's complex history woven into a chaotic headdress. That poster may rightly proclaim to be Cuba. Portocarrero, the best known Cuban painter after Wilfredo Lam, always remained true to his inspirations and never descended into propaganda, although he stayed in Cuba after the Revolution, while Lam lived mostly in Europe. You may still purchase copies of the *Soy Cuba* poster, printed from the original litho, at the Taller de Serigrafía René Portocarrero.

My irritation is even worse because Cuba's very own movie directors were so much better than the imported false gods of Soviet cinema. Tomás Gutiérrez Alea's *Memorias del subdesarrollo* gives a striking and nuanced image of Cuban society in the early 1960s, when all the contradictions set off by the Revolution became apparent. There is real soul-searching there, and pain and loss and confrontation between real people on real issues, not between stereotypes and archetypes.

28. TRAFFIC LIGHTS OF HISTORY

Nowhere in Havana is the existence of a strong pre-revolutionary middle class more obvious than in the Vedado neighborhood, situated between Centro Habana and the Río Almendares.

In Centro Habana the urban neglect looks truly desperate at times, also because this brick and concrete jungle has few green oases. But in Vedado, the edges of the elegant mid-sized family houses are softened by overgrown gardens. Beneath the shade of their own leaves, the patiently spreading roots of laurels and banyans pierce and lift the sidewalks, making the stone seem alive. There are palaces here, too, especially along Paseo between Línea and the Plaza de la Revolución, but Vedado's real life is hiding in the grid of side streets where comfortable houses with an endless variety of balconies and verandas seems to exist in one enormous leafy labyrinth.

The two main thoroughfares of Vedado, Línea and Calle 23, are linked with many such streets. Calle 12 stands out.

From Línea, it runs straight to the monumental gates of the Cementerio Colón, Havana's equivalent of Paris's Père Lachaise. We'll visit the cemetery and its celebrities later – a necessary visit, for many of Havana's ghosts and demons operate out of Colón.

This stretch of Calle 12 has a number of traffic lights. The most important one forces you to a longish stop at the corner of Calle 23. Looking to your right, a bas-relief runs around the corner of the building facing both streets. It commemorates Fidel's proclamation of socialism on this very corner on April 16, 1961. And his quote: "of the humble, by the humble, for the humble." When you look at the traffic light again, hoping for it to change, the gates of the cemetery loom ahead of you. In these two glances, you get a very real perspective on *socialismo o muerte*.

Driving again, you ask yourself, was this a threat or a promise, or a canny combination of both? And was the street corner for this statement chosen on purpose? Living long enough in Havana, you stop believing altogether in coincidences, as there always seems to have been a plan. Was Fidel saying: make a left turn here, people, or else go straight to you know where? Propaganda may mostly be a blunt instrument, but tattooed on the flesh of this city, it acquires its subtleties.

The first traffic light on the same stretch, closer to Línea, was more irritating as it was an extra slow one, apparently giving undue priority to a random side street. The traffic light was recently removed, but you'll see that that side street still has a military control point at the corner and access remains prohibited. Why?

If a visitor asks that question to a respectful elderly taxi driver, chances are the answer will be that here lived *la combatiente* Celia Sánchez.

Celia Sánchez was Fidel's companion and perhaps his great love during the early days of the revolution in the Sierra Maestra. She remained his right hand after the taking of Havana, looking – or so the legend says – at all the letters and requests he received, and writing or dictating the answers. She died in 1980, and Fidel was said to be devastated. Her apartment became a shrine where he was rumored to come regularly, to meditate or listen to her ghost. Maybe those were the unlikely nocturnal escapades into the city? Hence the checkpoint and the slow traffic light. Okay so far. Even with all the legitimate mistrust one has to apply to political hagiography, I'd like to believe in this very humane face of the events.

But whenever you are thus stopped by a traffic light of history, while on an urgent errand for the living, as is often my case, impatience overcomes respect for those emotions. The poorly educated adolescent inside of me starts shouting: People, she's long gone, okay? She'll never walk along that street again, *capisce*? Please, wake up.

But you see, the past is still stronger here than the passing urges of the new generations. Celia's ghost rules this block, and you have to sit and wait for her pleasure to let you pass. The veneration of the past, applied to many other ghosts, is truly suffocating at times, especially when there are so many unresolved challenges for the living. It's upheld by the official newspapers, which often carry headlines referring to the 1960s, if not the 1890s. Granted, my impatience is disrespectful, and even immature at my age. But I've never trusted saints' lives written by true believers. So I tried to find out the truth for myself. By sheer coincidence, when I went to see a friend, her mother mentioned that she had known Celia well. "She was a very nice person, really a bit like an early hippy." There was even a poetic side to her origins: she was born in a place called Media Luna, Half Moon, in Oriente.

I am now a little more patient when passing by her block.

29. GHOSTS OF REVOLUTIONS PAST

La combatiente Celia Sánchez is now resting at Colón. There is also a monument in her honor in Parque Lenin (see Chapter 32), sometimes confusingly referred to as her mausoleum. She is at home among other combatants, in the cemetery's Pantheon of the Armed Forces.

Before entering Colón, as a Santería initiate you'll have to ask permission from Oya, mistress of the graveyard, in Cuban syncretism identified with the Catholic Virgen de la Candelaria. You'll pay a small fee, which you'll slide into the interstices of the bright yellow cemetery wall. To fully comply with procedure, you should also rattle the dried seed pod of a poinciana tree, but as that may not be at hand, we'll take a risk and skip this part.

Let me take you now to the grave that, for me, houses the most ominous of Havana's ghosts, and the one who is most active in my mind, bothering me constantly.

That's the ghost of Alejo Carpentier, who without any doubt or discussion is Cuba's greatest twentieth-century writer. His tomb is easy to find, two blocks to the left of the main cemetery gate in the lane next to the outer wall. It bears the inscription: "I was a man of my times, and my times were those of the Cuban Revolution."

Alejo Carpentier's message from beyond the grave
at Cementerio Colón.

Carpentier, born in 1904, died in 1980, when the Revolution was twenty years old. He had thrown his lot in with Fidel, to all appearances, and was rewarded accordingly. From 1966 until his death he lived in Paris as ambassador of Cuba to France. Due to his background, even in Cuba he always spoke Spanish with a strong French accent. The greatest of Cuban writers was of uncertain origins, about which he spread his own myth. He pretended to have been born in Havana, the son of a French architect and a Russian pianist. In fact it seems he came from humble origins in Switzerland, and that his family later migrated to Cuba, where he grew up in rural Artemisa, far from the refined environment of European intellectuals in the capital. As a boy he worked for a milkman in the small town of Alquizar. I never understood why he needed to lie about his childhood, because his modest background makes his later trajectory even more remarkable.

His masterpiece, *El siglo de las luces*, "The Century of the Enlightenment" (translated into English as *Explosion in a Cathedral*), is a long meditation on the risk of any revolution to lose its own soul, or even to bring about the changes it promises.

Using the spread of the French Revolution to the Caribbean as his paradigm, he vividly describes the arrival of the guillotine as the first tangible sign of a new era. One of the main characters says, in essence, that the French Revolution has failed but perhaps the next one will be the right one. He pleads to be saved from "Better Worlds" created only with words, and complains of the excess of words to which his times have surrendered. He says there is no promised land – except maybe for the one man can find looking inward. Of course all of this, including the reference to long speeches, refers to the Paris of the 1790s . . .

Now when I stand by Carpentier's tomb at Colón, his epigraph sounds to me like an excuse from beyond the grave: *I couldn't help myself*. Surely the distance from Cuba, and the knowledge of European history not rewritten by propaganda, had had an effect on him.

But why, then, did he remain faithful until the end? Wasn't that an intimate betrayal of his true insights?

The dilemma was this: Carpentier had suffered long years of exile from the political right, and if he didn't go on believing in the left, he would become politically and spiritually homeless. Those were times of clashing, contradictory truths, of the good guys vs. the bad ones. It's also possible that he wanted to give himself the most Cuban persona possible, due to his unclear nationality.

To many of that generation, there were no gray areas. In

France, a staunch Communist party remained true to itself, in spite of Stalin's ghost. An entire generation of French intellectuals was obliged to keep professing Marxism, even against their own better judgment, in order not to lose their academic credibility or their university tenure. The Cold War allowed a hugely simplified vision of the United States to provide the new Bad Guys, and to maintain an ongoing conflict with the fascism of the 1930s and '40s, long after Hitler had been defeated.

Seen from Paris, Havana standing up to the United States was a perfect paradigm to maintain and to justify this attitude.

It has been given to my generation to see all so-called absolute truths in politics revealed for what they were and are and will be. This was not the case for Carpentier, who stubbornly held on to a final illusion. This was and is true of many Cuban intellectuals, who may yet have to pay the price for the mental slaloms they have imposed upon themselves in order to maintain fifty years of acquiescence. In a world today made up almost entirely of gray areas, intellectual adherence to unchanging truths has become a professional hazard.

Gabriel García Márquez is said to have been so impressed by *El siglo de las luces* that he tore up the first draft of *Cien años de soledad* and started over. Yet, in my humble view, he didn't get the true message from Carpentier's masterpiece (infinitely superior, in my personal taste, to the verbose magical realism of the idolized Colombian, winner of the Nobel Prize). I frequently saw García Márquez in Havana enjoying privileges granted by the Cuban establishment grateful for his support. Had he joined the ranks of the Cuban intellectuals in surrendering without reservation to the "excess of beautiful words" subtly denounced by Carpentier? After García Márquez's passing, in April 2014, Cuba granted him the last honors as one of her heroes. When I saw him for the last time, at a late-night concert at the club El Gato Tuerto close to the Hotel Nacional, I asked myself if deep down in his own conscience, he could justify his persona as a great humanist, knowing all the deeds and side-effects of Revolutions. The same question may be asked, sooner or later, of two generations of Cuban intellectuals, and it haunts me every time I hear Carpentier's whispers.

30. MUCH LOUDER GHOSTS

Alejo Carpentier's ghost is discreet. Other monuments at Colón are less so. Least of all, the monument to the victims of the Maine.

Here's the story: The U.S. battle cruiser *Maine* exploded while at anchor in the Havana harbor on February 15, 1898. It remains one of history's mysteries whether this was an accident or a terrorist attack, and if the latter, whether manipulated or not. The suspicion that it was a manipulated event remains, because the explosion provided a pretext for the United States to enter the ongoing Cuban independence struggle against Spain. This intervention became the Spanish-American War of Randolph Hearst and young Teddy Roosevelt. Since this determined Cuba's incomplete independence as a quasi-U.S. protectorate under the Platt Amendment, and later the Revolution's anti-Americanism, it's not a metaphor to say that the echoes of this explosion in 1898 are still with us today.

The monument at Colón is now an empty epitaph. The remains of the 261 victims were disinterred and brought to the United States as early as 1899, and now rest at Arlington National Cemetery. On the Malecón, another grand monument erected in 1926 commemorates the event. The American eagle at its top was removed after the Revolution and a copy of it is now at the U.S. ambassador's residence in Havana, only waiting to return to its perch, as U.S. diplomats in Cuba sometimes joke. I always wonder, wouldn't it be better for the eagle to stay put where it is, legitimately at home, rather than spread its wings over the Malecón again?

The Maine's was not the only loud bang of its kind in the Havana harbor. In March 1960, the Coubre, a French freighter carrying a shipload of arms from Antwerp, Belgium, likewise exploded in the port while being unloaded. At least 75 people died and 200 were wounded. Fidel immediately blamed the United States, but there are other conspiracy theories about the event, including that it was a terrorist act by Algerian independence fighters. (The struggle against France, with extreme violence on both sides, was then at its worst.)

Fidel would tell me musingly, during a dinner in 1998, that he knew the quality of all the good Belgian weaponry lost to Cuba that day. Where to get arms must have been constantly on his mind back then, as the threat of invasion was always present. And when he made his April 1961 speech at the corner of 23rd and 12th that we visited earlier, one of his most telling statements was that the Revolution "would henceforth hand out guns instead of voting ballots." It's said that Cuba's close and enduring relationship with North Korea is based on the fact that the Kims never refused arms to Havana. During an embarrassing episode in July 2013, the North Korean freighter Chong Chon Gang was caught in the act of smuggling vintage Cuban MIG fighter jets through the Panama Canal, allegedly for repairs back home. The planes and other weaponry were naively stacked under bags of sugar, as if none of the parties had ever heard of a scanner, or simply didn't care. The UN Security Council intervened, as this was a breach of a weapons embargo against Pyonyang. But Cuba got lucky: other simultaneous events in the world drew more attention, the United States did not want to complicate the secretly ongoing talks with Cuba by insisting on sanctions, and the case was dropped for all practical purposes. Cuba will still get her guns, for as a quote from Fidel on some walls still proclaims: "*Todo cubano tiene que saber tirar, y tirar bien*" ("Every Cuban needs to know how to shoot, and how to shoot well").

Of all these weapon-shipping stories, the Coubre explosion produced the most lasting side effect. The iconic portrait of Che Guevara by Alberto Korda, one of the most enduring images of the last century, was shot during a memorial service for the Coubre victims.

31. NAPOLEON IN CUBA

If Alejo Carpentier was right in seeing the French Revolution as an omen of all the later ones, who better to illustrate his point than Napoleon, the ultimate imperialist posing as a rebel?

Napoleon's own track record with the Caribbean was a particularly bad one, as he was responsible for reintroducing slavery after it was abolished during the idealistic phase of the Convention in 1798.

Napoleon was also responsible for the betrayal, kidnapping, and early death in miserable captivity of Haiti's independence hero Toussaint L'Ouverture. But Haiti wrought vengeance upon his family: his beloved sister Pauline's first husband, General Leclerc, died during the doomed French expedition against Haitian independence.

Pauline is said to have discovered her later uninhibited sexuality in Haiti's sultry climes. A stereotype? She had no qualms about flaunting her sex appeal, as her topless sculpture as a Roman seductress by Canova illustrates; but her brother felt guilty about his part in Haiti's struggle later on. His handling of the slavery issue was apparently the only thing troubling his conscience during his last exile on St. Helena.

Cuba's national hero José Martí had no doubts about it. He visited Paris in 1874 and again in 1879 and met with the then world-famous actress Sarah Bernhard and with Victor Hugo, who saw Martí as a great man indeed. Martí also visited Napoleon's grave, absorbed the atmosphere surrounding it, and dismissed the Emperor's ghost as that of a vile imposter: *el corso vil, el Bonaparte infame*. When French intellectuals desperately try to contrast Napoleon's humanism with Anglo-Saxon mercantilism, they are alas completely mistaken when it comes to Caribbean history. When Martí meditated by Napoleon's "sterile red marble tomb," he saw him for the imperialist he was, and hence as a natural enemy of the freedom Martí would give his life for. For Martí, Napoleon's triumphal flags were drenched in the blood of conquered peoples. Fidel also visited the tomb, in March 1995, apparently without any of Martí's objections, although he always saw himself as Martí's successor ("What Martí promised, Fidel fulfilled.") Even today, Paris aspires to be the natural counterweight against overwhelming U.S. influence in the Cuba of the future.

In sharp contrast with Martí's disgust, Napoleon's ghost was enthusiastically conjured up in Havana by Julio Lobo, the pre-revolutionary sugar king and avid collector of Napoleonic memorabilia. A self-made, high-living member of the sacharocracy (originally called Wolf, a German family name he translated literally into Spanish), Lobo apparently had imperial ambitions, even down to imitating Napoleon's signature arm-in-vest posture.

On October 11, 1960, Lobo was told by Che Guevara (who was at that time president of the National Bank) that his reign was over, and that all of his mills and factories would be nationalized. He fled Cuba on October 13, leaving behind his collection of Napoleon memorabilia along with his other treasures (he also owned an El Greco, among other masterpieces). The Government took the collection and later transferred it to a grand mansion next to Havana University, the Casa Orestes Ferrara, where the Museo Napoleónico is still housed today. I knew it in a somewhat dilapidated and abandoned state in the 1990s, but *la princesse* Napoleon, aided by the French Embassy, later made a refurbishment possible, and today the collection is adequately cared for.

Among the artifacts of more or less true historical relevance is a copy of Napoleon's death mask and a lock of his hair, certified as authentic by a letter from a consul at St. Helena.

It's a little known fact that Napoleon's last personal physician, his fellow Corsican Francisco Antommarchi, died in Cuba in 1838. Since he witnessed Napoleon's passing, the death mask now in the Havana museum is supposed to have been among his possessions.

The lock of hair has a story of its own, as there is a conspiracy theory about the British slowly poisoning Napoleon in his last exile, a theory sometimes said to be proven by the high arsenic content detected in the surviving hair samples.

What did Fidel, often targeted for poisoning by what he saw as the new Anglo-Saxon Empire, think about this detail?

32. THE ORESTES FERRARA SECRET

There is yet another fascinating secret related to Napoleon's Havana museum.

The palatial building where it is housed belonged before the Revolution to Orestes Ferrara, a political henchman of President Machado in the 1930s. Machado is one of the former leaders most despised by Cuba's revolutionaries.

In January 1959, the *barbudos* were approaching Havana. Fulgencio Batista had fled. There was fear of chaos and looting, as desperate hangers-on and shady enforcers of the fallen regime were still around, and feelings of resentment and vengeance were running high.

Apart from the human cost, many of the highly educated revolutionaries within the capital were also concerned about Havana's art treasures. The city was full of priceless works and artifacts, accumulated since colonial times by governments, aristocrats, and the newly wealthy. It's said that Havana had the highest per capita concentration of grand pianos of any city in the Americas or even in the world. At the time of Batista's flight, the American actor George Raft was in bed with Miss Cuba 1958 in a suite in the Hotel Capri. He would later give his personal version, reliable or not, of the vandalism and the looting that started around three a.m., when Batista's departure became known.

In stepped Natalia Bolívar Aróstegui, a scion of the oldest Cuban aristocracy, fearless and athletic, a champion swimmer and a revolutionary of the first hour. She was also a Santería initiate, and in later life would become the intellectual high priestess of Afro-Cuban traditions, publishing several standard works on the subject.

Natalia, with the commanding presence of an aristocratic revolutionary, made sure none of the art collections were disturbed. She also took a particular interest in the Ferrara mansion. It was at risk because it stood just next to the university – always a hotbed of rebellion – and because it was closely associated with the hated former president Machado. She made an amazing discovery in the mansion.

There was a secret tunnel, running from the house all the way under the Vedado neighborhood to a hidden seaside exit under the Malecón wall, where a speedboat could be moored for a quick departure.

In the worst years of Cuban politics, marred by violence and corruption, even the closest allies of Machado (Cuba's president from 1925 to 1933) had to take their own personal precautions.

Natalia and her companions explored the full length of the tunnel, which was over a mile long. They used divers' oxygen equipment as a precaution, but the tunnel was intact and they suffered no mishaps. It was Natalia herself who told us this story, during a memorable dinner at my house in Siboney in 2015. In her eighties, she's still as feisty and original as ever. But when I tried to check the facts with Cuban officials, they were very skeptical and even denied the existence of the tunnel. I still believe Natalia, because her story had the flavor and immediacy of real-life experience.

There are more stories about the secrets under the surface of Cuba's capital. Under the Hermanos Amejeiras Hospital – a building originally planned as the central bank – vast vaults intended for Batista's gold are said to exist. Other rumors say that enormous underground shelters to protect 10 percent of the population in case of nuclear war were built in the 1960s. In certain neighborhoods in and around the capital, mysterious entrances to this or that section of the underworld can be seen, continuing to feed the urban legends. In a city with so many layers of history, it's only normal that more layers exist beneath our feet. One may add that, according to geologists, most of Cuba is standing on hollow coral reefs.

Orestes Ferrara's tunnel may only be a modest example of Havana's secret underground, but still stands as proof of how fickle and dangerous Cuban politics could be.

The entrance to the tunnel, in the floor of one of the main rooms in what is now the Napoleonic Museum, was sealed off, but for all I know, the tunnel still exists. But there are no more such easy getaways.

Immediately after his meeting with Che Guevara, Julio Lobo tried to hide some of his treasures in another secret passage under his office in Old Havana. But the house was surrounded by police the next morning and hermetically sealed.

The legend of many such treasures hidden in houses in Vedado and Miramar remains vivid. I know of at least two cases of discoveries of gold bars and jewels. Lobo understood right away that the Revolution was there to stay, but many of his class regarded it as a folly that would soon blow over, hid their valuables when they fled, and planned to return.

But Havana's greatest subterranean secrets are her military tunnels.

Shortly after the Revolution, the leadership developed a very specific doctrine of national defense. Cuba could never hope to resist a full-fledged U.S. invasion, which often seemed likely and at times unavoidable, with classic warfare. Fidel pinned his hopes on a threefold strategy: as much camouflage and subterfuge as possible, spreading out troops and equipment widely and thinly over the entire island's territory, and continued resistance by autonomous units if a central command could no longer operate. It was essentially a bureaucratically sanctioned *guerrilla*. The ultimate aim was to make a U.S. invasion such a costly operation in terms of U.S. losses that it would be a pyrrhic victory at best.

Hiding all heavy military equipment underground to avoid

early detection was thus part of the doctrine. The enormous network of shelters filled with mostly vintage 1960s tanks, planes, and artillery is still there, underfoot.

33. THE CAVE AT THE END OF THE WORLD

The then-president of the National Bank who gave Julio Lobo the bad news has become a universal icon.

No image is more popular on Havana's walls or on visitors' T-shirts, than Che Guevara's heroically stoic face gazing into the distance. What was he seeing in the clouds, on that day in March 1960 when they buried the victims of the Coubre explosion?

Two and a half years later, he was holed up in the Cueva de los Portales in the Sierra Candelaria in Pinar del Río, west of Havana. Unknown to most, this is one of the crucial locations of twentieth-century world history. But first this.

About half of the girls I knew in college had a Che Guevara poster on their dorm wall. Together with an equally iconic Jim Morrison, he must have overseen countless losses of virginity: sexual freedom was spreading fast in precisely those years. The girls were often innocent of politics and saw only the man. He himself, rather a prude, would certainly not have appreciated being made part of the sexual revolution.

The maker of the picture, Alberto Korda, famously took pride in not having made a penny in royalties from this image, which *Time* magazine declared one of the most recognizable and enduring of the entire twentieth century. That's the Cuban spirit at its best and its purest. As a creative person I'm a defender of my rights, but Korda created a historic image for the public domain, a much nobler endeavor.

Cuba is still very defensive of any commercial use of this

image outside the island. That's a losing battle, as both the creativity and the poor taste of much advertising will unavoidably prey on such an image. And the public domain is not treated with any respect anymore. It's open season on any image belonging to our collective consciousness or subconscious. Even within Cuba, recent attempts to use Che's image and name as a brand of aftershave were seen as political sacrilege, and the transgressors got into serious trouble and were publicly shamed.

The image as such will surely outlive its original political content. Who was the man behind them?

Che Guevara settled in the Cueva de los Portales during the Cuban missile crisis in October 1962.

The crisis was then in its most crucial phase. A massive U.S. invasion of 120,000 troops was expected along the north coast from Tarara in the Playas del Este all the way to Mariel, forty kilometers to the west of the capital. But most of the Soviet missiles and their warheads were concentrated much farther to the west, in the hills of the Sierra Candelaria. This modest mountain range forms the spine of the province of Pinar del Río, separating the interior from the coastline. Its lush tropical vegetation offers camouflage, but of course the launching pads had long been discovered and exposed by U.S. spy planes and were sure to be hit first if it came to war.

Che Guevara was to be in charge of that western front. But given all of the above, his choice of headquarters was remarkable. The Cueva de los Portales is quite impressive as a set of high-ceilinged, connected caves with theatrical geological details; but the system, cut by a river, is wide open at both ends along the riverbank. It would have offered no protection whatsoever against nuclear war.

The spartan set-up Che lived in during those crucial days

is still preserved. Above his sleeping quarters, a set of concrete stairs leads to a platform where there is a desk. Supposedly here, while waiting for the endgame, he wrote an article that was posthumously published by the army magazine *Verde olivo* in October 1968. It's one of the scariest pieces of writing produced by the twentieth century. It says, in essence, that the people will march unafraid into the nuclear holocaust, as the final redemption of the just.

The man had become an apocalyptic prophet, yearning for the end of the world in a lonely cave. After reading this personal version of the apocalypse, one sees the writing platform in the cave, at the end of its high staircase, as a sacrificial altar where all of humanity could be given over to martyrdom in the name of one man's self-justification.

One can only guess what had driven him so far, so fast, so deep: a craving for the absolute; the disappointments of political power, once conquered; disgust with the world; a loathing of life or oneself, because we are here way, way beyond optimistic heroism transforming the world, as the Revolution had seen itself. He had reached the extremism of denying reality. Or perhaps he had become the prisoner of his own image, as captured by Korda, and there was no way back? A shortcut to the iconic immortality he was indeed going to achieve. Peace was surrender. Now it was total war or nothing. Was he living one of those dangerously exalted moments when war becomes just that – suicide, individual or collective – a kamikaze moment, the fatal urge to burn all bridges?

We can never truly enter another person's mind, but isn't that the direction all the known facts point to?

All of this happened in what is, beyond the fatal cave, a true paradise. The entire region is now an unspoiled biosphere reserve stretching from Mocha to Soroa, an hour's drive west of

Havana. The remnants of the missile pads and the shelters are slowly returning to the texture of the overgrown valleys and the exuberant hillsides, becoming part of a future archeology of one of the twentieth century's most dangerous moments. From an ancient coffee plantation high in the hills in Mocha, and from the Castillo de las Nubes in Soroa, there are splendid views of the surrounding plains, in a vast silence rich with birdsong. Just one of the entrances to the secret tunnels of the launch pads is marked at the entrance of the park.

All the beauty of the world could no longer seduce or sedate the prophet in the cave. Blind to it, he was writing his testament of final redemption by hellfire.

After this postponed apocalypse, he sought new adventures: in the Congo, and finally in Bolivia.

A very personal aside: while Che was praying to the god of total war in his cave, I was living in Antwerp with my grandmother. She had survived the misery and deprivation of two world wars, and she was certain now that World War III and a Soviet victory in all of Europe were upon her, as she patiently explained to her ten-year-old grandson. She was a fearless realist: "The Russians won't be any worse than the Germans." Her main concern was to hoard enough coffee and sugar for the next four years of rationing. This, then, was my earliest connection with Cuba and Che Guevara.

There are still conspiracy theories claiming that Che wasn't killed in Villagrande, Bolivia, in 1967, as per the official version of his death. The British journalist Richard Gott, who knew him well in his glory years as a globetrotting revolutionary diplomat, saw the body shortly after his murder and reported some doubt about its identity, "because he was much smaller and thinner than I had recalled."

A senior colleague of mine who had known Che in Havana

shortly after the revolution also shared his doubts. He told me that the dead body in Villagrande had a much fuller beard than Guevara had been able to grow. Richard Gott, however, added that it might be normal that Che looked shrunken after his deprivations in the Peruvian jungle. Yet the rumor that he died of a severe asthmatic crisis while he was still in Havana, whether or not in disagreement with Fidel, still persists.

Incidentally, the colleague who expressed those doubts was killed in the terrorist attack on the Brussels airport in March 2016. It may seem irrelevant, but it touches me in a strange way that he was on his way to Miami to visit his in-laws, who had gone into exile there from Havana.

34. CONVERSATION IN CAFÉ DEL ORIENTE

The Cuban forensic doctor Jorge González, who between 1995 and 1997 was charged with retrieving Che Guevara's remains in Bolivia, told me in abundant detail how he had gone about this task. He did so with a mixture of humor and deep emotion, and I have no reason to doubt the fundamentals of his story.

Dr. González told me of his adventures in the classy Café del Oriente on Plaza San Francisco, on a cool, breezy, luminous Havana winter day, when this part of restored Habana Vieja looks its best. The contrast between the tale and the surroundings was enormous. The tale belonged to the heroic past of the Revolution in black and white images, of deeds by bearded men and feisty young women in muddy clothes, moved by blind faith in the justice of their cause. But here and now Havana was so beautiful and elegant, filled with a colorful crowd of tourists uninterested in tragedy. It was so different from what Che and his men had wanted and dreamed of that there was something painful about this contrast, too.

The doctor is such a good raconteur that I didn't interrupt him, even when I had doubts or questions about certain details.

El Che and the six companions murdered along with him – four Cubans, one Bolivian, and one Peruvian – were originally buried next to a river. When that river flooded its banks, the graves were exposed and the remains reburied elsewhere. Eyewitnesses to the second burial were hard to find. The main one had been an aged German priest living nearby, who had since left the country and could not be located. With endless tact and diplomacy, Dr. González managed to identify the three military drivers who had been involved in the reburial and, eventually, to make them talk.

". . . when we had finally located the graves with some degree of probability, it was the last but one day of the time we had been allowed for our search by the Bolivian officials. To save time we had to use a bulldozer. I was afraid it would destroy everything, but I also reasoned that the bodies would not be in shallow graves, after the exposure of the first site. So I ordered the bulldozer to dig just a foot or so deeper at each go . . . at a depth of about four feet, the teeth of the excavator got a grip on a leather belt. It was half decayed and broke immediately, but I was jubilant . . .

Now we kept digging with archeological care. The skeletons were revealed. It appeared that they had been reburied in one tangle, just as the bodies had fallen when dumped straight from the military truck.

It was easy to identify Che's remains, because it was known that the Bolivian military had hacked off his hands to send them to Argentina to identify the fingerprints. This primitive method had been used because at that time there was no refrigeration available in remote Villagrande to preserve the body . . ."

But as a forensic scientist, Dr. Gonzalez added, he wanted a more trustworthy form of identification.

This was made possible because Che had used a dental prosthesis sliding over his natural teeth to alter his appearance while traveling incognito on secret missions. Thus there were accurate dental records, always the most reliable identification of a skeleton.

The hacked off hands became a story in their own right. After the research in Argentina, they were allegedly returned to Cuba via mediation by Chile's president Salvador Allende. They are still kept in Havana but are never on public display, this detail being too gory and intimate.

According to Dr. Gonzalez, the hands were hacked off together with the cuffs of the shirt Che had worn, the cuffs still showing the star of his rank as *comandante* . . .

I had a question at that point, because in the last picture of Che's body I'm familiar with, he is shirtless. Would he have been dressed again before his hands were cut off? Again according to Dr. González, the skeleton was also still wearing the olive green parka showing the seven bullet holes of the execution. His tobacco pouch was in one of the pockets – when deprived of cigars, Che was a pipe smoker. I had similar questions about those details.

But my questions remained unasked, for at this point Dr. González's story became very personal and emotional. He said that immediately after the discovery, three different feelings overwhelmed him. First, the satisfaction of a duty accomplished under near impossible circumstances ("like a woman after giving birth"); next, the pride of having contributed to something much greater than himself, something of global importance; and third, gratitude to the Revolution for having allowed him, a man of humble origins, to become the scientist who could accomplish this feat.

I left it at that out of respect for his emotions, but urged him to publish his story. He said he had recorded every detail in his field diaries, and that there is film footage of some of the episodes, including the spontaneous honors rendered to the caskets by the local population while they were driven to the airstrip for their eventual repatriation.

The remains arrived in Havana in October 1997, exactly thirty years after the events. They were buried in the grand Che memorial in Santa Clara, where Che had won the last battle of the Revolution, clearing the road to Havana.

Che's ghost is still present at various locations in Havana. For tourist purposes, a house outside the Cabaña fortress is designated as his home – just next to the Cristo de la Habana, who looks like his older brother. The ghost also inhabits the remote suburb of La Coronela where his 1965 expedition to the Congo was secretly prepared. And then there's the dreary office at the National Bank, well known to me, where he must have felt the increasing boredom of administrative power urging him on to new adventures. Those were doomed in advance, in Congo as well as in Bolivia.

The ghost of 1962 in the cave remains the most disturbing and the most eloquent, but to me at any rate, the humble and miserable death in Villagrande redeems the man in a better way than the arrogant Che longing for the apocalypse.

Dr. González's emotions in the Café del Oriente reminded me of the ceremony in October 1997 at which I was present, when a massive crowd of *habaneros* came to pay their respects to the caskets at the Martí monument. They were lining up all the way down the slope of Paseo, as far as one could see. It felt like a spontaneous event, rare of its kind in this city, truly *los humildes* coming to pay their respects to their hero. My privileges allowed me to pass in front of the crowds, and I felt uncomfortable and unjustified when I saw the many weathered faces and tired shoes of the real Havana up close.

35. PALACIO DE LA REVOLUCIÓN

Because the 1962 apocalypse didn't happen, and the cloud of a U.S. invasion evaporated, life in Havana went on, and her leaders had to keep, clothe, feed, and organize her further.

Back from the shelters, they now got comfortable in the Palacio de la Revolución.

The Plaza de la Revolución is overseen by the giant monument and obelisk to José Martí. Behind the obelisk lies the compound where all the real power of revolutionary Cuba is concentrated: here are the vast ceremonial spaces of the Revolution Palace, the offices of the government and the Communist Party. By way of checks and balances such as exist here, facing the Plaza from the opposite side is the Ministry of the Interior, the all-seeing eye. Total power comes with paranoia, but perhaps here the fine art of the watchers watching the watchers has reached new levels of sophistication.

Inside the government compound, the offices of the Party have their own entrance. Security is tight, no doubt, but also discreet, and visitors are welcomed here with the best mixture of respect and informality, not in the least with sinister glances or invasive controls.

The government offices hold the meeting rooms from whence the economy is run by remote control. The metaphor is adequate, for official Cuba still clings to belief in a push-button economy. The legislative powers are not here. For the longest time, the National Assembly met in the convention center outside the city, as if it were just one more occasional congress. That's changing now: the grandiose Capitolio in the city center is coming out of a lengthy restoration process and will house the legislature again, one of the visible facts of new institution building in the making – as a constantly housed Congress is gradually becoming a counterweight for the Communist Party's Central Committee.

From the outside, the buildings in the compound on the Plaza present a rather harsh, martial aspect. The entire complex is pre-revolution. It stands on the highest ground in the city, where a Spanish regional center of the Catalonians once stood. The original buildings are said to have been intended for the Supreme Court under Batista. The Revolution did an excellent job of rejuvenating and humanizing the grand ceremonial halls. They hold interior gardens with giant ferns, and colorful national works of art including ceramic walls (one by René Portocarrero) and cheerful stained-glass windows. Rather than a tropical Kremlin, it's a display of the exuberance of the national soul – or at any rate, of Cuban political power as it wants to be seen and to define itself.

It's unexpectedly luminous. The much less accessible spaces of the watchers, at the opposite side of the Plaza, contain and concentrate the shadows.

The checks and balances represented by the MININT building, behind the grandest Che-by-Korda sculpture of the entire city, are very specifically Cuban. In fact, one could say that there are three branches of power: the Party, the Armed Forces, and the Ministry of the Interior. Under Fidel, the Party always came first, even though he wore military fatigues for most of his public life. When Raúl took over, there was a clear power shift to the Armed Forces, including in the economy. But the MININT was always there, casting its mysterious shadows. Even when decision makers or reformers were at work late at night in the Palace on one side of the Plaza, another window on the opposite side stayed lit. Havana never sleeps without surveillance, be she rich or poor, powerful or humble. She is always jealously watched. The empty Plaza at night feels like one enormous contradiction. A million people could converge here moved by the relentless willpower of one man, but in the silence and the emptiness it now feels as if energy has dwindled and the city has been abandoned by her gods.

But never by the MININT. Seen from the empty Plaza at night, an enormous indifference hangs over the anonymous neighborhoods full of haphazard buildings and uncollected garbage that spread out in every direction, especially towards vast sections of Centro Habana and El Cerro. The lives in those barrios were certainly touched by what happened on the Plaza, but not exactly as they hoped. Now night itself feels like the ultimate weapon of surveillance.

It's said that under the Plaza there is a vast military shelter. Are both sides of the real power thus secretly connected after all? Yet, for Cuba's future, the relationship between the army – always authentically linked with the people – and the shady forces on the other side, will be a crucial question.

36. WHO'S THE TERRORIST?

After the announcement of the diplomatic normalization between Cuba and the United States, the question of terrorism immediately came to the forefront of the discussions. Cuba was still on the State Department's list of states sponsoring terrorism. Havana had long been arguing that this was absurd. Between the 1960s and the 1980s, every freedom fighter in the world had been someone else's sinister terrorist. I myself lived through endless discussion at the United Nations resulting in the impossibility to ever negotiate a multilateral treaty banning terrorism, for the simple reason that it was out of the question to agree on a generally acceptable definition of such misdeeds.

Moreover, Cuba herself had repeatedly and undeniably suffered terrorist attacks. There was the 1976 explosion of the Cubana airliner above Barbados, which killed all passengers on board. Havana argued that the alleged instigator of that attack, Luis Posada Carriles, wanted for extradition in several countries, had always been protected by the United States. I witnessed three bomb attacks against hotels in the city in July and September of 1997, which killed one person – a young Italian tourist – in the lobby of the Copacabana Hotel on Primera Avenida in Miramar. The man responsible for those attacks, apparently a Salvadorian mercenary by the name of Raúl Ernesto Cruz, was later captured and sentenced to death in 2005, but he benefitted from the general moratorium on the death penalty as of 2008, and his sentence was commuted to life in prison. I doubt that the man would have been executed anyhow: he could have been useful as a witness or as a pawn in some exchange. That probably saved his skin. In 2003 the pathetic pirate wannabes of the Lancha de Regla had been sent *al paredón* not by their crime but by politics; in this case, the opposite happened.

Keeping Cuba on the terrorist-sponsor list became even more of an anachronism when Havana became the seat and guardian of the peace negotiations between the Colombian government and the FARC (Fuerzas Armadas Revolucionarias de Colombia), parties to one of the longest-running civil wars on the planet, predating even the Cuban revolution and long since unwinnable by either side.

I followed this negotiation from up close, as I was a good friend of the ambassador of Norway, the other guarantor of the peace process beside Cuba, and because the European Union pledged to provide massive financial support for the implementation of the peace process. I was privileged to attend the signing, in Havana, of the final ceasefire between the parties on June 23, 2016.

Both the FARC and the other Colombian *guerrilla* army, the ELN (Ejército de Liberacón Nacional) maintained liaison offices in Havana, and their representatives, although moving in a shady zone of parallel diplomacy, had favored access to the old guard of the Cuban establishment. Not surprisingly so. The FARC were very dear to the hearts of the old revolutionary *comandantes*, because they had built a state within the state in Colombia, and could thus at the same time govern and be rebels – a paradox impossible to maintain in Cuba, where the establishment controls everything under the cover of permanent *rebeldía*. Also, by remaining in essence a rural movement, the FARC had stuck to the roots the Cuban revolution had been forced to give up once Fidel entered Havana. The successful autonomous territory governed by the FARC probably made the Cuban leadership even more nostalgic for their days in the Sierra Maestra.

By early 2015, the negotiations had advanced enough to make Cuba's mediating role the main argument to allow the United States to take the country off the blacklist – a necessary condition Havana had put forward to go ahead with the diplomatic recognitions. Cuba was de-listed in May, and the embassies opened in July in D.C. and in Havana on August 14. Just like the embargo, the terrorist label hadn't worked. They had isolated the United States rather than Cuba, as President Obama would recognize again during his 2016 State of the Union.

37. PARQUE LENIN

The park named after the greatest of all communists lies south of the city confines, about twenty kilometers from downtown Havana. While it may be seen as Havana's green lung, due to the distance it fulfills that role in a different way than New York's Central Park. Havana's own Parque Central, bordering Old Havana and Centro Havana, is more of a vest-pocket park by New York standards.

During weekends, Parque Lenin has its amusement rides, horse riding, rodeo, a miniature train, and other attractions. But it's above all a grand extension of unspoiled open spaces, a luxury for most city dwellers, and certainly for a majority of

Havana's pseudo–Frank Lloyd Wright architecture:
Las Ruinas in Parque Lenin

habaneros, who often live in such cramped quarters that they constantly hurt their elbows against encroaching walls. On weekdays the park is deliciously deserted, and one may roam its expanse undisturbed.

Open meadows alternate with thick bamboo groves as you proceed on the central avenue.

The avenue runs by the imposing Frank Lloyd Wright–like architecture of the restaurant Las Ruinas, ingeniously built over the ruins of an ancient plantation house, and basking in a sea of pink-blossoming trees in the month of May. Inside, at the top of the stairs, there is yet another colorful work by the versatile René Portocarrero, in this case a large stained-glass wall. For now, Las Ruinas stands abandoned like the set of a forgotten futuristic movie.

On a discreet byroad of the central avenue, in front of the rodeo grounds, you pass a small art gallery devoted to the pre-revolutionary painter Amelia Páez, and the mysterious Peña Literaria, built to be a small library in an underground passage. Was it intended to keep readers safe under U.S. bombs? Right past it, to the left, a well-kept lane leads to an impressive plaza, shielded by rows of pine trees, in the middle of which stands an enormous monument to Lenin, his heroically upward tilted profile emerging from titanic grayish boulders. Long ceremonial steps lead up to it.

In the surrounding silence, this commitment to a faraway icon feels unreal. You look around you, taking in the whispering treetops, the absence of any worshippers. It's at the same time heavily political and unexpectedly calm. At first it feels uncanny and contradictory – what function does this enormous monument, in such a quiet place, fulfill? Does this kind of exclamation set in granite really exist, if it's not continually celebrated? How can propaganda go mute?

The end of history: Lenin unseen and
silent in his own park.

Next, even more strangely, the entire scene becomes *reassuring*. Oh yes, we know who Lenin was, and what he did and stood for. He will have had his moment. He's silent now. But this monument won't be toppled. It's frankly too beautiful and at the same time too absurd. It belongs to the breathing of the spaces around it. It's a refuge against history, showing that all its sound and fury must pass.

On Saturdays, along the road leading to the monument, beer stalls and barbecues are set up, the rodeo is on across the street, and loud crowds completely ignore the mute giant behind the next grove of trees.

38. PLAYAS DEL ESTE

Get the kids into an *almendrón, vamos a la playa!* The most
tired Spanish phrase of non-Spanish speakers defines Havana's
most popular escape from the summer heat, the ineffective
fan in your narrow bedroom, your prying neighbors jealously
inspecting your new shoes, the exhaust fumes, the flames and
the ashes of the ancient oil refinery in the port, the busloads of
disappointingly stingy and often undereducated tourists, and
all the other marvels *la capital* holds for its inhabitants.

You cross the 1950s tunnel under the bay. It's still a good-
looking piece of engineering, although legend has it that it
delayed Fidel's arrival in January 1959 because the tanks taken
over from Batista's disintegrated army could not fit through it,
and had to reach the city by a roundabout trajectory via Regla
and the Vía Blanca. The Túnel de la Bahía is also directly responsible for the moving of the harbor to Mariel, as it limits
the depth of the old port channel to about eighteen meters,
too shallow for large post-Panamax container or cargo ships.

Emerging from the tunnel, you follow the monumental
and well kept six-lane Vía Monumental past a grandiose and
abandoned stadium, past clusters of poinciana trees exuberantly blooming between May and July. The stadium and other
installations nearby were built for long-forgotten Panamerican Games, a prestige project in hard times, now poetically
quiet or miserably forlorn, depending on your point of view.
But the nearby athlete's village has become a vibrant community, just next to Cojimar.

Cojimar itself is still a quiet seaside suburb with somewhat
mysterious vibes. In his Cuban years, Ernest Hemingway had
his routines here and kept his fishing boat, the Pilar, docked
here. There is a small monument to the writer in a pergola

next to the old Spanish fort on the local Malecón, the east-ernmost outpost of Havana's fortifications. On the steps of the pergola, the unavoidable cluster of old men dressed in *guaya-beras* and smoking their soggy cigars hangs out in deadly bore-dom waiting for the invasion of tourists that will unavoidably kill the real life of this neighborhood forgotten by time, in-cluding mangy dogs, dirty flotsam around the fort, and all its other grimy ingredients.

Farther east, on either side of the highway, are the vast social housing apartment complexes of Guanabacoa and Ala-mar. The buildings look somewhat forbidding from the out-side, but the apartments are mostly very decent and a far cry above the endless shantytowns girdling many other cities in this part of the world.

Here as elsewhere, notably in New York City, providing collective housing with dignity has been a challenge bravely undertaken and kept up, in spite of the unintended side ef-fects. Cuba has no gangland culture – yet. How long this and other phenomena can be kept at bay with the new openness and freedoms is a tantalizing question. Are the authorities in denial about those issues as it sometimes seems, or are they discreetly preparing for them? The surrounding Caribbean and Central American societies are not exactly peaceful, and are armed to the teeth with illegal weapons. And Cuban soci-ety, with its mixture of Latin and African blood, is certainly not peaceful by temperament either. Threats of "*Te voy a matar a machetazos*" ("I'll kill you with my machete") come easily in drunken rows; a funny one once overheard was "*Te voy a dar hasta que llore la foto de tu carnet*" ("I'll beat you up till the picture on your ID card weeps"). Peaceful Havana is not. It's just that the lid is securely kept on.

By now you have reached the turnoff to Playas del Este

on your left, and you follow a narrower highway where the public jammed into old and new cars and contraptions of various descriptions, the motorcycles with sidecars containing entire families, are already anticipating beach fun. On the side-lanes under the trees, more girls and boys are on their way on horse-pulled carts. Occasionally a woman rides side-saddle as a motorcycle passenger, a brave elegance in this traffic. Unabashedly sexy chicks try to make it faster to the beach by hitchhiking, known as *pedir botella*, targeting rental cars with T (for tourist) license plates — *un tur* in Havana slang.

All of this humanity on the move converges on the several miles of fine white sandy shore between Santa María del Mar and Guanabo. On the beaches, families and groups of friends go tribal, establishing campsites that soon become reassuringly messy, toddlers having fun for half an hour before the ever-faster little girls turn on the spoiled little boys who take refuge with mamá. Rum and beer flow freely, vendors peddle tamales and guava pastries, the unavoidable combo comes to sing "Guantanamera" to the tourist who has been lured here by a one-night stand, a fake Mexican *mariachi* band sweating profusely in baroque outfits finds more favor with the locals — and the beach police keep watch, in league with the shadiest over-tattooed-and-gold-chained characters around, so as to make sure that only the right bad people get to do their thing.

Even repainted in cheerful yellow and blue, the old Soviet hotel in Playa Santa María cannot deny its unwelcoming soul. The much better Hotel Atlántico, farther east again, shares a beachfront with several thatched *ranchones* where you can get a *comida criolla* and a coconut. Still farther east, the entire zone of beach and dunes towards Guanabo is mostly deserted during the Cuban winter. The road behind the dunes ends abruptly by what was once a wooden bridge, washed away by floods, but still leaving the area known as Puente de Madera. During the cold spells in winter, the beach here can be covered in thousands of poisonous bluish jellyfish called *agua mala* (bad water). Their little balloons under the vast sky and the Magritte clouds then turn the entire vista into a surrealist painting, as if the clouds have been mating and multiplying on the sand, and the little ones are waiting to ascend.

But the area holds many other surprises. Among the harsh bushes of coastal vegetation just behind the dunes, there are countless discreet ruins of former pavilions of fun and grace, now abandoned to hasty sex and the corresponding graffiti testimonials.

The grand and gated villa complex of Tarara, once mostly rundown but now about 50 percent restored, in the 1990s housed hundreds of children from the Ukraine, suffering from cancers resulting from the Chernobyl disaster. It was an unforgettable sight to see those bald kids having fun among the semi-abandoned houses and on the beautiful beaches, either being cured or passing their last weeks surrounded by care and friendship. During her own most difficult times, Havana still surrounded them with genuine solidarity. It was such a Cuban scene, this mixture of decay and love and the refusal to give up.

39. JARDINES DE LA TROPICAL

Parque Lenin and the Playas del Este are Havana's favorite outings. But earlier generations could have fun closer by. In the now abandoned Jardines de la Tropical, in the neighborhood known as Puentes Grandes, I can satisfy my taste for real urban jungle, not the concrete variety.

Roaming the neighborhoods we have already visited yields an incredible store of imagery of urban life and survival, but the literal urban jungle exists upstream along the Almendares River, in what was once known as the Valley of San Gerónimo, till the brewery La Tropical built an amusement park here in the early 1900s, designed by the Catalan art-nouveau architect Ramón Magriña.

A deep, lushly overgrown valley separates this onetime amusement park from the city. At its edge, an industrial dam still provides power for an ancient paper mill that would belong to industrial archeology anywhere else. The central pavilion of the park is a vast, art-nouveau inspired artificial rock house, overlooked by a now mostly inaccessible Moorish castle, and surrounded on all sides by fairytale-like smaller pavilions in various states of ruin or partial survival. Exploring the off-limits deeper reaches of the park, more derelict pavilions reveal themselves, and circles of small benches, and mysteriously painted walls with Chinese motifs. I gained unexpected access to the Moorish castle when U.S. punk-rock-cabaret diva Amanda Palmer filmed a beautiful video clip there just before Christmas 2016. I was amazed to discover that the interior is completely intact, with all the elegant details of a mini-Alhambra.

In the abandoned park behind the castle, the sunlight that filters through the vines and creepers creates an explorer-coming-upon-a-ruined-city-in-the-forest feeling. Underfoot, empty bottles and other more unmentionable residue of urban adventure are buried in deep layers of decaying leaves. Once upon a time small outlying counters sold Cerveza Tropical here – the trademark survives here and there like ancient writing in a lost temple. At the very end of the path, a padlocked gate protects the dam and its industrial machinery, and a lone goat is tethered to the remnants of an ancient generator.

40. TWO SHORES OF ART DECO

As illustrated in the Jardines de la Tropical, the Art Nouveau movement reached Havana mostly via Catalan architects – the Catalans were successful entrepreneurs in the early years of Cuba's independence. But the movement didn't leave that much of an imprint on the city's architecture as a whole. It was more successful in decorative detailing – ironwork, floor tiles – and in large amounts of imported objets d'art, vases and statuettes, and sometimes beautiful locally produced copies of European Art Nouveau furniture.

Everything is politics in Cuba, and architecture is certainly often a political signature. The grand buildings of the colonial past have found respect again. But systematic neglect of some of the other architectural epochs and styles may have been at least unconsciously political.

After 1960, the construction of a new world and even a new man required a new architecture.

It has to be said to Cuba's credit that few, if any, megalomaniac super-projects were undertaken. Thus the country and especially Havana were spared the architectural horrors and bombast of many another communist capital. The new architecture became more authentically socialist, pouring enormous quantities of concrete to build schools, housing, clinics, and sports facilities. In their design, those buildings could be rather sterile or sometimes playful, but they certainly were and are functional.

Traces of abolished middle-class elegance: the entrance of
landmark art-deco apartments in Vedado

The past architectural epochs that became politically incorrect, or at least irrelevant, were some of the best expressions of Cuban opulence, good taste, and connectedness to
universal architectural movements. Take the art-deco style,
the one following Art Nouveau as the style en vogue.

If you think you've seen the best of the tropical art-deco
movement in Miami's South Beach, now think Havana. There's
an incredible treasury of the best examples of the style spread out
all over the city – in private houses, former commercial spaces,
and especially in neighborhood theaters and movie-houses.

Only very recently has the value of this been recognized, and a few restorations undertaken. Many of those buildings were completely integrated designs, as was the custom. The architect designed the building, the furniture, the light fixtures. Take a good look at the theater at the corner of Prado and Colón. This is the masterpiece of Cuban art-deco architect Saturnino Parajón. It is the archetype of countless smaller theaters all over the city. Other impressive examples of the style are the austere yet elegant Casa de las Américas on Calle G (Avenida de los Presidentes) just off the Malecón, and the badly neglected but still eye-catching grand apartment building on Calle 13 y L, just off Línea in Vedado. The headquarters of the Cuban Freemasons, on the corner of Salvador Allende and Calle Belascoaín, is also an art-deco masterpiece of grand proportions. The masonic emblems on the roof have survived. The clock with astronomical signs on the façade, and the world map on the side, only partially.

The Revolution deeply disapproved of the sophisticated bourgeois life and leisure reflected by those decors, and most of those living it have fled. I don't believe the pale imitations they found in Miami Beach could ever make up for their loss.

41. RUM AND CIGAR WARS

The most beautiful art-deco building in the whole of Havana is the Edificio Bacardí on Avenida de Bélgica on the frontier between Havana Vieja and Centro Havana. It's emblematic not just for its splendidly restored architecture, but also for the U.S.-Cuba rum wars.

Cuba, the United States, and rum go back a long way – in the twentieth century alone, at least as far back as Prohibition. The Caribbean rum-running route, with Cuba so close to

Florida, was probably one of the biggest suppliers of speakeas-
ies all up the East Coast. Triangular trade in rum between
Cuba, New England, and Europe dates to the U.S. colonial
period.

After the Revolution, Cuban brands of many products,
but principally rum and cigars, became the object of complicated trademark disputes, later also involving third parties as
international joint ventures set up by the government started
to market Cuban brands worldwide – except, of course, in the
United States.

Former owners of nationalized brands fought back with
their own third-country products. Well-known Cuban cigars were imitated from Guatemala to Santo Domingo, legitimately from a legal point of view, perhaps – but still only
creating poor substitutes for the real thing. No doubt good
tobacco is grown all over the region, but only a Havana is a
Havana in the end – with the added temptation, especially for
many in the United States, of a forbidden fruit.

In pre-revolutionary Cuba, the Bacardí family was rum
royalty. They had to leave their building behind like so many
others, but took their name abroad and started their new ventures with a vengeance. If Bacardí became synonymous with
rum in the U.S. thanks to politics and strong advertising, the
Cuban brands thrived internationally.

As a long-term resident in the Caribbean I will refrain
from publicly judging the merits of individual island vintages.
The sugar cane may be the same everywhere, but the taste,
smoothness, and afterglow of rums is vastly different from
Barbados to Haiti, from Jamaica to Cuba. Let's just say that
the smaller distilleries maintain secrets and traditions lost by
producers of mass-marketed rums. Cuba has major and minor
brands, and between them the differences are notable.

Symbiosis of grace and necessity: the perfectly restored Edificio
Bacardí watches over its neighborhood gone organic

Mass-produced rums sold in the United States are mostly
fit for cocktails and, to my taste, too harsh to stand on their
own. But that, of course, is subjective.

The brand wars between the Bacardí clan and the Cuban
government, with their French associates, started long after
the Revolution, in the 1990s, when Bacardí purchased the re-
sidual rights of the original owners of the Habana Club brand
in the United States. The U.S. Congress then stepped in to
protect the unclear Bacardí claim, although the trademark
had in the meantime been registered in Cuba's name. The
case went all the way through the court system in the U.S.,
without the Cuban side gaining satisfaction. The World Trade
Organization also ruled on the case, in Cuba's favor.

In commercial terms, the amounts of Habana Club rum
produced in Puerto Rico and sold under the pirated label in

the United States are insignificant next to the huge success
of the Cuban/French joint venture, but this is a case akin
to those of Havana buildings, fueled by resentment distilled
into pure hatred. Hatred or at least very deep resentment of
the nationalizations carried out by the Revolution is still an
ingredient in U.S.-Cuban relations, albeit only for a minority
among U.S. politicians. But to the wealthy Cuban families
who were despoiled of their investments and at the same time
of all the trappings of a unique and opulent lifestyle, that hatred is almost a birthright.

When it comes to the Cuban cigar brands, trademark piracy also happened for Cohiba, although that is an undisput-
edly post-revolutionary brand on which no justifiable foreign
claim can exist.

In fairness, intellectual property rights pertaining to foreign products or productions are not always respected in
Cuba, either. Piracy of more than one kind thrives.

But as rum and tobacco are part of the island's soul, on the
Havana side these cases are seen as wars of national resistance.

42. WAVES OVER THE WALL

Some say that there are two Cubas just as there were two Ger-
manys: a capitalist one in Miami, and a socialist one in Havana.
Of course I disagree – there is only one real Cuba, and it's not
in the United States – but as a metaphor for blending two very
different societies and economies, it may be interesting to consider. Can the Malecón sea wall be seen as a remote cousin to
the wall that came down in Berlin in 1989? If so, the opening of
the U.S. embassy on that very Malecón on August 14, 2015, was
a symbolic breach. But as Cuba is an island state, the wall won't
come crashing down – we still need to keep the ocean at bay.

By a set of coincidences, I've had a professional relationship with the Miami Cuba as well. In 2004 the then-mayor of Miami, Manny Díaz, a second-generation Miami Cuban, presented me with the symbolic key to the city. This was in part a recognition of consular duties in Florida, but also and maybe more because he liked to converse about Havana whenever I visited him. Something similar had happened earlier in Brussels, when Paul Cejas was U.S. ambassador to Belgium under the second president Bush. He was from a prominent Cuban family and had himself lived in Havana till he was sixteen. He, too, liked to hear all about life in Cuba. It felt very strange to have lively discussions about his native city with the ambassador of the *Imperio*, which was so despised in Havana. Even for a high-ranking representative of the hostile United States, Havana held a lasting fascination. Ambassador Cejas, now retired and a sponsor of higher education in Florida, visited his original homeland with a group of U.S. academics in 2014, and so became part of the growing people-to-people diplomacy that was active long before the December 17 announcements.

In a Carlos Varela song evoking a Sunday family dinner in Havana, an empty chair is said to belong to a sibling sitting ninety miles away. Those ninety miles between Havana and the closest point in the United States, Key West, or Cayo Hueso in Cuban (also, by the way, the name of a Havana neighborhood), have become a permanent metaphor of closeness and separation alike. Till the December 17 statements, the Malecón wall could be seen as the last barrier of the Cold War, much more tangible than the infamous DMZ between South and North Korea. But the comparison between the Malecón and the Berlin Wall is only partially tenable, because a sea wall will always be necessary.

Thirty-foot waves routinely wash over the Malecón wall at times of rough seas. That's when we say that the ocean spirit Yemaya is angry, and that the spirit of the deep, Olokún, is disturbing her.

But those waves abate as soon as the sea gets friendly again. Waves of change and attitudes rolling in from Miami may be more difficult to absorb, and may take longer to calm down.

What will they bring? Cash, gold, cars, phones, microwaves, ACs, flat-screen TVs, mountain bikes, playstations . . . All of this expensive *pacotilla* is to be seen already in massive, plastic-wrapped bundles at the Havana airports as the luggage of visiting Miami family members coming in on the ten or so daily charter flights and, as of late 2016, on the much cheaper regular commercial flights, not just from Miami but from New York as well.

The thirst for these items is unquenchable, and proof that the people want things, not words.

With the things come the attitudes and the rising expectations. Consumption is a civic duty in capitalism, as it's the only way to keep the system going. That wave will be unstoppable, whatever havoc it may create for the *cubanía* rooted in ideas of self-sacrifice and disdain for individual material success. That religion won't stand the chance of a snowball in hell. The official discourse is that Cuba is creating a sustainable and prosperous socialism; but even economists working within the establishment point out that the government wants a prosperous country but not prosperous individuals – and that just won't work in the real world. Of course the government will have to stand in the middle to avoid the emergence of a society consisting only of billionaires and paupers. That will require enormous skills of subtle governance never needed or practiced in a command economy. Isn't post-

Soviet Russia facing precisely that challenge with all its social consequences?

The Miami *cubanía* is one of hard work and success; it has also been one of solidarity and mutual support. Today it is losing the resentment of its old guard. There is entrepreneurial spirit in Cuba, dormant for half a century but never wiped out. Strengthened and supported by Miami cousins, it may go far if given enough freedom. But this will not be for all Cubans. Will it be possible to realize those changes in attitude and culture without creating a lost generation?

Even in highly disciplined Germany with the strongest work ethic in Europe, the blending of West and East took a quarter of a century and still left behind an army of lost souls no longer needed or welcomed in the new society.

The old European joke about the communist economies was: "we pretend to work, and they pretend to pay us." A new one came up after German reunification: "I haven't worked a day in my life; on top of that, now I'm unemployed."

The waves crashing over the Malecón from Miami will hold all those challenges.

43. *PATRIA ES HUMANIDAD ES PATRIA* (HOMELAND IS HUMANITY IS HOMELAND)

The Cuban-American visitors arriving at the specially adapted Terminal II of José Martí Airport in Havana are greeted there with a famous quote from the national hero: *"Patria es humanidad"* ("Homeland is Humanity"). It stands in large lettering on the tarmac side of the terminal building. "Welcome home," in a way – but those three words are filled with deeply ambiguous meaning here. The Cubans arriving here have run away from their homeland. On board the planes, the landings are highly emotional to those who have not returned for decades, and are greeted with a mixture of applause, tears, and prayers. I've often sat among those passengers, thinking my own thoughts about identity and rootlessness, and sometimes explaining the real Cuba to a Miami Cuban sitting next to me.

In the small terminal, the slow procedures to clear the vast amounts of luggage and plastic-wrapped *pacotilla* get into gear. There is a VIP service available for a fee, for those hoping to speed up the inspections.

As a lifelong frequent flyer, I have developed a complicated love of airports. They can leave you with deep frustrations when you have to line up or when you get stranded or lose your luggage. But they also feel like spaces where globalization and common humanity really work, and not just for the happy few. Nowhere is a truly universal human society more real and tangible and more democratic, in spite of all the barbed wire, frontiers, passports, visa, and uniforms always trying to limit our God-given freedom to roam the planet.

But Havana's airports give me exactly the opposite feeling – of being rooted. Even while the country is losing more than 50,000 emigrants every year, mostly to the United States, the deep attachment to the native or ancestral soil is always evident.

The old Jose Martí terminal was converted into Terminal II after the first modern terminal was built in 1999 as Terminal III. It was financed by Canada, always a good neighbor to Cuba, and nowadays a source of a million tourists each year.

After the introduction of numerous charter flights from and to the United States, the older terminal became dedicated to the comings and goings of the Cuban diaspora.

When the new airport opened, and travel was still very

restricted for most Cubans, it became the focus of weekend family outings of *habaneros* unable to get on a plane, but admiring the new marvel as a building, a monument to progress – and a place where the several bars and shops were always well stocked for the tourists' sake.

The restrictive travel law included the requirement to obtain an exit visa, the *tarjeta blanca*, or white card. It was seen as the ultimate control of citizens' freedom of movement, and it was prohibitively expensive for many, at that. It was abolished in January 2013. Almost every citizen became free to travel unhindered, even the majority of the most vocal dissidents.

The move was politically very astute: granting international freedom of movement to Cuban citizens restored a basic right the United States and the Europeans had long been pressing for, and at the same time it shifted the onus onto them, by forcing their embassies and consulates to turn down about 30 percent of all visa applications, so that they were now the bad guys. We who had lobbied for years for travel freedom were surprised by the very liberal content of the new law, and its equally liberal interpretation.

It's easy to spot a flight leaving for Havana at any airport, be it at Madrid, Miami, Tampa, or JFK. You spot the largest concentration of plastic-wrapped bundles of voluminous luggage, accompanied by the liveliest crowd. These back-and-forth movements of a human and material exodus represent humanity on the move in a very specific Cuban way. It extends to the compact crowds of family members waiting outside Terminal II in Havana – they are not allowed in. In the sticky heat, rubbernecking relatives sweating it out are trying to spot an auntie or an uncle, and to size up the volume of the expected loot, while quick-eyed semi legal taxi drivers search for the hapless victim without a greeter. When the two crowds finally mingle, however Cuban they are on both sides, and however tearfully they fall into each others' arms, the Miami relatives are easily recognized by their clothes, their jewelry, and their bicoastal body language.

When the Cuban revolution began exporting itself to Africa and elsewhere, it reversed Martí's quote: All of Humanity is my Homeland.

Terminal II doesn't feel like just any airport. It's the gateway between two vastly different societies, two different worlds, which nevertheless have in common their deeply Cuban humanity. Martí's quote and its reversal both feel right here.

44. HAVANA'S PALESTINIANS

The Malecón wall is the tangible frontier between two Cubas. But an invisible line divides the island itself right across the middle.

The eastern part, Oriente, always feels different from the capital and the western half of the country, defined by Havana's cosmopolitan spirit and the city's Paris-in-the tropics look. But Oriente is the oldest and the deepest Cuba – it's where Spanish Cuba began her history. Santiago, five centuries old in 2015, was the first real colonial capital of the island, as the Spanish arrived from the east. Havana was founded only when the expansion to Mexico and Peru shifted the major sources of riches to the west.

Cuba's patron saint, la Virgen de la Caridad del Cobre – sexy *Ochún* in Santería, her colors yellow and gold, sunflowers her favorite offering – is housed in the church of the same name near Santiago. Ernest Hemingway also donated his Nobel Prize insignia to her, in an attempt to placate her spirit, as we'll see later.

Oriente is much more Caribbean in feel and outlook. It's also much more Afro-Cuban in population.

The Castro family are also *orientales*, from Birán. Deeply rooted in the racially diverse Oriente they are not. The father of the Castro brothers was a Spanish soldier who stayed on in Cuba after the war of independence.

Oriente was also the breeding ground of the Revolution. The dramatically aborted and bloody attack on the Moncada barracks in Santiago in 1953, prelude to all that was to follow, is still commemorated by Cuba's major public holiday on July 26. National heroes are buried in Santiago. Fidel Castro's ashes joined them there, in the Santa Ifigenia cemetery, on December 4, 2016. It will be the final resting place for all the surviving protagonists as well. The Sierra Maestra mountain range sheltered the early stages of the armed rebellion, and it was thanks to the support of the local population that the revolution was ultimately successful. The July 26 movement was the cradle of the entire uprising, and also explains an ever-present slogan on the walls: "Siempre en 26." Cities compete every year to be the seat of the commemoration.

In spite of this permanent recognition of the importance of its eastern half, this part of Cuba is also the poorest. How come?

Back to 1960.

When the exile of the bourgeoisie happened, even middle-class black Cubans would not have readily emigrated to the southern U.S. states where the civil rights movement was only just beginning. The longer-term consequence of this was unforeseeable. When remittances started to flow from Miami, they came mostly from white emigrants, and benefited the Afro-Cuban communities of the eastern half of the island far less. The influx of remittances is now enormous – anywhere between three and five billion yearly, by far the most important item on the balance of payments. Oriente, the older, more traditional Cuba, is missing out. This, in turn, creates internal migration to the capital in search of a better life. *Habaneros* routinely refer to migrants from Oriente as *palestinos*, internal refugees.

Thus the east-west division is an economic frontier and, however delicate a theme this is in Cuba, something of a racial line as well. The theme is delicate and has to be approached very respectfully – for Cuba is authentically the least racist and racially conscious society in the Americas, a welcome relief from many aspects of skin color sensitivity elsewhere.

Other gifts from Oriente became part of the national soul. During the Haitian independence wars in the early nineteenth century, an influx of French speaking creoles brought French family names, large-scale coffee growing, and eighteenth-century aristocratic dress and dances, all of which are still alive in the culture of Santiago de Cuba.

There also came from Haiti via Oriente a wave of Freemasons, who discreetly built lodges all over the island, in spite of repressive Spanish laws. By the middle of the twentieth century, the lodges were so rich and powerful they raised the spectacular art-deco headquarters building we have already visited on the major intersection in Centro Havana where it proudly stands today, with Masonic symbols still on its roof. The Revolution did not take kindly to the Masons, as a secret society with its own rules and allegiances. This mistrust was probably unjustified, but the Revolution was jealous. As we have seen, the Masons went underground – where they met the more secretive of the *santeros*, such as the all-male Abakuá societies, and sometimes merged rites with them. It's fairly

Masonic insignia: like the *santeros*, the Masons went
underground but never gave up; their symbols stayed
proudly on the roof

common, today, to see a Santería initiate in white and wearing all the necklaces of his chosen master spirit, also sporting
a Masonic ring. In the Colón cemetery in Havana, impressive
Masonic tombs remain undisturbed.

Within Cuba, universal history's migration of ideas, peoples, and beliefs from East to West – probably a pseudo-
scientific idea, but still an intriguing one – was played out
on its own scale. Thus we should respect the *palestinos* arriving in the capital on their personal quests, blending Cuba's
East and West and infusing a truly Caribbean fire into Havana's mix.

The ongoing story of the *palestinos* around Havana as a
metaphor for much older Cuban history we'll come across
later.

45. NEXT YEAR IN HAVANA / JERUSALEM

From these very special *palestinos* we move on to another remarkable community.

The temple and congregation Beth Shalom, located in Vedado, maintain the traditions of Ashkenazi Jewish life in Havana. The community is small, about 1,500 members strong, only a fraction of what it was in the first half of the twentieth century.

But not before. There are far more ancient Jewish communities in the Caribbean, most notably in Jamaica and Curaçao. In downtown Kingston, Jamaica, stands the synagogue of the oldest Sephardic community in the Americas. The original temple was destroyed by a 1907 earthquake, but many of the seventeenth-century tombstones survive, bearing mostly names of Portuguese origin.

The Havana community is not nearly as old. Due to the presence of the Inquisition in the Spanish colonies as of around 1570, the Jews and the forcibly converted *marranos* or New Christians, still deeply mistrusted in Spain and Portugal, often fled to the Protestant colonies, where they thrived. It took till around 1900, after Cuba's independence, before Havana was safe for Jewish immigrants. There is a Sephardic synagogue in Old Havana, but most Jewish immigration here came with the wave of people fleeing the pogroms in Russia and Poland via European ports such as Hamburg, Bremen, and – very prominently – Antwerp. In 1906 the new community purchased land for its own cemetery in Guanabacoa just across the bay from Havana, where it's still located today. There is even a monument to the victims of the Holocaust.

Next, as of 1920, when the United States began to apply a restrictive quota to Jewish immigrants, Cuba and some neighboring countries became an anteroom for Eastern European Jews hoping to eventually reach Ellis Island and beyond. But then history again produced one of its unexpected side effects.

Some of the refugees from Russia and Poland stayed behind in Antwerp, where they gradually set up a flourishing diamond trade and industry. The Nazi occupation of Belgium saw various degrees of persecution of the Jewish communities and – controversial to this day – different degrees of collaboration with the Germans by local authorities. In Antwerp, with

Improbable Havana encounters: Grave of a Jewish
refugee from Antwerp at the Guanabacoa cemetery

a large and highly visible community – many Antwerp Jews were and are staunchly Hassidic – persecution and collaboration by the local police became intense as of 1941. Many of the diamond community managed to flee, and many chose or were forced to settle in Havana. The large influx of diamond cutters and traders meant Havana took over from my native Antwerp as the world hub of the diamond trade for a number of years. The community settled mostly in the same Vedado neighborhood where the Beth Shalom temple stands. It soon had its own social life and its own school. The diamond cutters set up shop, training and employing many Cubans. This forgotten chapter of Jewish history is only now being documented, with many witnesses of the generation that grew up in Havana still alive and cherishing vivid memories of their tropical years after the dramatic escape from gray Antwerp streets patrolled by sinister uniforms and collaborationist informers.

Most of the community dwindled after the war, when the migrants settled either in the United States or in Mexico or Argentina, and Jewish life in Cuba became very discreet after the Revolution. As for other religions, worship was all but prohibited when Cuba officially became an atheist state. On top of that, the community remaining after the peak in the 1940s mostly had close business ties with the United States that became unsustainable when Fidel Castro began his systematic confrontations with Washington and nationalized all U.S. assets as of the summer of 1960.

In spite of all this, Cuba did not break diplomatic relations with Israel until 1973. The synagogue was closed, but the library and the archives of the Beth Shalom community were respected. The building of the Unión Zionista de Cuba, on Prado, was taken away in 1979 and became the Unión Arabe de Cuba, still in existence today. Yet even in those difficult times, Cuba occasionally authorized Jews to migrate legally to Israel, while making ordinary travel all but impossible for other citizens. As there were attempts by non-Jewish Cubans to abuse this escape route, the authorities sometimes even appealed to the elders of the Beth Shalom community to establish the faith credentials of the emigrant.

This situation only changed in 1998, again as a wondrous side effect of history. When Cuba accepted a visit by Pope John Paul II, for reasons we'll explore later, it became the new state doctrine to avoid a return of the Catholic Church as the exclusive religion in Cuba, as had been the case under Spanish rule. To underscore religious pluralism, the synagogue was reopened, together with other houses of worship. As everything in Havana is done according to a plan, the onset of this new religious freedom came in 1992, when the constitution changed the island from an atheist to an agnostic state. To further underscore their point, Fidel and Raúl in turn visited Beth Shalom at Hanukkah. Although religious pluralism is now officially recognized, non-Catholic Christians, especially smaller groups of evangelicals, complain that the social position of the Catholic Church is too prominent. They are sometimes still harassed, but the Jewish community and Beth Shalom are left in peace. When the synagogue was restored in 1998–1999, the congregation transformed from Orthodox to Conservative. The original women's gallery was turned into a classroom for religious instruction. But there is still no resident rabbi.

Cuba still has no diplomatic relations with Israel either, a fact that the elders of the Beth Shalom community deeply deplore. And whenever I go there and see the spirit and the attitudes, especially of the young members of the community, it strikes me how similar Cuba and Israel are in many respects.

Improbable Havana encounters:
bicitaxi and Islamic Andalucía

There is a common spirit of resistance and survival against all odds, a stubborn sense of identity to be cherished. They even share a desire to create a warrior state, a kind of modern day Sparta with a cheerful and tough and combative youth.

It seems like one more paradox to me that Cuba cultivates such close ties with the Islamic world, sometimes condoning theocracy in the name of respect for sovereignty. Should not Cuba, with her agnostic spirit, her free and healthy attitudes toward sex, and her strong and emancipated girls and women, share my own yearning for a truly modern Islamic culture?

Also, living in Havana as long as U.S. enmity lasted, may help to understand somewhat how threatened Israel feels in its own region.

In 2013, 180 members of the Beth Shalom community emigrated to Israel, partly thanks to Canadian mediation.

In a further remarkable twist of history, Beth Shalom was the community that cared for Alan Gross, whose liberation on December 17 of 2014 was the key to U.S.-Cuba reconciliation.

Cuba created its own diaspora after the Revolution. Yet even in exile, Cubans maintain their patriotism much like a religion. For over half a century, many of them have been saying or thinking at every new year: "next year in Havana," just as Jewish people all over the world wished each other for centuries, "next year in Jerusalem."

46. *CANTOS DE IDA Y VUELTA* (SONGS OF COMING AND GOING)

The forgotten history of the Jewish communities in Havana illustrates once again how connected to the rest of the world the island has been at crucial times.

The entire Spanish colonial empire needed Havana as its commercial hub. The original sister city on the other side of the Atlantic was Seville, where the colonial administration – the Consejo de Indias – was located, and where to this day all the archives of the colonial era are to be found in the Archivo de Indias. But as the Guadalquivir River gradually lost navigability due to progressive silting, the trading houses moved to Cádiz on the Atlantic coast. In fact, this brought the colonial trade closer to the Spanish cities where the entire colonial adventure started. Columbus set out from Palos de la Frontera, just north of Cádiz.

Mariners plying the transatlantic trade brought Spanish music and traditions to Havana. But they brought much more than that, of course. Let port cities communicate, and the rough edges will emerge.

When in the early twentieth century Fernando Ortiz examined the seedy underbelly of Havana – *la hampa habanera* – he came to the conclusion, as we have seen earlier, that the Afro-Cuban gangs of the capital – *los negros curros* – had taken over much of the slang and the customs of the Andalusian underworld of gypsies, smugglers, soothsayers, card sharpies, knife-players, witches, and clandestine abortionists. Any vicious knife in Havana today is still called a *sevillana*. This Spanish underworld was itself a by-product of repression and social control in cities where the Inquisition held sway and where forbidden life, gone underground since the expulsion of the Moors and the Jews, could never be fully wiped out. Havana welcomed all of it, and added her own flavors. And in reverse, African rhythms were brought to the gypsies of Andalucía, mixing *rumba* with the traditional flamenco. This phenomenon is called *cantos de ida y vuelta*, "songs of coming and going."

In Santería, the motherly ocean spirit Yemaya is camouflaged as the Catholic Virgen de Regla. The little church of that saint, just across the bay from Havana, and reached by a small ferry – *la lancha de Regla* – houses a statue of the black virgin, the original of which is in the church of Chipiona near Cádiz. The Chipiona statue is said to have come from Africa in the early days of Christianity. The local clergy is sometimes irritated by Cubans showing up there in full Santería regalia, but sometimes they relent and allow the *santeros* to tell their tales of Yemaya. Even a conservative Spanish Catholic priest has to acknowledge this remarkable feat: his object of veneration with its double African and European identity, following the transatlantic slave and trade route, ends up at the focal point of the entire Spanish empire, there to bring solace to whites and blacks alike.

Another curious remnant of the transatlantic days in Cádiz are the stores called *ultramarinos*, "overseas" shops surviving from the days when colonial imports were sold there, and whose ancient walls and countertops have absorbed centuries-old smells of coffee and rum competing with the *pescaíto frito* (as "little fried fish" sounds in *gaditano* dialect) in the streets outside. The word became so embedded that nowadays it may refer to any surviving old-time grocery store. And next to the Plaza de la Catedral and the Plaza San Juan de Dios, two alleyways sum up an era: the Callejón de los Negros, and the Callejón de los Piratas.

The long umbilical cord between Cuba and Spain was never cut, and this makes for a unique post-colonial situation. Under Franco, emigration to Cuba lasted all the way until the Revolution. In Havana, the clubs and associations regrouping Spanish immigrants according to their region of origin always remained active and highly visible, building palatial headquarters and even collective mausoleums in the Cementerio Colón. You'll find some of the clubhouses among the finest buildings of Old Havana along Prado and around Parque Central. Some of the Spanish republicans who had found refuge in Havana later saw Batista as their next Franco, and joined the ranks of the clandestine revolutionary cells in the capital.

Then, in 2003, the Spanish *Ley de Memoria Histórica* granted Spanish citizenship to the Cuban survivors and descendants of the Franco dictatorship. More than 150,000 Cubans were issued Spanish passports over the next ten years, and the figure is expected to go up to close to half a million – about 10 percent of Cuba's active population.

This is not just symbolic, or a rediscovery of family ties. Those Spanish Cubans will vote, in Cuba, for multiparty elections in Spain, and they may even, with the narrow electoral margins determining victory in a Europe in political turmoil, determine the winner.

The ancient back-and-forth of the *cantos de ida y vuelta* is taking on new and unexpected forms.

There is one last intriguing similarity between Cádiz and Cuba. When Napoleon had conquered most of Europe and his brother was ruling in Madrid, the city of Cádiz alone never fell to him, in spite of a protracted siege. On the contrary: all the liberal and anti-imperial forces of Spain united in Cádiz and adopted the Constitution of 1812, a forerunner of the political freedoms Spain would finally only come to fully enjoy after Franco's demise in 1975. The liberal current soon spread to the colonies, and ten years later all but Cuba were free. Not before the first great liberator of South America, Francisco de Miranda, had died in a cell in Cádiz where, after the fall of the Bonapartes, a reactionary monarchy had been restored.

The role of Cádiz in all of this recalls Cuba's stubborn resistance against the United States. Like Cádiz standing up to Napoleon, Havana never fell under the siege of what was called *el imperio yanqui.*

47. *MULATAS DE RUMBA & PUELLAE GADITANAE*

Still in Cádiz, as of the nineteenth century, early Cuban *rumba* mingled with gypsy flamenco to create the roots of contemporary Andalusian music, later spread all over the world by the great Paco de Lucía, assisted on the bass by the fabulous all-around Cuban musician Alain Pérez.

But the musical fame of Cádiz is infinitely older, and connected with Havana via one more mysterious bypath of history.

When the great French illustrator Gustave Doré traveled through Spain in the 1860s, recording life in the raw, he produced one of his most enduring images. A seductively narrow-waisted girl dances flamenco barefoot on a tavern table, under the hungry wolf's eyes of a pack of men ready to draw their *navajas* over her.

As Cádiz dances to the mixture of austerity and exuberance of flamenco, so Havana has been dancing for centuries to the sensual rhythms that became the *guaracha* and the *rumba*. When Doré was seduced by the wasp-waisted and sure-footed dancer, the mutual exchanges between flamenco, *rumba*, *guaracha*, and *guaguancó* were in full swing. By then, faster and faster steamships were traveling the *ida y vuelta* route between Cádiz and Havana, and styles in dance and music mingled ever deeper. It's my regret that Gustave Doré never made it to Havana to leave a visual record of the taverns there. But the scandal-courting *mulatas de rumba* had even more identical sisters in Cádiz's remotest history.

In imperial Rome, the poets Juvenal and Martial recorded the fame of the shamelessly sexy dancing girls from Gades – Cadiz – simply known in Roman theaters and house parties as *puellae gaditanae*. We even know the name of the greatest star: Telethusa.

How is it that over so many centuries, Cádiz and Havana have both created such fearless firebirds, able to set us ablaze with their seduction? What determines such magical coincidences? In the 1950s, in the famous outdoor nightclub Tropicana, a show presented the modern-day Mulatas del Fuego at their best. The later salsa superstar Celia Cruz made her debut as a sedate singer surrounded by their fiery antics.

Rafael Alberti, the greatest Spanish poet to go into exile in Latin America from Franco, fondly recalled his native Cádiz and her dancing girls. His daughter Aitana, in her youth one of Picasso's muses, and a writer herself, happens to live near my office in Miramar, Havana.

When her father evoked Gades, he may not have been thinking of the beautiful nude statue symbolizing the city and standing in the port, looking out over the ocean. The sculpture by Juan Luis Vasallo was made under Franco in 1948. The grand bronze copy was placed over the port only in 1989.

When in Cádiz, my European home, I often sit at Gades's feet thinking about the other side. Almost inevitably, the oldest *canto de ida y vuelta* will have been about a sailor with a lover in both ports. Gades, shading her eyes with one hand against the intense light of the Costa de la Luz, stares after him or is waiting for his return, but Havana is a dangerous rival.

Gades's sister in Havana is La Giraldilla, the emblematic statue on top of the Castillo de la Fuerza, said to represent Inés de Bobadilla looking out in vain for the return of her husband Hernando de Soto, lost in Florida.

The ultimate *canto de ida y vuelta* between Cádiz and Havana was by and for the great flamenco dancer Antonio Gades, who chose Cádiz's Latin name for his pseudonym, and whose ashes were transported to Havana after his death in 2004, according to his last wishes.

48. ALMA MATER

More about a very different statue.

Havana is justifiably proud of her university – not just the institution, but also the set of buildings of the main campus, on a hill at the Vedado end of Calle San Lázaro. The monumental stairs of the *escalinata* lead up to the statue of the Alma Mater, and behind her to an architectural oasis of mixed neo-classical and art-deco details. Here even more than elsewhere in the city, the contrast between the solemn décor and the liveliness of its users is striking.

The students are not just getting their academic training here. Walking under the trees, sitting on the steps, discussing in circles on the grass, they also have to decide where they stand in this society, how to swallow the Marxist courses that are compulsory in any faculty, what future their degree will hold for a job and an independent life, whether to stay in Cuba or to leave their beloved country in search of opportunities – so many more things than similar bright youngsters have to face in less complicated countries.

Among a typically Cuban multiracial group – not brought together for college advertising reasons here – a lively discussion between a girl and a boy is in progress. The girl, very decidedly, sums up the challenges. The boy, in spite of his *supertoca'o* half hipster, half punk outfit, stands for allegiance to the Federación Estudiantil Universitaria, and has just participated in the yearly *marcha de antorchas* (a torch-lit parade) past the *escalinata* on José Martí's birthday, affirming that the nineteenth-century writer's philosophy, *el pensamiento martiano*, is not just the future for Cuba but the light for an entire unhappy and unjust world today. This disproportional affirmation is one of the sometimes endearing, sometimes irritating aspects of Cuban insularity.

"Jorge, this coming May I'll be an industrial engineer, right? I'm offered a government job in Santa Clara. What am I to do? I'm living with my granny in Vedado, my boyfriend lives around the corner. The salary I'll get doesn't even rent me a room in Santa Clara – those go to the *yuma* tourists who pay for one night what I earn in one month. They say that the factory can offer me lodgings, but there is a waiting list and you know what that housing will look like. I like clean clothes and running water. Tell me frankly now, Jorge: am I going to bury myself alive away from my family? *Por Dios!*"

Jorge doesn't stand down easily. The Federation has liberalized some of its attitudes. Thirty years ago, Jorge's tight jeans would have brought him public shame for sporting *ropa enemiga*. Havana today can pretend to love John Lennon (sitting in bronze on a bench in a Vedado park), but the anti-jeans squads in the 1960s also inspected boys' haircuts in the popular Rampa hangouts, and condemned you to the scissors if your hair reached below the ears. Conscious or not of this past, Jorge continues to defend his FEU: all that's wrong in Cuba is due to *El Bloqueo*, but things are improving *sin pausa y sin prisa*, steadily but without haste. We'll get internet next year, the Party will take care of us.

"Jorge, you know I respect you. You're an idealist and that's noble. But I see what happened to my dad, twenty years ago. He was also told that everything would be getting better, and he believed it and refused to leave when all his friends did. Now he's a bitter man who just lost his job at the Unión Eléctrica like tens of thousands of others. He has no money to start a little business as a *cuentapropista*. His friends in Miami won't send him any, because they argue that he blew his chance to follow them in the 1990s. Now he sits and gets drunk and repeats that he's the moron left behind *para apagar la luz del Morro* – to turn off the lighthouse after everyone has gone . . . Jorge, *mi hermano*, that's not going to happen to me!

I want a life! And then I'm not even mentioning the worst thing, that the degree I've been working so hard for, is on sale for a hundred and fifty *fula* (dollars) to any good looking illiterate chick . . ."

"Now you're exaggerating even more! OK, you can buy a certificate in bookkeeping or hospitality, but not our diplomas! You badmouth everything because you don't get an iPhone and a flat-screen TV. You want *stuff*. We have ideas and ideals . . ."

Our girl is dressed on the sexy side of hippy, but with nice style and taste. Now she eyes Jorge suspiciously. It occurs to her that maybe his conformist politics are just a trick to get away with his quasi-punk persona uncensored. How clever would that be . . . She remembers seeing a group of *chivatos* (informers) coming off a MININT truck early one morning on the backside of the Kid Chocolate boxing gym, just past Parque Central on a block of much wheeling and dealing. They looked like the perfectly decked out, gold-chained, gold-toothed pimps and dealers they were camouflaged to be – and then yet again, maybe they were, too! – when off duty. Do you ever know the real motives of even your best friends, in today's situations? She shrugs.

"You know me better than that, Jorge. I'm not a materialist. Don't reduce me to your slogans . . . I'll frame my diploma and hang it on a wall and that's it . . ."

Our girl is now seen by Jorge as a *facilista*, one of many graduates looking for easy solutions in the parallel economy rather than to put their real skills into practice for a quasi-symbolic salary.

"What you gonna do? Babysit visiting *yumas*? Repair cell phones on the sly? Work as a waitress or . . ." (the next step is implied).

Observing this from a European perspective, I see it with a sometimes painful understanding, as creating jobs for a new generation of bright college kids has proven to be just as challenging in the E.U. in recent years.

Looming behind the arguing students, the Aula Magna with its grandiose painted frescoes is an impressive space, where distinguished foreign visitors are often invited to speak. Politicians who are critical of the country may use this forum to expand on ideas for reform. The authorities take it in stride – the speaker has been assigned this pulpit so as to allow the Cuban side to describe the ideas proffered as academic speculation. Spanish foreign minister Margallo was not given this opportunity here in 2014, and his lecture about the post-Franco political transition in Spain, at another location, was seen as highly subversive, since the subtext of applying the entire experience to Cuba was all too obvious.

The university and the ministry of higher education are the guardians of orthodoxy. On the Havana campus, the torch of Marxism-Leninism is supposedly handed over to the next generation. The Federation of University Students is one of the key mass organizations affiliated with the Communist Party. Understandably so, as the campus was also one of the hotbeds of revolt against Batista, and repression against students was harsh and deadly. Fidel himself started his trajectory here as a student leader. One of his co-students from those days in the late 1940s remembered details: how Fidel always dressed formally, preferably in pin-stripe suits; how he got a reputation as a daredevil, riding his bicycle into a wall at full speed; how his character was already then a mixture of idealism and reckless activism, little tempered by scruples when the ends justified the means. Like the students today, the future *comandante* defined his personality here, more than absorbing a higher education – he studied law, but was never very successful as a lawyer, and politics soon became his all-consuming passion.

But he did have his moment in court, taking up his own defense at the trial after the failed Moncada attack in 1956. He turned the tables on his judges: his long statement became a blazing indictment of the Batista regime. It was later circulated, first as a clandestine pamphlet and then as a classic of revolutionary literature titled *La Historia me Absolverá* – translated in English as *History Will Absolve Me*.

Given what a bloody event the Moncada episode had been, the sentence was surprisingly light, whether it was an effect of the young Castro's eloquence or because Batista's forces had been uncontrollably cruel in the immediate repression after the attack. The entire affair became an embarrassment for the regime, and it was best to put away this annoyingly well-spoken and well-connected young lawyer for a while without harming him. He was whisked off to the model prison on the Isla de Pinos, now the Isla de la Juventud. But it was getting late for Batista: in the halls of the university, unrest and revolt were spreading further.

On the grand *escalinata*, more bloody episodes of repression played out. This happened, tragically, under the welcoming statue of the Alma Mater at the top of the stairs. This then is the story of the statue itself, a 1919 work by Mario Korbel, for which a daughter of the Havana aristocracy modeled. When the statue was ready, the family was scandalized to discover that the breasts of the girl were prominently visible, and, as legend has it, the sculptor was forced to admit that he had put the well-born face on the body of his *mulata* mistress.

In contrast with more staid examples elsewhere, Havana's

Alma Mater is as seductive as she is protective and nourishing. This and future generations of students will need her embrace as they set out from the campus.

49. GOD'S CROCODILE

Conversations like the one just overheard may be going on behind the Alma Mater's back. But as we've learned on the Plaza de la Revolución, most of the time Havana is being watched more closely. In Catholic countries, up to my own generation, children were terrorized by an eye-of-God image in a triangle signifying the Trinity, while in school we were taught that God sees and knows everything, even our most secret thoughts. In bars and other public places, God's all-seeing eye was often accompanied by the warning "God is watching: no cursing here!"

It seems at first all but unbelievable that the Revolution introduced its own eye of God, with a logo all too similar to the old Catholic one.

I invite you to go and see it freshly painted on a wall just past the embassy of Spain on Calle Agramonte, facing the old presidential palace and the *Granma* Monument, where the boat in which Fidel landed is on display in a glass shed next to an eternal flame. That particularly telling sign may be painted over, but the logo is repeated on thousands of other walls in the capital and all over the country, and always reminds me of the spying God of my childhood. The triangular logo on the wall has improved on the Catholic all-seeing eye with a machete, and brings home the same point a little less subtly. What does it stand for?

In September 1960, just after all U.S. assets in Cuba were nationalized and the true course of the revolution was irreversibly set, Fidel wanted the unconditional support of every man, woman, and child. On the steps of the presidential palace – Batista's hastily abandoned old lair – he now announced the creation of the CDRs, the Comités de Defensa de la Revolución. Watchful committees were set up not just on every city

The CDRs are watching, even you kids!

block, but soon even on every floor of apartment buildings. This was the last straw for the middle class. Fiery rhetoric was one thing, and the nationalization of companies seen as neo-colonial – including United Fruit, flagship of the U.S. presence – was another step many Cubans could still agree with, but for many the loss of all privacy was intolerable. The massive exodus of entire social groups was the next step.

The CDR logo still stands for the same organization today. The controls may have weakened, especially in the capital, to the small-time annoyance of elderly and mostly female *chismosas* (busybodies) watching the comings and goings of their neighbors, and calling our Havana a whore with their stares or their grunts when she has new shoes, or especially a foreign lover.

Yet especially in more populous neighborhoods and certainly in the provinces, the network remains alive, and it still holds its own congresses and hands out its own rewards. Occasionally it still organizes pseudo-spontaneous *actos de repudio* – public shaming – in front of the homes of dissident activists. But in fairness it has to be said that the security most *habaneros* still enjoy in their city is also due to social control and the self-restraint it entails. The network is also active at the times of elections, to turn out the voters – because in a one-party system, voter participation (or indifference) constitutes the real test.

Cuba wouldn't be Cuba if it hadn't also tried to give the CDR presence a more playful twist. To bring home the point to the Revolution's children, a different logo was designed: a cartoon crocodile or the *caimán* (alligator) said to have the form of the island. The crocodile has popping-out all seeing eyes, above a supposedly friendly, just short of menacing, grin . . .

As for God's triangle, we may be reminded that both Castro brothers were educated by Jesuits.

The exodus caused by the all-seeing eye triangle and the grinning crocodile is documented in a very straightforward way in the Cuban classic film *Memorias del subdesarollo*, by the great director Tomás Gutiérrez Alea. Havana lost the vitality of her freethinking and independent forces. There followed a massive move toward social equality and the painstaking creation of a new and obedient elite. This was successful insofar as the revolution overcame tremendous adversity and subversion, but it still feels like a lost victory now, when the ever so slow and painful way back to a new generation of independent thinking and behavior has to be found to assure the country's future.

50. *LA FÁBRICA* (THE FACTORY)

If the bright students at Havana University find it difficult to define where they stand, how is it then with the young creative talent with which the city is bursting in all fields – music, painting and the graphic arts, sculpture, film, theater?

It's one of my convictions that this young creative Cuba will have to take over tomorrow to keep the island on the world map where the revolutionary generation has placed it so visibly with its politics and imagery of utopia. However disrespectful the old guard would find this idea, Cuba is a strong worldwide brand, and it will be necessary to think in those terms and to build on it.

The Havana arts scene received a big boost with the opening, in 2013, of the Fábrica de Arte Cubano in a vast warehouse near the Puente de Hierro over the Almendares, just on the crumbling edge of the Vedado neighborhood. The Cuban

Arts Factory is an initiative of Cuban rock star X (Equis) Alfonso, the son of a musical dynasty including the founders of
the group Síntesis, known for rocking renderings of traditional Yoruba chants.

X and his crew turned the abandoned space into a multi-
disciplinary meeting point, combining music, photography,
film, architecture, design, and fashion all under one roof,
and attracting a young and hip crowd for parties and performances. The art on display is cutting edge, with strong doses
of irony and tongue-in-cheek social criticism, sometimes of
downright provocation, but with content mostly thoughtful
and playful at the same time. In a way, the constant testing
of the flexible boundaries for artistic freedom has made for
mature expression of subtle opinions, because the artists on
display here don't want to deny their *cubanía*, or to be quoted
abroad as being overtly subversive.

The great challenge is to remain true to one's country
even while criticizing it, without playing into the hands of its
enemies. That's demanding a lot especially from young artists,
who have to add this challenge to their creative talents and the
dialogue with their private demons, but at the same time it
hands them a responsibility they are living up to: to define the
rich talents of the future Cuba in a non-disruptive way, not as
attention-grabbing egomaniacs. They have my deep respect
for the way they are handling that difficult task.

51. MERCENARIES

The government-controlled press jealously defends its monopolies in Havana. The communist party newspaper *Granma*
is still named after the boat Fidel and his small band of followers landed in 1956 to start the Revolution. There are other

papers: the organ of the Union of Young Communists, *Juventud Rebelde*, and that of the state-sponsored labor unions, *Trabajadores*, this last one maintaining at times a somewhat autonomous voice on the economy. Still, even the contents of this paper are based on the principle that there is never a divergence of interests between the State, as the main employer, and the workers.

To talk about this, I visited the headquarters of the umbrella Union – the Central de Trabajadores de Cuba – and argued that in Europe, and especially in Belgium where I grew up, there was and is a tradition of powerful unions and collective bargaining, making organized labor very much an essential part of the political landscape.

"But ambassador, you come from a model of social conflict between groups and classes; we practice a solidarity model, in which all interests converge."

"Even when millions of jobs will no longer be in the public sector?" I tried to argue.

"Even so. Because that's the way it is and always will be."

When I was a kid and asked my grandmother the reason for this or that, and granny didn't have an immediate explanation, she used to say: "How come? From the comings of coming!"

I still haven't overcome my inquisitive habit, and the answers I get from the Cuban establishment often seem to echo my grandmother's pun.

But what is the reason behind this rejection of common sense arguments, and the stance that nothing will ever change? To me, it's not arrogance. Isn't it rather a fear of the inevitable changes the future will bring? Cuba has put itself forward in world politics, but it's a small and fragile country after all. Keeping up the defiance with hundreds of thousands of people in uniform, and a plethora of flags and medals and parades, can perhaps be seen as the only way for Cuba to cling to a heroic self-image.

I honestly see no real threat in the dissident community: some headstrong individuals questioning the system, quite a few of them elderly ladies. While it's true that most of them get some foreign support, and can thus be branded counter-revolutionary mercenaries, isn't the harsh way they are often treated rather like "using a sledgehammer against a butterfly," as the London *Times* questioned the 1960s drugs trial against the Rolling Stones?

The dissidents stand up for rights we consider elementary: freedom of speech and freedom of assembly. With the threat of a U.S. invasion long behind us, what harm can they really do? On top of that, by opposing the Cuba-U.S. rapprochement because it legitimizes the "regime" in Havana, most of the vocal dissidence has condemned itself to political irrelevance by a cramped adherence to the status quo that justified their existence. Not just as a diplomat but also out of deep love for the country, I am convinced that the necessary changes will have to come from within. From within the country, to start with: for, by, and from Cubans in Cuba. But even from within the existing structures, as they are the only ones to work with, barring a social collapse no person of good will can hope for. The United States would be the first to suffer from Cuba in the very unlikely event it became a failed state. Not only would this bring a massive influx of refugees to south Florida; it would also give free rein to the cocaine trade to use the island as a very convenient transshipment point. To Europe, such an unwelcome disaster would be a moral defeat, a failure to lend a helping hand to our Cuban friends to reach a better future. I am sometimes asked about this risk, but let's simply discard the scenario. So evolution from within and from within the existing institutions it has to be.

Not that reform from within the system is easy.

The Cuban constitution of 1976, as revised in 1992 and 2002, declares that the system is eternal in its fundamentals. Article Three defines the "irrevocable character of socialism and the revolutionary political and social system," excluding "any return to capitalism." Likewise, the procedure established to revise the constitution, in article 137, repeats the same dogma.

As a lawyer by training, and also gifted with a little common sense and some experience in this world, frankly such statements tend to make me smile. Everything always changes, that's the very flow of life. Institutions change or adapt to their societies or simply disappear. The parks of the world are full of forgotten monuments to beliefs that were once eternal.

Cuba's best-known independent blogger, Yoani Sánchez of *14ymedio*, has gained wide international recognition but is still seen as a pariah at home by official Havana. In the run-up to President Obama's visit in March 2016, she launched a simple plea. While welcoming all the symbolism of the visit, she asked: "please, allow us to clean up our own mess." I burn my fingers every time I have contact with *14ymedio*, but how could anyone disagree with this message?

52. BLOGGERS' BREAKFAST

Havana still considers any contact with the dissidents as forbidden, and imposes this prohibition on visiting VIPs. A rare exception was made for President Obama during his March 2016 visit, but when this was invoked as a precedent, the official reaction was: "There is only one President Obama." But there is a fringe of intelligent activists who have managed to find a gray area where they can operate without falling under the sledgehammer.

I have learned a lot from interacting with them. For my own symbolic reasons, I'm having breakfast with a group of them on the eve of a May Day parade in Havana. May Day is still celebrated in Havana with all the hoopla of a great proletarian parade, as if the collapse of the communist camp elsewhere in the world hadn't happened. Or, in Cuban establishment logic, precisely because it has, leaving the island proud and lonely at the last barricade.

I'm going to watch the parade to look for possible subtle changes in the slogans, or in the order of appearance of the historic leaders on the balcony of the Plaza de la Revolución, still practicing the tired Kremlinology of generations of diplomats at many a May Day in Moscow.

May Day on Revolution Square

By contrast, the girls and boys I'm breaking bread with on the eve of the yearly parade make up a lively and good-looking group of college graduates in their mid-to-late twenties, of all races: two girls who are documentary filmmakers; a serious-looking, prematurely bald, white economist; a strongly motivated and very vocal Afro-Cuban, cut to run for political office in any more open society; and a few more quiet, pensive types.

While meeting them, I wonder how they see me, the diplomat, bearing in mind the various options. As a naïve accomplice of a system they hope to change from within? Or a true friend of the country they love?

That they deeply love their homeland becomes clear immediately. For that reason, they accept acting with a caution I never feel to be cowardice. They proudly repeat that they are not dissidents. These youngsters seek no outside support. They want to fly on their own wings. Their greatest fear is to be cut off from their deep Cuban roots. What they really want is to stand on the shoulders of the true achievements of their revolutionary elders.

They tell their tales: how they travel the island with hopes to set up a digital literacy campaign, honoring one of the Revolution's proud accomplishments of the 1960s in eradicating illiteracy, but also showing their elders how far the country has now fallen behind by refusing to grant access to worldwide connectivity. How they would bring laptops to even the humblest barefoot kid and the most isolated *guajiro*, to open up a new Cuba and a new world to them. How they try to show their documentary film in provincial towns, sometimes helped, sometimes not, by local Party and government officials.

I feel deeply moved by their intelligence, their sincerity,

Three continents: a white-Indian maiden, past symbol of the
Americas, sits in front of the Asociación Yoruba de Cuba,
headquarters of African Santería

and their enthusiasm. They are so deeply Cuban, and yet their
stories are so different from the official discourse. I tell them
that they are restoring my faith in their country, and that it's
up to them to define the Cuba of the future, beyond the tired
definition of a country that opposes anything American, by
digging deep into their own talents and making clear to the
world that there was a Cuba before the Communist Party, and
there will always be a Cuba, with all the riches of a national
character that goes beyond official statements.

The Cuban establishment's greatest claim is to represent
the whole and all of Cuba. This is questionable when looking
at sheer numbers, to begin with. The Communist Parties in
all countries where they once ruled never represented more
than a fraction of the population, and it's no different in Cuba.

The official notion is, of course, that the Party is not a political party as it is known in other countries, but rather a moral vanguard. How believable is such a notion today, if it ever was anywhere?

But the claim of one institution to represent everything within its fold is the real situation. In the face of that, these youngsters are patriots in the best and brightest sense of the term. They just love Cuba, and being Cuban, and are also well aware how exceptional their country is and always has been. We return to the same paradox we started out with in these reflections: how to save that Cuban exceptionalism and sense of destiny, when so much of that has been monopolized during the last half century by one group and one voice?

Churchill wrote, in the darkest days of the Cold War: "in the end, human life will evolve in so many ways not comprehensible to a Party machine."

53. PRIMERO DE MAYO

Off then to the May Day parade. I leave Siboney before dawn, and cross an entire city where all traffic has been halted or diverted to grant passage to the buses bringing in the marchers from all over. Deprived of the routines of her inhabitants – either mobilized or in hiding – the entire city in the pre-dawn shadows is turned into a ghost town with a heavy police deployment, traffic lights still giving rhythm to the void.

On the Plaza I find a reserved seat on the cold stone benches under the José Martí monument. With some hidden yawns I enjoy the sights and sounds of the musicians setting up on the stands facing the tribune, the foreign delegations arriving with their flags. Security has become tighter than I remember from previous occasions, even for the privileged. There is even a metal detector, still a rare implement in confident Havana. A large and enthusiastic delegation from Venezuela is already waving its flags, while daybreak paints the sky in long streaks of yellow and purple between the effigy of Che Guevara on the MININT building and the equally grand but more recent one of Camilo Cienfuegos on the building to the right. Cienfuegos, the best loved of the revolutionary *comandantes*, was mysteriously lost at sea when his plane crashed in 1960, precisely at the time when the revolution radicalized and became estranged from some of its prominent supporters.

At right angles with Cienfuegos, looking somewhat like a revolutionary mullah with his long beard and wide-brimmed hat not unlike a turban, a large poster of the pre-revolutionary black union leader Lázaro Peña is affixed to the National Library building, and looks surprisingly like president Obama for a short moment in the uncertain light. The fiercely independent union leaders from before the Revolution were later granted political sainthood. They were among Cuba's earliest declared communists, especially the longshoremen's union, led by another black man, Aracelio Iglesias, who was murdered in 1948. But I sit there asking myself how the revolution would have handled an independent syndicalist with his own power base. Who cares to remember that Lázaro Peña, so proudly displayed here, was totally opposed to the takeover of the unions by the government in 1960, and was treated with downright hostility?

Meanwhile, the enthusiasm of the Venezuelan delegates is shared in a more sedate manner by a crowd of Argentinian trade unionists. The political left in Argentina has strong emotional links with Cuba via Che Guevara, of course. Even bad boy *futbolista* Diego Maradona had a Che tattooed on his shoulder during one of his coke-rehab episodes in Cuba.

Next to arrive are the Brazilians, no champions of dawn, and developing their own somewhat superior enthusiasm. To this observer, it feels like they're saying: okay, brothers and sisters, we all love each other, but we're doing better, see? Brazil's own economic worries, next to those of Venezuela and Argentina, started later, and in May 2015 president Dilma Rousseff was still Havana's best new sugar mama.

Spanish, French, and even British contingents now also position themselves. Solidarity rules, however different European unions are from the Cuban ones.

Coming from Cádiz, officially declared Europe's capital of unemployment in 2014, I understand that to these visitors, the bosses, the capital, and even the bourgeois socialists have become the enemies yet again. But what remedy against that is to be found in Havana? How naïve can they be? After we saw the east European workers paradises exposed for what they really were, waving your union flag here feels misguided and sad. Let Havana present herself as an unrepentant communist for a few hours, but you don't have to pretend, since you know better. Doesn't the United States, the capitalist archenemy, have strong and vocal trade unions, especially in New York? It's almost reassuring that I find out that some of the delegations will be off for a week in Varadero after the parade. That, at least, is a true conquest of European socialism. I suggest that some of the future marchers from Europe read up on the history of the Cuban labor movement before their next visit.

In the meantime, the Cuban marchers who have been bused in since four a.m. are waiting in compact blocks on the downward slope of Paseo, still invisible to us on the tribune. They patiently and obediently regroup under the slogans praising their eternal rebellion, maintaining the ideological fervor with a swig of rum on the sly.

The leadership now appears on the balcony above the tribune and takes its correct order. No change in rank or presence. I learned this observation as a youngster watching similar parades in Ethiopia, where the situations were far less innocent. At each occasion, a few more colonels of the military junta were missing, eliminated during shootouts around their conference table. Here it is much more civilized – only a race against time for the elderly leaders.

When the parade gets moving from down on Paseo, the band in front of the tribune plays the *International*. A flag-waving Argentinian faints and falls over from emotion, his flag immediately taken over by a comrade, like on a battlefield. The man is carried to an ambulance. The band now intones a popular *rumba santiaguera*, the sun is rising above Camilo Cienfuegos, while the MC with a voice echoing over the vast space of the Plaza maintains an enthusiasm hardly present in the crowd marching under its banners and papier-mâché symbols of ministries, state corporations, and mass organizations. Luckily there is the lively music by the excellent band, and I hum the lyrics of my favorite tune to myself: *y la cucharacha baila con la lata* – "even the cockroach is dancing with the tin (of condensed milk)." No hidden meaning, of course.

As soon as a marching group has passed the tribune and turns to the left, passing between Cienfuegos and Iglesias, it quickly breaks ranks, throwing away the small paper flags and other propaganda toys, and disappears to a bus, a bed, or a beer.

54. THE PEN & THE SWORD

As a writer, one works literally with a very literal medium. However cautious you may try to be, sooner or later you have to put things in black and white. Photographers, painters, and movie directors may suggest things with images, but at the risk of losing one's self-respect, the true writer sooner or later has to call things by their name. When facing the choice between respect and telling the truth, should a writer always go for the truth? Ideally, truth can be told in a respectful way.

How does the printed word fare under revolutions? At the end of the day, no enforced orthodoxy can ever sit well with a real writer. We've seen how the great Alejo Carpentier worked around it. The Union of Writers and Artists, UNEAC, is an essential pillar of the Cuban political establishment. Cuba maintains a strong cult of the book and the written word, while sternly controlling what goes into print.

In the United States and elsewhere, Cuban literature is still identified with writers like Guillermo Cabrera Infante, whose *Tres Tristes Tigres* is seen as a Cuban Joycean masterpiece. Cabrera Infante had been with the Revolution in the early stages, but defected in 1965. Like others in the same situation, his work then became taboo, and his very name is virtually unknown to the Cuban public today.

Some great literary talent went into exile after 1960. The writers who stayed had to adapt. They saw enough possibilities to work around difficult themes in allegorical ways or concentrating on history or poetry, which remains unusually popular with Cuban audiences. Day-to-day reality in Cuba was largely avoided in the printed word. But it found its way into scriptwriting and onto the screen, thanks to the truly independent spirit of the late Alfredo Guevara (no relative of Che Guevara) as head of the national film institute, ICAIC (Instituto Cubano de Arte y Industria Cinematográfica), and his fearless star director Gutiérrez Alea.

Then came the *Período Especial* – the painful crisis-management phase after the implosion of the Soviet Union, roughly from 1994 till 1998–1999. What many saw as the death throes of the Revolution did loosen social controls as the establishment was seeking a way out of the crisis. Gutiérrez Alea directed *Fresa y chocolate* and *Guantanamera*, both based on material and themes officially seen as sensitive if not downright subversive: homosexuality and the Cuban male, as well as the dead weight of bureaucracy. Cuban cinema broke out of its bonds: in 1994 *Fresa y chocolate* was nominated for an Oscar.

It looked as if Gutiérrez had taken advantage of the temporary helplessness of the system, while Havana enjoyed her short spell of relative anarchy. But much earlier, in the staunchly controlled environment of 1968, he had directed his classic *Memorias del subdesarollo* (*Memories of Underdevelopment*), in which he shows the exodus of the Cuban middle class as it was lived from within that class. What he examines under the surface is the attachment of many intelligent Cubans to their nuanced outlook on life, which could not be captured in one-sided slogans attempting to explain everything. I always saw the title of the movie as deeply sarcastic. Other, more politically correct interpretations prevailed. Since the main bourgeois character of the story is represented as egocentric and morally empty, the film could also be presented as a criticism of that pre-revolutionary class. But the ambiguity is typical. Seeing it as I do, this merciless homegrown self-portait of Havana in her most dramatic years, utterly destroys the superficial propaganda of the Soviet-inspired *Soy Cuba*. Incidentally, I met Edmundo Desnoes, author of the book on which the movie is based, in New York in 2016. He too, like Cabrera Infante, had fled conformism and censorship in 1979, after originally identifying with the new Cuba.

Gutiérrez's very last production, *Guantanamera*, on the surface is a romantic comedy, but the very humor is subversive. The script is a tragicomic road trip around the transportation of a dead relative in a coffin over the length of the island, for burial in Havana. It could be seen as an allegory of the mummified system and the dead weight of an otherworldly bureaucracy the family has to deal with, using the subterfuges and inventions of real life under the slogans. It's rumored that Raúl Castro was enraged when he saw the film and wanted it banned. Alfredo Guevara then offered to resign from ICAIC, but Fidel himself intervened, and he stayed on till his death in 2014. In this instance, freedom of expression won the day over censorship. Nevertheless, the Cuban film director Rigoberto López told me that, in those same years, an excellent script about the rivalries between Cuban and French pimps in Havana around the time of the First World War and the then-thriving trade in white sex slaves was rejected for production. The theme was considered too delicate, given the blatant prostitution then prevalent on the Malecón and the Quinta Avenida.

Out of the same cracks in the system grew the two most prominent new writers within Cuba: Pedro Juan Gutiérrez and Leonardo Padura.

Gutiérrez, after a nondescript career as a good boy writing for the official press, morphed into an unrepentant pornographer in the stlye of Henry Miller, chronicling salty, casual sex in the sweaty walls of Centro Habana. His *Dirty Havana Trilogy* was published abroad, thanks to a set of circumstances, after censor-ridden Cuban publishers turned him down with all the offended and highly ambiguous disgust of a nun in a sex shop. Noboby captures like him the raw life of the grimy *barrio*, fat and warts and all.

Next to Pedro Juan Gutiérrez, who is now hugely enjoying his bad boy status, Leonardo Padura cuts a decidedly more distinguished figure. He began his career writing short detective stories exploring many neighborhoods of Havana's underbelly, and graduated to more ambitious works reflecting on history and the human condition. Just like Gutiérrez, he found his way – and even more successfully – into foreign publishing. Official Cuba remains occasionally doubtful about both new literary stars. They travel freely like many Cubans now, and publish and speak abroad from Buenos Aires to Madrid, but can still encounter hurdles at home. Padura's monumental *El Hombre que Amaba a los Perros* (*The Man who Loved Dogs*), based on Leon Trotsky's exile and death in Mexico, initially sat uncomfortably with Cuban conservatives because the evils of Stalinism felt too close.

In most of Padura's tales, the star detective is Mario Conde, a semi-retired police officer who's brought back into the picture by his former superiors when they are at a loss to solve particularly mystifying murder cases. Conde's Havana mostly feels as grimy as Gutiérrez's. When the emasculated body of a corrupt former high official who fled to Miami washes up on the Playa del Chivo just outside the tunnel under the bay, the entire environment is described as "the river spitting out all of Havana's piss, shit, vomit and menstruations." Conde is obsessed with the internal rot of the system he has served as a policeman. He sees the imposition of Soviet-style politics on his country as an enormous lie and an even greater absurdity. He regularly drinks himself into a stupor to forget his own cowardice. When a dangerous hurricane threatens Havana, he is seen climbing onto the roof of his building to invoke the destruction of the city as an act of redemption.

But unlike Gutiérrez's characters, he also lives moments of a deep poetic melancholy when roaming Havana's streets and observing the slowly disintegrating grandeur of her ancient buildings. In *Paisaje de Otoño* (*An Autumn Landscape*, 1998), a murdered former high official turns out to belong to the administration of nationalized properties, giving Conde/Padura a choice opportunity to spit all his venom at imported communism. The tale is set in 1989, years before the disasters of the *Período Especial*, and its meaning is obviously that the entire system was doomed to betray itself from the beginning. Had not the great Alejo Carpentier, in his subtle messages from beyond the grave, said the same thing thirty years earlier?

In spite of some lingering distrust in official quarters, Padura's *El Hombre que Amaba a los Perros* (2009) received the critics' yearly award in Cuba and was even made available in the country at a subsidized prize. But in an ongoing game of back-and-forth, Padura's script for *Return to Ithaca* had the movie banned from the 2014 Havana film festival, apparently because the themes of exile and return, even when presented under a Homeric metaphor, were still too sensitive. As a French-Cuban coproduction, the movie was then programmed as foreign feature during the next festival set up by the embassy of France. A similar controversy emerged over *Fátima o El Parque de la Fraternidad* about Havana's transvestite subculture. After some lobbying, the movie was shown outside the official program of the 2014 festival and was a resounding success with the public. But that same year the film *Conducta* (by Ernesto Daranas), a very harsh tale about the daily life of a schoolboy with a drug addicted mother in a poor neighborhood, was an enormous hit with Havana audiences, precisely because it showed uncensored situations *habaneros* are all too familiar with in their real lives.

Padura's Mario Conde detective stories have now been turned into four feature-length film productions as well. Apart from the intrigues showing much of Havana's underbelly, the city itself becomes the protagonist of the tales, revealing its most unexpected secret alleys and passages next to its surviving elegance. The indefatigable Pichi (Jorge Perrugoria) plays Mario Conde.

In a complicated and shifting environment, talent will always be testing the limits and pushing the envelope. Creative Havana is way ahead of the politics of the moment. In the other visual arts, ironies and double entendres about the system have long been tolerated by and for an elite, but cinema as a mass medium is monitored more closely.

Padura's novel *El Hombre que Amaba a los Perros* coincided with the publication of *Stalin's Nemesis, The Exile and Murder of Leon Trotsky*, by Bertrand Patenaude of Stanford University. This book is not just a page-turning minute-by-minute factual account of Trotsky's stay in Mexico and his death, but also a complete and merciless debunking of The Old Man's illusions about the Soviet Union as such, and not just of Stalin's hijacking of the utopia. Will the conclusion that Stalinism was just the logical consequence of Leninism and of communism in the real world ever be applied to Cuba? Padura's book, celebrated by the Instituto Cubano del Libro, is after all a work of fiction, and a long and intricate one at that. It was unlikely to stir up counterrevolutionary feelings. In that same book, Padura attacks the "lamentable, empty, and complacent" literature produced in Cuba in the 1970s and '80s, "under the ever-present weight of suspicion, intolerance and national uniformity," and confesses: "I should have preferred, like Isaac Babel, 'to write the silence.' "

In their direct and visceral flashes of daily life in real Havana, Padura's Mario Conde detectives may be far more corrosive.

The writer Pedro Juan Gutiérrez, putting down his rogue mask for a few moments, told me that the publishing of erotica is a barometer of freedom. Revealing the solid intellectual within, he pointed out that thanks to the Church and the Inquisition there were no such books in seventeenth- or eighteenth-century Spain, while they were hugely popular in France and Britain.

It takes time to recognize that eventually the pen *is* mightier than the sword. Meanwhile, Gutiérrez confirmed Mark Twain's naughty pun – *The penis* mightier than the sword.

Fortunately Havana was spared the bombast of communist realism in the arts and architecture. Where it flourished and continues to flourish, though, is in the official printed word. The old guard at *Granma* and at the government press agency, Prensa Latina, maintain a uniquely verbose and at times melodramatic writing style, even beyond the normal Latin exuberance. In a witty and subtle criticism, a young Cuban artist once calculated the weight of all the printing ink spent on "the excess of beautiful words" (here is Alejo Carpentier again), in a project he called *The Weight of History*.

55. *PRIMA BALLERINA ASSOLUTA*

Let's move on from these grimy novels to a noble and elegant art form: classical ballet. I'm invited to a performance of the Ballet Nacional. I drag myself there out of a sense of duty, as I have no patience for ballet and even less for the kind of pompous romantic music that habitually accompanies it.

The performance is being held at the Sala Avellana of the National Theatre next to the Plaza de la Revolución – an enormous space, second only in capacity to the 7,000-seat Teatro Karl Marx. The Gran Teatro on Parque Central – the elegant nineteenth-century opera house one more commonly associates with the ballet – is being restored.

The Ballet Nacional is one of Cuba's international claims to transcendent culture. Rightly so, as the troupe is highly respected abroad and frequently goes on tour, exposing the young dancers to the constant lure of foreign contracts, a temptation oddly shared with Cuban salsa musicians and baseball players. But even with the occasional defection, the country has a constantly renewed, more than ample pool of talent to fill the stage.

The theater is packed. Occupying seats of honor in the middle of the balcony, we have a sweeping view of the stage and the entire space. The conversations and the expectant humming before the performance come to a halt when a door to the right-hand box opens, and the queen of the evening is escorted to her seat: Alicia Alonso, *prima ballerina assoluta* in her nineties, completely blind, her timeless Nefertiti profile offset by a white turban. She graciously acknowledges the standing ovation she receives and takes her throne. A nervous and sweating little man sitting to my left takes out a well-worn notebook and a bitten pencil just as the lights are dimming and the performance is starting.

The music and frankly the dancing bore me as ever, but I'm fascinated nonetheless. By you know what?

The costumes.

In a city where it has long been problematic to get a shirt or even a button for a shirt, and where even now the selection in retail clothing is between a polyester *guayabera* from a state store (if you manage to convince the sleepy salesperson to sell you one) and the tackiest semi-clandestine imported faux Gucci bling jeans straight from the Chinese container in Panama, the beauty of the costumes, and the care for detail they show, is simply amazing. And the variety of the outfits, since tonight's program is a patchwork of the great classics, with all the characters dressed accordingly, from Russian princesses and princes to Italian peasants. And in no small numbers: at some points in the performance there are fifty or so dancers onstage. I can only imagine the stubborn determination required to make and to maintain all these costumes, to get the fabrics and the zippers and the buttons and the stockings and the gold thread and the fringes and the tassels and all the rest.

During the intermission, the queen is holding court backstage in perfect English for the visitors. "The dancers must be very honored that you're here," one ventures as an opening. "No, they're dead nervous," is the deadpan reply, "for they know I see everything."

Okay, now I get it: my nervous neighbor with the notebook takes down each ever so slight slip of the toe or grip of the hand of everyone onstage, and whispers his report in the queen's ear during the interlude. Seeing her profile up close, its demanding and unforgiving aspect, one understands that she's still perfectly capable of pronouncing professional death sentences on this or that member of the troupe. Her spy has to decide between absolute loyalty to his queen and the survival of young talent.

Yet I'm thinking, in spite of her surveillance system during the performance, maybe it's better for Alicia Alonso that she can't see many of the details of the ballet's school on Prado in Habana Vieja, where the original splendor of a palatial headquarters is mixed with the decay of fifty years of inadequate and patchy maintenance, and where the front desk has degenerated into the shabbiness of a shaky little table manned by a disinterested fat woman and a dead plant. But to do justice to the school, the students of all ages and colors are beautiful and lively and in high spirits, whether barefoot or on points. As always and everywhere in Havana, it's not about the walls, it's about the people.

Queen Alicia, prima ballerina eterna, with her fragile body and her unforgiving pharaonic profile, belongs to eternity already. She is her own monument. But she got her building too. On the first of January 2016, the beautifully restored Gran Teatro just across from the Capitolio on Prado, was solemnly reopened under its new name of Gran Teatro Alicia Alonso.

Cuba's most successful dancer since Sra. Alonso's heyday, Carlos Acosta, became a star of the Royal Ballet in London but never turned his back on his country. He was rewarded with a palatial mansion in Siboney, just around the corner from where I lived from 2012 till 2017.

56. LE PARISIEN

From the noble environment of classic ballet, let me next introduce you to an unapologetic tourist trap: the Le Parisien cabaret at the Hotel Nacional.

It's a daily show not comparable in setting with the more famous grand open-air decor of the Tropicana, the temple par excellence of pre-revolutionary Cuba's decadent elegance. But the Parisien show, for all its kitsch, and the *mulata* bodies gloatingly observed and filmed by Varadero tourists during their one-night Havana experience, holds some surprises of unvarnished reality.

The performance opens with scenes evoking the arrival of the Spanish conquistadors in the pagan paradise of Cuba's native Taíno and Siboney population. There are quite graphic simulations of rape and brutal enslavement. The tourists are still gloating at the generously exposed bodies of the mistreated "Indian" beauties, but to the well-informed spectator the scenes are unexpectedly crude and real. Next African slaves are brought in, and again sexual violence and the whip are the main feature for several tableaux. These parts, however whirling and kinetic, walk a fine line, but it never feels as if they cater to titillating or sadistic instincts. They just tell a real story.

Next, though, everything comes together. A multiracial Cuba born out of all the misery of the first encounters can now give free rein to an exuberant and provocative lust for life. This part culminates with a long scene in honor of the *orisha* Changó, with the rhythms for the dancers provided by authentic *batá* drummers, and the splendid outfits in Changó's colors – red and white – are embroidered with his symbol, the double axe, *oché* in Yoruba.

This concludes the best part of the show, and the rest is tailored to tourist tastes. The dancers of both sexes end the performance running through the audience, so the public gets a tantalizing up-close taste of the near-nude bodies sweating and panting from their acrobatic choreographies.

The show is a very Cuban performance, and I would hate to see it watered down and sanitized into a provincial Las Vegas derivative.

57. HATUEY & HURACÁN

The Parisien show vividly illustrates the confrontation between the Spanish and the native Cubans. The conversion of the "pagans" camouflaged the conquistadors' lust for gold and easy sex. All of them were direct heirs of the Reconquista of

Arab Andalucía – completed with the fall of Granada in 1492, the very year of Columbus' first voyage.

Modern Spanish history is beginning to admit that the Reconquista was in fact a vicious civil war between landsmen of different religions, just like the 1930s civil war between socialists and fascists. What we now call ethnic cleansing followed close upon the Reconquista, and Spain drove out and deported her Muslims and Jews en masse. Then the Inquisition made sure the imaginary *limpieza de sangre* – the purity of "old Christian blood" – was upheld with unrelenting terror, perpetrated in close collaboration with the Dominican friars who were soon nicknamed, in a Latin pun on their name, *Domini Canes*, "God's Dogs."

The Inquisition soon expanded to the Spanish colonies, where it lit the same pyres as it had in the motherland. It's all the more remarkable, therefore, that a dissident Dominican friar, Bartolomé de Las Casas, authored the first great anti-colonial pamphlet, describing the entire colonial undertaking as a genocide. In his *Brevísima relación de la destrucción de las Indias* (1552), Las Casas devotes a chapter to Cuba. It's the earliest eyewitness account of the atrocities.

His best-known story is about the Indian cacique Hatuey. When on the pyre and ready to be burned alive, he is told that he can still save his soul by a conversion in extremis. He then asks if there are Spaniards in the heaven his soul will go to. "Of course," says the executioner. "In that case, no thank you."

Hatuey has remained a national symbol in Cuba, with his imaginary profile used for advertising a beer brand (no longer available in Cuba but still sold in Miami) and, of course, Cohiba cigars. The resistance of the Taínos and the other native group, the Siboneys, became a paradigm for anti-colonial politics. Indio Hatuey is also the name of Cuba's best known weather station, in the province of Matanzas. As if to make up for the death on the pyre of the brave cacique, by some odd coincidence the weather station named after him systematically records the coldest weather in Cuba's subtropical climate – once approaching freezing point in February 1996.

While traveling the length of the island, Las Casas claims to have witnessed mass suicide and child murder by the native Cubans, in order to escape slavery. The figures he gives are impossible to check. On one occasion, he cites the death of six to seven thousand slaves in the mines within three months. The figures for other islands – Jamaica and Puerto Rico – are even more radical: he says that a population of six hundred thousand souls was reduced to a few hundred.

Las Casas also recounts a visit to the newly founded (1519) city of Havana. He has given the caciques his personal assurance that no harm will befall them, and immediately upon his arrival, the soldiers sentence twenty-one leaders to the pyre. He says that he helped them escape with great difficulty, and that next the Indians fled to the mountains in large numbers. In this instance, that would mean west, toward the Sierra Candelaria. This is the first recorded instance of slaves turning *cimarrón*, or runaway. To this day in Cuba to take to the mountains, *pa'l monte*, means to go to the wilds, even when they are in fact flat terrain.

It's possible that this one incident explains why Havana's Indian roots disappeared early on. But it leaves other intriguing traces. Fleeing to the west of the city, the Siboneys had to cross two rivers, the Almendares and the Quibu, which offered some protection from their pursuers. Seeking safety across those rivers would be repeated in Havana's history. And the westward flight of the Siboney may, after all, justify the present-day name of the westernmost suburb of the capital.

Las Casas's pamphlet gave rise to long debates and soul-searching in Spain. It also created the *Leyenda Negra*, the Black Legend of Spanish atrocities, cleverly exploited for propaganda by the other colonial powers who were just as bad, if not worse. Las Casas's passionate advocacy on the Indians' behalf also led to the introduction of African slavery — probably the largest ever tragic side effect of a humanitarian endeavor.

A more moderate interpretation of the relations between the Spanish and the native groups holds that the Taínos and the Siboneys were simply absorbed into the Cuban population. Most of the settlers were men only, and took local wives or concubines. This theory finds some support in eighteenth-century chronicles that still find scandal in Spanish men living in sin with Indian women. Apart from the scarce archeological record they left, the most enduring traces of the original Cubans are in the many places still named in their languages, from Guanabacoa next to Havana to Baracoa at the far eastern end. And of course the words for tobacco and hammock (*hamaca*), not forgetting the Taíno storm god *huracán*, father of all hurricanes.

Unlike countries like Peru, Ecuador, Guatemala, and Bolivia, Cuba has become decidedly un-Indian. Still, Havana likes to present herself as the meeting point of three races. In a reminder of the cigar-store Indian popular in the United States, traditional tobacco brands and cigar bands love to display a good-looking supposedly Indian maiden, invariably with suspiciously Caucasian features. The godmother of all such *indias finas* is the statue next to the Parque de la Fraternidad, obviously modeled after a white girl in spite of her feathers and arrows. Was she, like the original Alma Mater of the statue at the university, also the sculptor's mistress, only less prudish? The statue was originally placed in 1892, to commemorate the fifth centennial of the "discovery" of the Americas. It was officially called La Noble Habana but people knew it as La Fuente de la India – The Indian's Fountain. In a way certainly not intended at the time, the white Indian girl illustrates the mingling of the races in her own fashion.

Official Cuba still tends to subscribe to the *Leyenda Negra* and the genocide. It's a welcome political theme to mix with the slavery question – and the claims for reparations – still prominent in the 2014 closing documents of a regional summit held in Havana. The combined slavery and genocide issue is a unifying factor between the Caribbean and Cuba's best friends on the continent – Ecuador, Bolivia – and a handy tool for Cuba's very professional diplomacy in the region. It was mostly Cuba's clever maneuvering in the Community of Latin American and Caribbean States in 2014–2015 that bypassed the outdated Washington-based Organization of American States (from which Cuba was banned after the Revolution), and convinced President Obama to recognize that Cuba was the key to better relations between the United States and Latin America.

58. *TODO EL MUNDO CANTA*

Huracán and the other Taíno gods have left Cuba (although his mighty fury still visits regularly) but they were never really replaced by the severe, inquisitorial Catholicism from the motherland. Much of the Catholic clergy remained peninsular (from the Iberian peninsula), among other reasons because celibacy didn't work any too well for local priests falling under the spell of the sexual freewheeling Havana was so famous/infamous for during the eighteenth and nineteenth centuries.

The chronicles compiled by Fernando Ortiz illustrate this abundantly. He sums it up as follows:

"Havana was known for her libertine pleasures on the portside and in the neighbouring barrios – El Manglar, Los Sitios [still known by the same name today] where sailors enjoyed all the fun they had missed for months at sea and mingled with the colored dancing girls (*negras y mulatas de rumba*) and the whores of three races in shacks serving as taverns and dance halls, amid card games, tobacco, and strong liquors, all to the most sensual and exciting music that was ever designed to stir up uncontrolled passions from the very guts of humans . . . (. . . *al son de la música mas sensual, excitante y libre que las pasiones sin freno lograban arrancar a la entraña humana . . .*)"

It sounds so much more visceral in Spanish. And to conclude: "Havana deserved to be called the Babylon of ruffians."

The same chronicles dwell on the fact that the convents were just as infested with sex and gambling, and that with a few honorable exceptions, monks lived in sin with their colored girlfriends and were as addicted to the *monte* card game as the rest of the city. Similar patterns of behavior could be found in virtually all the colonies, but Havana as the great colonial crossroads won the best of the bad reputations.

Cuba's Catholic bishops found it necessary to decree that it was forbidden "to drink chocolate and to smoke tobacco in church, to sleep under the altars or in the confessionals, to allow women to stay for the night, to hang up indecent images, and to play cards or dice games in the cemetery . . ." It appears that the Catholic hierarchy, with scant support from a corrupt officialdom getting kickbacks from all the vices, desperately tried to maintain a white Christian veneer on the wild city. The almost obsessive reprehension of interracial sex is just an illustration of how mixed and brown the real city was fast becoming.

Meanwhile back in Spain, the Catholic Church had become an essential part of a fossilized and deeply corrupt establishment, impoverishing the country rather than enriching it in spite of all the gold and silver flowing in from Havana. There was a short break of enlightenment under the Bourbon King Charles III (Carlos Tercero), when the totally degenerate Spanish Habsburg monarchy had died out. Carlos Tercero is even recognized as a good king in Havana today – the very first shopping mall opened in Centro Habana in the 1990s was even named after him. Here Havana discovered the newest religion: spending and consuming – for the happy few.

The blind conservatism of the Catholic Church in Spain obviously opposed with all its might the Cuban struggle for independence, seen as a dark plot by Republican Freemasons. Spain tried to repress Cuban independence with a very dirty war that included terror tactics and even concentration camps. The reaction of some of the clergy in Cuba was more diverse, and some local priests blessed the revolutionaries. Felix Varela, a prominent priest and intellectual, became a campaigner for independence and an end to slavery in the 1820s. He died in exile in the United States, but is now rightly revered in Havana as a great precursor, and the imposing cultural palace of the Catholic Church near the cathedral is named after him.

In spite of the deep family ties, the rejection of the Spain of the colonial wars remains very much alive today. Not a coincidence: Fidel and his *guerrilleros* in the Sierra saw themselves as the direct heirs to the *mambises* (singular *mambi*), as the fighters of the independence wars against Spain called themselves. They, in turn, upheld the tradition of the *cimarrones*, the runaway slaves who had taunted the colonial establishment for centuries with their settlements in the wilds. This fact explains why the news on the front page of the official newspaper *Granma* is so often from the 1890s. It also illustrates how Fidel in the Sierra, and especially Che in Bolivia, saw themselves as an absolute moral vanguard, saints of a religion of their own, starting out with only a few followers and ending up by conquering absolute power. Again it's not a coincidence that even during her most atheist years, Havana still worshipped José Martí as The Apostle. In a related way, the utter neglect suffered by Havana since the 1960s may be due to the founding myth of the revolution being that of resistance in the wilds; the city was never a natural environment to the *barbudos* themselves, even though they had a strong following among urban intellectuals.

The Catholic Church bounced back forcefully in the Havana of the early republic, as of the early 1900s. It remained socially prominent, and controlled quality education: the Castro brothers went to the Jesuit college of Belén. But in the meantime, for the untamed Havana under the white upper and middle-class surface, Santería had been further codified and had spread as the true religion of the people and of mixed-blood *cubanía*. Not that formal religion was ever Havana's forte. Pre-1959 attendance at services was generally under 5 percent. Yet in the 1980s and '90s, between 80 and 85 percent expressed belief in the divine, if not in any particular religion or deity.

The Revolution became officially atheist or rather, became a religion unto itself. Much of the Spanish clergy disappeared. Much of the white bourgeoisie, who had filled the churches, emigrated. Fidel was reportedly formally excommunicated from the Church by Pope John XXIII in 1962. Some Cuban-born clerics were sent to re-education camps. This was the case of Jaime Ortega, then a young priest in Matanzas, in 1966–1967. The largest Catholic boarding school in Havana, Villa Marista, became a dreaded interrogation center of the Ministry of the Interior. Havana never refers to this center by name, even in whispers. It's called Todo el Mundo Canta – "Everybody sings," to sing in the universal slang meaning to confess to anything.

After his liberation, Jaime Ortega remained active in various parishes, and kept up his personal resistance. He would later become a cardinal and the head of the Cuban Catholic Church. His own experiences had made him very attentive to the anti-communist crusade of Pope John Paul II.

When Fidel, for his own unfathomable reasons, sought reconciliation with the Vatican during the *Período Especial*, Ortega became the driving force behind the first ever visit of a pope to Havana, in January 1998.

59. WHO'S THE BOSS?

To warm up the crowds for the visit, the statue of the national patron saint La Virgen de la Caridad del Cobre was taken on an island-wide parade from her sanctuary near Santiago. Of course this became a resounding success, especially in Havana. Ochún is her dearest sister and her greatest protectress. More than a saint, an African spirit, or a psychological archetype or model, she's like family to many. The Catholic Church, by now, had become wise enough to coopt Santería for her own benefit.

But the Church found it difficult to produce posters and flyers, in a country almost without free printing presses, where at times even a Xerox machine was considered a tool of subversion if it fell into the wrong hands. Mexican bishops came to the rescue and sent large quantities of posters proclaiming "Jesucristo es tu Señor." When these somehow made it through customs and began to appear behind windows in the city, the CDRs counterattacked with their own poster that said *"Aqui mando yo!"* ("I give the orders here!").

European diplomats with frequent access to Fidel in the run-up to the visit advised him "to have mojitos with the cardinal" – a suggestion he took with rather ill grace, and not just because he didn't like mojitos. The cardinal for his part, for all his suave persona, had never forgotten his early experiences under communist rule.

While the government insisted on inviting the Pope for a state visit, the Vatican held fast that this was a pastoral pilgrimage – not by the head of state of the Holy See, but by a crusading preacher. The authorities nevertheless restored and prepared a grand guesthouse, a spectacularly pink neoclassical palace facing the Palacio de Convenciones in Playa, which the Pope refused to occupy.

60. THE HOLY SPIRIT ON THE PLAZA DE LA REVOLUCIÓN

I witnessed from up close Fidel's welcoming speech at the airport. It was a masterpiece. He fully played the gracious host to his visitor, while at the same time mercilessly destroying the Church's historic track record in Latin America.

In spite of this, the visit became a success for both sides. The Comandante went to mass on the Plaza de la Revolución, and sang the *Ave María* with the rest of the crowd, after looking over his shoulder to ascertain that he himself had attracted much larger crowds in his heyday. In a highly comical moment when he arrived below the stage with the altar, the concelebrating bishops produced small cameras from beneath their vestments and enthusiastically filmed the Cuban heretic. The Pope himself was very frail and almost without a voice at times, but the crowd constantly encouraged him with loud slogans of "Juan Pablo, Hermano, amigo de los cubanos," and "Juan Pablo Segundo, amigo de todo el mundo." Already at the airport, the irritation of his untamed spirit at the betrayal of his body had been evident, when he slapped the hand of the security agent who tried to help him step into the popemobile. Now he visibly absorbed the energy of the chanting crowd, and the exchange reviving a very old man and giving him back his voice turned the mass into a spiritual experience even for an agnostic like myself, albeit not the one intended. When a sudden gust of wind stirred the pope's white robes, he jokingly improvised in the middle of a trailing sentence that the Holy Spirit was passing. The crowd's enthusiasm climaxed.

At the end of the service, cheap blue plastic rosaries were handed out, creating the same near-hysterical mobbing and grabbing as New Orleans Mardi Gras beads – and probably coming from the same factories in China.

Just before John Paul II left the country, God and the Devil made a pact: the Pope condemned the U.S. embargo, and in exchange Cuba admitted more foreign Catholic clergy. Afterwards, the evaluation of the "success" of the visit on the side of the Catholic Church was restrained. There had been an expectation of more access to the media and to the schools in the aftermath of the visit, but that didn't happen.

61. WINNERS AND LOSERS

The visit, with its successful crowd control, also turned into the re-taking of Havana's streets after the years of tolerance for flashes of anarchy. The exuberance of the nightlife was greatly tuned down. I cannot say that I was happy with this development, as much of my own intimacy with the city had been gained thanks to her more libertarian years.

By 1999 the cleanup was complete, including new special police units with gray berets, well equipped with high-tech communications gear for often invasive ID-checks on the streets. Jesus won the day, but Fidel carried the season. Havana had to behave herself again or, as of old, at least to pretend.

Cardinal Ortega had come to realize that Cuba was not another Poland, and that the mere presence of an already tired and ill John Paul II would not foment a counterrevolution. He became much more cooperative with the establishment than his early experiences with the system had coached him for. The government, from its side, recognized the social role of the Church. In and outside Havana, the Church and its affiliates – Caritas, the San Egidio Community – have taken over some social duties the government finds hard to uphold, especially care for the elderly and the homeless, although under official policy, that last category doesn't exist.

Catholics and their priests and bishops in the provinces sometimes supported and sometimes opposed the Cardinal's actions and policies. Quite a few saw him as too close to the government. The National Conference of Bishops, bypassing the Cardinals' personal authority, in 2013 published a harsh condemnation of the social and spiritual consequences of fifty years of communism, only partially camouflaged in the sugary devotion normally coating such pastoral letters. Quite surprisingly, there was no official reaction – illustrating that the Catholic establishment now enjoyed a wide margin of freedom.

Ortega's enemies within the Catholic community won't

forgive his distancing himself from dissident groups such as the Damas de Blanco, whom he accused of abusing church services for propaganda purposes. The Ladies in White started their movement as spouses or mothers of political prisoners, but after the prisoners were released in 2005 and for the most part went into exile, they continued their actions as a more general protest against oppression.

They used to attend mass every Sunday at midday at Santa Rita Church on Quinta Avenida in Miramar, before marching up and down a stretch of the avenue – from Calle Treinta to the Malecón tunnel and back – heavily escorted by plainclothes security recording every face and every move, and sometimes intervening harshly when the Ladies in White deviate from the tolerated route of their event. The marches were discontinued after the third papal visit, by Pope Francis in September 2015, and Ortega retired as head of the Catholic Church in 2016. But he is still very much a political player, now as an elder statesman, especially since he was the personal messenger between the Vatican and the White House for the U.S.-Cuba diplomatic reconciliation. The Damas de Blanco continue to oppose the Cuba-U.S. thaw, thus placing themselves at loggerheads with the leadership of the Church, as Pope Francis himself was instrumental in the diplomatic breakthrough. It looks very much as if they've chosen the wrong side of history – but standing up for fundamental rights may be beyond politics and even beyond religion. In spite of their bravery or their recklessness in seeking repeated arrests in support of those rights, the Damas de Blanco are also known for their vicious internal fights and personality clashes.

This affects their credibility, and they are by no means a viable political opposition movement, as some in Europe and the United States like to believe.

The Catholic Church has retained or regained some socially conservative traits from its long history in Cuba. The advances in women's and LGBT rights, for instance, are not looked upon kindly by many of the clergy. Catholic social activists, who had benefitted from the Church's protection to open debates about the future of the country, began to feel stifled by backward-looking dogma. But the picture is mixed: the Church now also runs the only non-governmental institute of higher education, as well as a very successful business school, and a bright younger clergy is also active, biding its time in the cardinal's mostly obsequious entourage.

The changing of the guard at the top of the Church provides a glimpse of its future role in Cuba. The new leader of the Church as the archbishop of Havana is Juan de la Caridad García, formerly bishop of Camaguey. Next to a very political Ortega, he is decidedly more "pastoral" and much more discreet. The social role of the Church has been consolidated further, but Catholic grassroots dissidents and somewhat rebellious local clergy are mostly left to their own devices.

62. JACOBINS & DINOSAURS

When Raúl Castro gradually took over from his brother (2006–2008), he developed an unexpectedly close relationship with Ortega. This allowed the Church to mediate for the release of a large group of political prisoners in 2005. Later, during regular weekend lunches, Raúl would tell the Cardinal that he himself favored faster reforms in the country, but that he was held back by "Jacobins and dinosaurs." Ortega himself shared this humorous quote with me. There are certainly quite a few Jacobins – revolutionaries to the death à la Robespierre during the French Revolution – among the old guard. But we note that the president himself definitely doesn't want to go down in history as a dinosaur.

When I sat in on a private meeting with Raúl in March of 2015, he went even a little further. He said that during the phone call that led to the December 2014 reconciliation, President Obama had told him that he continued to reject a one-party system. "But Señor Presidente," Raúl said he answered, "there are really two parties in Cuba: Fidel's, and my own."

63. OTHER CHURCHES, OTHER GODS

Besides the social recognition of the Catholic Church, and the renewed street controls, there was a third consequence of the Pope's 1998 visit. It was soon made clear that the Church could not lay claim to the religious monopoly it had enjoyed in colonial times. As we have seen already, the Beth Shalom temple was reopened, and in Habana Vieja, under the stewardship of Eusebio Leal, two orthodox churches – Russian and Greek – were added to the restored monuments. There soon came more tolerance for Jehova's Witnesses and Adventists, although evangelical Christians had always been the focus of much negative propaganda even while, according to our detective Mario Conde, there was already a notable if marginal evangelical subculture in Havana in the 1980s, appealing mostly to small-time criminals in search of redemption.

Smaller evangelical groups still occasionally run into trouble today, as they are sometimes seen as unregistered cults rather than legitimate denominations. There are occasional complaints about the destruction of their places of worship – but then again, they may be in breach of zoning laws or otherwise technically illegal. The deeper cause may be the fear that foreign missionaries catering to those groups will be politically on the far right. In spite of these occasional frictions with small groups not registered with the Protestant Council of Churches, future Christianity in Cuba may well be evangelical rather than Catholic, like elsewhere in the region. The Office for Religious Affairs of the Central Committee of the Party continues to oversee the licensing of churches, as it were. As with so many other issues in Cuba, anyone operating outside the established controls may be in for trouble. U.S.-based churches and missionaries will follow in the wake of political normalization, but so far most Pentecostal and other such missionaries come to Cuba from other countries in Latin America. They may find some willing ears in generations adrift either philosophically, economically, or both, but I pray to my own gods that Cuba be spared the absurdities of born-again or other fundamentalist religions, and that the lay spirit of the country will survive.

So far there is no grand mosque in Havana, although there is an expanding Muslim presence, due to a growing number of Arab embassies and cooperation with the Gulf States. Sovereign funds from Arab states have become important financiers for public works in Cuba, in the absence of soft loans from the World Bank, the IMF, or regional development banks. A building site for a mosque to be financed by Saudi Arabia has been identified and signposted for several years now, but no works have started, apparently due to political and dogmatic rivalries within the Muslim community. The site is right next to the poor Jesús María barrio in Havana Vieja, at the edge of the port. There is little doubt that it will feel out of place in this neighborhood of feisty and scantily clad girls. Even official Havana has reasonable doubts about women's rights in the Muslim context, and about the segregation of the sexes, an unnatural and unwelcome situation in any Cuban environment. For evening prayers during Ramadan, the city historian allows a gathering at the cultural center Casa de los Arabes in Habana Vieja, which is otherwise mostly a place to taste some humus and tabbouleh (when available), or watch a Cuban interpretation of Middle Eastern belly dancing. But the Cuban girls, like when they do their version of flamenco, can't repress the Caribbean body language, and even when fully decked out in Lebanese garb, they shake more booty than belly. The staunchest Muslims would disagree anyway.

I hope the Cuban authorities keep a keen eye on any future mosque, so as not to end up with the deadly intolerant Salafist intrusions I know only too well from the grand mosque in Brussels, located just next to my offices there. It became a hotbed of hateful propaganda – with well-known consequences. In the growing religious fervor in Old Havana, a garden devoted to Mother Theresa of Calcutta was added even before she became a candidate for sainthood. Her white and blue robed order is active in the city. To extend the blessings to a famous and attractive sinner, next to it a garden dedicated to Princess Diana was also opened, the Jardín Diana de Gales.

In the crumbling depths of the Barrio Chino, our detective Mario Conde again discovers near-forgotten shrines of ancestor worship, somehow kept in operation by the stubborn elders of the community.

As for the Masons, the building of the Gran Logia de Cuba de A.L. y A.M., Constituyente de la Confederación Masónica Interamericana, proudly stands where we've seen it various times already, at the crossroads of Salvador Allende and Belascoaín. We've also seen the secret connections between the Abakuá *santeros* and the Freemasons, and you'll find undisturbed masonic tombs at the Colón Cemetery. The mantras of the Revolution, endlessly repeated on Havana's walls, are in their own way the liturgy of a religion, and a very dogmatic one at that. Like the Catholic Church at one time, the revolution has declared its doctrine infallible. Social work in Cuba, as well as political dialogue, has to take into account the strong attachment – some say the fetishism – of vocabulary acceptable within the dogmas. In Cuba there are no consumers, but there is "the citizen and his/her economic behavior." There are no socially vulnerable groups – as everyone is supposedly still taken care of – but we can acknowledge "individuals in vulnerable situations." There is, God forbid, no idea of political transition. There is not even a process of economic reform, instead there is "updating of the socialist model." And so on. Churches and their affiliates have become quite good at negotiating these constraints, just as result-oriented diplomats have to do daily.

Havana pulled off her newest feat of religious diplomacy by hosting in February 2016 an encounter between Pope Francis and the Russian Orthodox patriarch Kirill, announced as the first ever encounter between the heads of those often antagonistic churches. This was made enormous front-page news, for somewhat mystifying reasons. How many Russian Orthodox Christians are there likely to be in Havana? Is even the Russian Church part of the old guard's comfort zone and Cold War nostalgia, like their ancient Soviet tanks and MiGs? Is it because the staunch nationalism of the Moscow patriarch is also a bulwark against the decadent West? All of the above, most likely. Or, with a longer-term perspective, can Havana be a meeting point between Russia and Western Europe, a much needed crossroads at a time of uncomfortable borders and relations in Central Europe? That would be a grand ambition – but don't put it past Cuba.

64. *MISIONERO DE LA MISERICORDIA*

The visit by Pope Benedict in March 2012 felt very much like an interlude in the Havana/Holy See relationship, just as this Pope's own reign was a mere transition from the forceful John Paul to the soft-spoken diplomat Francis. If Havana had given a hearty welcome to the fiery pontiff who some believed had overthrown European communism, she could handle the first German pope with his checkered past and rather sour countenance. Benedict consolidated but brought nothing new. He met with Fidel, though, and the meeting was said to have illustrated the aging Comandante's growing interest in spiritual and cosmic themes. As a matter of fact, such meetings of visiting VIPs with the older Castro were used as PR devices to underscore that the man was alive and well, mentally lucid and intellectually active, despite frequent rumors to the contrary. The last such publicized meeting Fidel had, with the president of Vietnam, took place on November 15, 2016, in the morning. In the afternoon he was supposed to meet with visiting Canadian prime minister Justin Trudeau. When that meeting didn't take place despite close family ties between the Castros and the Trudeaus, this was the first indication of the final stage. Fidel died two weeks later.

While he continued to intervene in political debates once in a while, and published "reflections" in *Granma*, in his retirement the Comandante certainly had time to reflect on religion too. In the 1980s, Brazilian theologian Frei Betto published a book called *Fidel y la Religión*. Betto is still a hero to some leftist Catholics in the region nostalgic for liberation theology, and he has found new followers with the anti-globalists. But he was never very influential beyond his circle of admirers, and he did not grow in my own esteem when I witnessed a conference of his in Havana in early 2014, where he gave an apocalyptic depiction of Western civilization as one big orgy of drugs and prostitution. As a professional representative of such a decadent West, I sat wondering where else in the world a civilization was on a better spiritual path. In China? In Russia? The doubtlessly well-meaning Betto came across as one more incurable nostalgic of the 1960s in the totally different Latin America of today, the real Cuba not excluded. As for his book on Fidel and religion, the Comandante's track record with the Church showed that he had used religion, like any clever politician, when and where it suited him. As far as I was concerned, no whitewash was needed.

The third papal visit was that of Francis in September 2015. The first Latino pope to Cuba is not only that. He's also a countryman of Che Guevara, and the skillful diplomat who, together with the equally discreet and modest Canada, made the reconciliation with the United States possible. Francis came as a "Missionary of Mercy." But Catholic dissidents were first disappointed, later enraged, when in spite of his slogan, the Pope refused to meet with them, and even more so when, as they argued, "beggars and the homeless had been removed from the streets of Havana to give the city a better aspect." In fairness, there are not many beggars or homeless visible at any time in Havana, certainly not to someone who has lived in New York City in the 1980s. But be that as it may, the dissidence was bitter.

This spilled over for a moment when the popemobile arrived for the mass on the Plaza on Sunday, September 10. Three activists managed to break through the security measures and to approach the Pope. They were dragged off in full view of the crowd assembled for mass.

This service otherwise became a sedate affair, and had nothing of the vibrancy and the deep emotions of the 1998 mass celebrated by John Paul. Ochún had been brought over again from Santiago and stood next to the altar. But while she must have admired the willpower of the ailing John Paul, she may have been disappointed when Francis, in his homily, was extremely diplomatic and clearly saw it as his mission first and foremost to maintain the privileges the Church had gained in Cuba. The announced missionary revealed himself rather as God's supreme ambassador. The same prudent tone had prevailed from both sides as of the Pope's arrival at the airport, in sharp contrast with Fidel's oratory fireworks in 1998. In a near repeat of the passage of the Holy Ghost, the pope's skullcap was blown off as he descended from the Alitalia papal plane, but it felt like a very different omen.

While ignoring the Catholic dissidence, Francis had a meeting with youngsters at the Félix Varela Catholic cultural center. A large crowd of young *habaneros* had been assembled. Francis spoke well, and touched upon sensitive themes for Cuba's youth. But his discourse of neighborly love and opposing materialism sounded suspiciously like Cuba's old guard. I respectfully doubt that it will make much difference to most young Cubans' outlook on life.

With its regained position in Cuba since the late 1990s, the Catholic Church was also revealed to have remained very conservative on key issues. Some bishops almost share the government's fear of the internet as a tool of the devil. In a sexually liberated Cuba, the Church still preaches traditional morality, even though Pope Francis has shown himself to be personally more open to LGBT rights and the status of divorced Catholics. The fact that such reflections are even needed in this day and age sounds painfully outdated. More forward-looking Catholic activists who had been working for the Church magazine *Espacio Laical*, resenting the restraints of old dogmas, recently emancipated themselves from the clergy and set up an independent think tank called Cuba Posible. It has become the best forum for open-minded reflections on the future of the country, while skillfully retaining the respect or at least the tolerance of the censors.

When I recently discussed the Church's attitudes regarding gay rights with Mariela Castro, she argued that yes, there are very conservative forces there – but that the real Christians of Cuba's future will likely be Protestants who are much more open-minded. Besides, she added, accepting sexual diversity is first and foremost a simple question of humanity – of "touching hands," as she put it. That may in the end be the simple definition of real *misericordia*, beyond all religion.

65. MOZART IN HAVANA

Plaza San Francisco has become one of the liveliest squares in old Havana. It faces the cruise ship pier – the *Muelle San Francisco* of old – and lies between the church of the same name and the Lonja del Comercio, the restored former Chamber of Commerce building now housing company offices and the Havana CNN bureau. A bronze St. Francis showing affection to a near-naked boy, placed in more innocent times, to me now looks somewhat embarrassing. The church has been turned into a concert hall. In the front, where the entire transept of the original architecture went missing, its depth and perspective are convincingly suggested by a masterful trompe l'oeil fresco. This space is home to many of Havana's best classical concerts.

For Havana is not just good at drumming and salsa. There is an unexpectedly rich culture of classical music and musicianship here. It's in the San Francisco basilica that I love to hear my favorite piece of Cuban classical music: Guido López Gavilán's *Guaguancó*, at its best performed by the all-female Camerata Romeu. The piece is even the best soundtrack to this book, as it blends a deeply melancholic melody with the lively and insistent African percussion of the traditional guaguancó rhythm played by tapping the fronts and sides of the cellos. One of the young women lays her violin aside and, dancing with whirling braids, provokes the body-shaped instruments of her *compañeras*. It's the perfect meeting of all the sadness and all the untamed energy I feel in Havana.

In a courtyard just across from the entrance, on Calle Oficios, there is a contemporary monument to Mozart. It belongs there perfectly. Havana is a place for musical child prodigies, maybe most of all among the quick-witted street kids from the neighboring poor *barrios* hanging out here, lost in advance to Franciscan charity and cockily fending for themselves. Sports and music are often the only escapes from poverty here, as in so many other places. Musical education is a choice way to keep these kids from going bad. Bringing classical music to the rough *barrios* of Habana Vieja is also unexpectedly successful. A splendid Mozart festival organized a concert in the cathedral in October 2015. Many of the performers were from these very streets. The cathedral was overflowing with an adoring public, forgetting the humid heat and the frustrations of an entire week while listening to the masterful performances. The Havana cathedral (dating back to 1778) was built during Mozart's own short life (1756–1791), and he distilled timeless beauty from the war-torn Europe even as those wars reached Havana in 1762. Maybe a paradigm for our own times, I sat asking myself, sweating with the crowd and thus also transported to pre-AC ages when only a fan could bring some relief. Many of the girls in the audience had one, and I sat praising the fact that at least I didn't have to wear a powdered wig.

Through the open gates of the cathedral, the occasional street fight or the *pregón* (cry or proclamation) of a vendor regularly mixed with the music, as would doubtlessly also have been the case in the eighteenth century. Like in the *guaguancó*'s mixture of elegy and *alegría*, Havana made Mozart her own by adding the rhythms of her streets to his genius.

66. ART & POLITICS

But let's be realistic: Havana's streets will produce kids other than the next Mozart.

The 2015 Havana Arts Biennale was a great event by all standards: attracting a host of foreign artists and performers, blending *habaneros* seamlessly with visitors during car-free Sundays on the Malecón, and showing some of the most inspired and edgy Cuban art, as well. There has always been a great respect for talent in the visual arts, even when creations become politically edgy and touch upon themes not negotiable for public discourse – images and situations may say more than words. In spite of being a staunch Soviet ally for decades, in her creativity, Cuba saved herself from almost all the pitfalls of heroic social realism. The 2015 Biennale again had lots of politically inspired works and installations, showcasing the Cuban talent to give playful twists even to painful themes – boat people, the diaspora, the individual soul in the crush of collectivization.

A visiting foreign video artist, collecting images for future use, is interviewing kids playing on the streets in rough neighborhoods, asking them what they want to be when they grow up? She is venturing deeper and deeper in the cratered

The 2015 Havana Arts Biennale on the Malecón

streets of Centro Habana, till she comes upon a baseball game improvised with a broomstick and a ball of rolled-up old socks. She interviews the fans.

This eight-year old girl with a bright smile, missing a front tooth behind her beaded braids, wants to be a pilot. A more introspective boy takes longer to decide, but eventually shares that he will be a psychologist. The third kid is bare-chested, wearing Nikes several sizes too big, belonging to an older brother or else stolen at random. He's the cocky kind and his defiant eyes are much older than his ten or so years. He takes in the question, gives it time to sink in, while the interviewer insists: "what do you dream of becoming when you grow up?"

He spits in a crater in the sidewalk, slowly and deliberately, then faces the camera again and says one word: "Dictator!"

67. *PELOTA* (THE BALL GAME)

The improvised baseball game just witnessed for art's sake used to be a frequent sight all over town. Baseball is simply called *la pelota*, "ball." The yearly competition and the ups and downs of the white and blue Industriales team from the capital, and their main rivals from Pinar del Río, Santa Clara, and Santiago are still followed with passion on radio and TV by many, and may even induce some to read articles in *Granma*, because the sports pages – with winners and losers – are less predictable than the paper's politics. Through baseball, Cuba always remained connected to an entire Caribbean sports culture, together with Puerto Rico, the Dominican Republic, Venezuela, Panama, and even the Dutch Antilles. The Industriales give Cuban baseball a suitable socialist flavor, but the pre-revolutionary teams went by more colorful and more menacing names: Tigres de Marianao, Elefantes de Cienfuegos, Alacranes (scorpions) del Almendares, Leones de La Habana ... The other teams facing off Cuba in the regional Serie del Caribe championship often still go by similar names: Tigres de Licey, Lobos (wolves) de Arecibo, Leones de Ponce, Aguilas (eagles) Cibaeñas. The remaining Cuban tigers are the ones of the team from Ciego de Avila.

Of all things Americans left behind in Cuba after 1959, baseball was one of the strongest and most enduring. It remained the national sport. Being an aficionado of one of the star teams was a legitimate allegiance next to patriotism and Marxism; such not-frowned-upon loves were rare.

Also, next to salsa music, *la pelota* was the way into the cultural *nomenklatura* and could yield a star athlete the permit to own a private car, and to live in a house in Miramar or Siboney. There was still a strong element of patriotism in such relative stardom, as the financial rewards even for top athletes were very, very modest compared to what the U.S. major leagues would offer – and the siren song of million-dollar contracts beyond the Florida Straits was and is always present.

But by and large, Cuban athletes accepted standing proud under their flag to illustrate the fighting spirit of their island. Model *pionero* schoolkids during the weekends changed their red-and-white uniforms for little league outfits, and trained as pitchers, batters, and catchers under a talent coach's watchful eye.

In the 1990s, *la pelota* became an element in timid overtures with the United States, when the Baltimore Orioles played the Cuban team in Havana, generating disappointed hopes for more frequent exchanges, strengthening the million-dollar temptations for the Cuban players, and ending in a passionate discussion about the respective merits of aluminum as opposed to wooden bats. Nothing more came of it for a long time, but as in the case of ping-pong diplomacy with China under Nixon, baseball politics with the United States did have a future. Defections of Cuban players to the U.S. league happened with some frequency, as late as 2016. While in the past they were branded traitors with all the usual hyperbole, the reconciliation with the U.S. toned this down, and there was even an official brotherly visit from two of them accompanied by U.S. baseball officials, allegedly to work out an orderly transfer system. But the temptation of the million-dollar contracts in El Yuma is still very much there. Like in Central Park on weekends, *habanero* little league kids are coached by daddy, who is delighted if his son swings a mean bat, or does well as a pitcher or a catcher, and likewise slouching off with a tearful loser when the talent is just not there, and the pipe dream of the future millions with dad as a coach evaporates in the dreary Sunday afternoon walk back home to reality.

At the same time, *la pelota* lost some of its glamour in more recent years.

Almost as a reaction against the status quo prevailing in all things, sports included, younger Cubans became more and more interested in soccer. Baseball was officially sanctioned as a national pastime. Both Fidel and Che Guevara had once played golf before the camera – but that was probably to mock the bourgeois privilege of the golf club, which was soon turned into the national arts school. But Fidel loved to bat and did so repeatedly in the Estadio Latinoamericano in El Cerro, "*la catedral del béisbol cubano.*"

Maybe as a side effect of the renewed family ties with Spain, and of the much relaxed foreign travel law as of 2013, Havana weekends for young males became increasingly dedicated to matches of Real Madrid or Barcelona. Probably the influence of Venezuela's *Telesur* TV station played an important part as well, since more soccer came on local TV via Caracas. Shirts and flags of the teams are flourishing, in a further display of non-traditional loyalties that still feels like a provocation in Havana's mostly prudent public behavior.

Like improbable haircuts, low-hanging jeans, fancy phones, and fading allegiance to revolutionary symbols and practices, *pelota* vs. soccer is now a generational issue between grandfathers and grandsons, with daddy's age group caught uncomfortably in the middle. Girlfriends for their part follow their *novios'* preferences, although they themselves may see more excitement in the newer game, and its *yuma* (foreign) *fútbol* gods, as well.

The 2014 soccer world cup gave this a big push. Brazil, the host country, was at that time Cuba's closest ally in the region, so how could anything that was wrong come from Rio?

There was, nevertheless, an official line about the loss of affection for *la pelota*: you see, baseball is a demanding sport as to equipment; you need a glove, a bat, a helmet, the right ball. All of that is expensive, and of course, due to the embargo, hard to come by. For soccer, all you need is a ball.

Hm.

Having lived for a long time elsewhere in the Caribbean, and seen barefoot kids play an immensely complicated game like cricket with improvised sticks and balls made of old socks, I'm somewhat skeptical about the official line. If kids want to play baseball, surely they'll improvise the implements.

So we have this strange situation where the Cuban establishment defends the most American of sports against a loss of love to a decidedly European and Latin American rival.

Right in front of the Capitolio, on the border of Habana Vieja and Centro Habana, the Kid Chocolate boxing gym is another survivor from pre-revolutionary times. Being located in a poor neighborhood, this place may also be many a ghetto kid's first stop on a dream road to stardom.

The gym is, again with typical Cuban political incorrectness, named for Cuba's greatest black boxing champion ever, Eligio Sardiñas Montalvo (1910–1988), who was a world super-featherweight champion in the 1930s.

Boxing is Cuba's new claim to Olympic and other types of athletic excellence. If the new "chocolate kid" is good

enough, he may qualify to join the official training camp outside the city, and move from his gritty background to professional coaching and grooming. And next?

A Cuban *pelotero* tempted by the United States may make
millions in one season. Will we also see Cuban boxers entering the glamour, show-biz glitter, real drama, and unavoidable
fraud of big boxing, Las Vegas style? And one Cuban making
100 million dollars in a single night on Pay per View? Imagine the temptations infusing Kid Chocolate's sweaty walls.

It was at the Cuban "baseball cathedral," the Estadio Latino-

The Kid Chocolate
gym, where a poor
kid from the *barrio*
can dream once
again of a career as a
multimillion-dollar
boxer.

americano in El Cerro, that President Obama concluded his historic visit to Havana, on March 23, 2016. As this was the day after the terrorist attacks on the Brussels airport and subway, the Cuba-U.S. game opened with a minute of silence for the victims.

Standing to attention in the presence of both presidents in the vast stadium, I mused on how strangely events had converged. The presidents of such old enemies together in the box, chatting like family, was an event in itself.

Cuba lost the baseball game, but the release of hundreds of white doves as signs of peace at the end of the event seemed to open a new chapter – if not for the world, at least for these two neighbors.

68. THE UNITED MOBSTERS

Baseball was not the only love imported from the United States. Modern-day gambling brought near industrial expansion and enormous glitter to an old Havana vice. At a time when Las Vegas was nothing but a dusty desert town, a downright invasion of neon lights, roulette and blackjack tables descended upon Havana. The U.S. mob ruled the industry in a close alliance with Fulgencio Batista, who turned himself from a more or less legitimate politician into a successful political gangster with his 1952 coup.

This alliance realized a dream the mafia had cherished in New Jersey and Chicago since Prohibition days: simply to run their own government, hand-in-hand with politicians charging a negotiated price for their part in the coalition.

The best known of the legendary mobsters, Meyer Lansky, left his landmark on the Malecón: the Riviera Hotel, a fifties-designed masterpiece. When entering its lobby, one is reminded of the style of the United Nations building in Manhattan – same epoch, same lines and curves, similar furniture. The Riviera's style is just a little more playful and opulent. Maybe the comparison is unflattering to the UN, but one can still envisage Lansky himself, impeccably dressed, crossing the lobby on his way to a secret conference somewhere upstairs or backstage, or in his private suite on the top floor, like a diplomat or a politician running his own city-state. Lansky lived in the nearby FOSCA building in solid bourgeois style with his wife, keeping his Cuban girlfriend Carmen in an apartment on Prado in the old city.

In the film *The Godfather*, the last nights of Batista's decadent Havana are vividly portrayed. For the purpose of the movie, Batista's last stand during the New Year's Eve ball of 1958–1959 was filmed in the caryatid room of the presidential palace in Santo Domingo, now used as a waiting area

Lansky-land: how the mafia king saw Havana from
his apartment in the FOCSA building.

for ambassadors presenting credentials to the President of the Dominican Republic. I inspected it with secret amusement while waiting my turn to meet with president Leonel Fernández there in 2006, dressed in the white suit-black tie outfit required by protocol, making one feel like a tropical gigolo from Batista days, when this palace was occupied by his local equivalent, the dictator Trujillo of even more sinister reputation. But Trujillo ended up being murdered by opponents, unlike Batista who died rich and safe in exile in Spain after a temporary stay in Madeira.

He had robbed his country dry upon departure, apparently also leaving with the gold stolen from the mob. When Lansky died in Florida in 1983, he had exactly fifty-seven thousand dollars in the bank, not the expected millions. There are still whispers about a hidden Lansky treasure, but it's more likely that Batista, the better gangster, swindled them all.

When the Revolution arrived, the roulette tables were smashed, and the croupiers swiftly denied their religion, not having much choice. On the streets, popular anger and vandalism next targeted the parking meters, as it was known that they were nothing but the private slot machines of Batista's brother-in-law Roberto Fernández.

As I have already mentioned, the American actor George Raft left an eyewitness account of the vandalism breaking loose around three a.m., when the president's departure became known. In the Capri, too, the casino was smashed to pieces. Raft says that he went down to the lobby to witness the events. Miss Cuba fled. The party was over. Shootouts on the streets converged around Parque Central, where a bunch of Batista henchmen known as Los Tigres stood their ground for a while, before they and other *sbirros batistianos* were dragged off to summary executions under loud popular shouts of *"Al Paredón!"* ("To the firing squad!"). A herd of pigs was set loose in the Riviera lobby, soiling its elegance with mud and shit.

In spite of these situations and events, Lansky still tried to reach a compromise with Fidel, but of course his reign was over. He not only lost his cash, but after Havana spat him out he literally became a wandering Jew, trying in vain to settle in England, the Dominican Republic, and Israel.

Lansky had been Havana's most dubious lover. In the love nest on Prado she let herself be pampered with pearls and gold and diamonds. But who knows? When Mr. Lansky went home to Mrs. Lansky at two in the morning, Havana may well have turned herself into a political cat woman to join a revolutionary cell meeting in the forbidding depths of El Cerro or Diez de Octubre. Or maybe she pawned the mobster king's gold in a discreet *casa de empeño* to finance bullets for the Revolution. Havana could always be anything and its opposite, and still remain true to herself.

The sequel is well known. The mob moved to Las Vegas, where they took a desert and covered it in glitter for the masses yearning to be swindled. It was a new age – loud, trashy, and tacky: the dark and elegant fascination of sinful Havana was never to be copied elsewhere. As with most things in Cuba under whatever circumstances, even its evil had style.

On the top floor of the FOSCA where Lansky lived, there is a bar and a restaurant. They offer a panoramic and even vertiginous view of the entire city as Lansky once surveyed it, and one can muse about the power he craved over it.

The musings may be badly framed by the one-man band sometimes performing disastrous karaoke tunes in the bar on a partly programmed keyboard, but you get the view, at least; and the middle-aged gentleman performing this sad substitute for music has to eat, too. One is tempted to bribe him to shut up.

When he took Havana, Fidel turned another recently completed hotel into his headquarters: the Havana Hilton, soon renamed the Habana Libre. The Riviera never changed names. It still stands, badly eroded from the waves crashing over the Malecón wall. It will forever be a monument to the era of "The United Mobsters," just like the UN building on 1st Avenue in New York weathers a Caribbean-born hurricane once every few years, and is a monument to even grander if much nobler illusions.

69. *UNA MAL CRIADA*

The Riviera was the UM headquarters in their best years, but the founding reunion of mob *capi* to establish their Havana reign had been held in 1946 at the Hotel Nacional. The management of that hotel contacted me in 1998, when the bars were being refurbished for the upswing in tourism. Without regard to their misdeeds, the mobsters got their portraits in tasteful sepia on the walls of the main bar. Anything was good for the new types of visitor, and the mob was part of Havana legends. But not to limit the fame to the infamous, the hotel also checked its records for less edgy celebrities who had stayed there. Winston Churchill was an obvious choice, having won the worst war of human history largely on champagne and Havana cigars. When the manager contacted me, he was asking for a portrait of King Leopold III of Belgium, who was reported to have stayed at the hotel more or less incognito with then–crown prince Baudouin in 1948. After some political doubts, I sent the picture.

It was scarcely up on the wall when I received a mysterious

phone call from an elderly lady with a raspy voice but speaking old-school Spanish. She requested an urgent meeting.

When I received her, accompanied by a friend who turned out to be a lady in waiting, she revealed herself to be a survivor of the ancient creole aristocracy. Their weathered appearance corresponded to the aspect of the crumbling palaces where the last of that class still held on. I knew how they often retreated from room to grandiose room, when ceilings started to collapse from internal rot caused by half a century of tropical humidity and slowly disintegrating plumbing in the walls. But they were stubbornly sitting out the adversities of history, just as monarchists in mothballs in Paris still wait for the recognition that the French Revolution was not just an enormous crime, but also a fatal mistake.

The name-dropping that peppered the lady's conversation sounded like the pompadour-style architecture of the sugar aristocracy: la Marquesa Justiz de Santa Ana, Ofelia Broch de Torriente, la Marquesa viuda de Pinar del Río, Estela Moas de Runken . . . It was also like turning the brittle and spotted pages of an almanac of the society balls before the revolution. I suddenly envisaged Havana as a white-gloved debutante, having turned into these tough and tanned *viejitas*, more resistant to time than their palaces were.

My visitor's point was that, yes, the King had visited Havana. But he had by no means stayed at the Hotel Nacional, but rather at her mother's house. Such historical misinformation required an urgent correction. And not only that: "When His Majesty passed, my mother wrote a very elegant letter of condolence to the Princess, his widow. She never received a reply. As far as I'm concerned, the Princess lacked education." The lady-in-waiting, translating this last accusation into a more down to earth formula, repeated: *"Una mal criada!"*

70. HOLLYWOOD HAVANA

When Coppola made *The Godfather* cycle, Hollywood had long been banned from Havana. Some stock footage of the city and the Morro lighthouse was used to evoke the arrival of the *capi* in 1946, and for the rest Havana could be more or less convincingly imitated in Santo Domingo or elsewhere. But a previous Hollywood generation had not just played hard in Havana like George Raft at the Capri, but had also worked there. Havana, with her looks and her climate, was the perfect set and the perfect extra. Hollywood would provide the stars.

But alas, miracles did not happen. In the 1940s and '50s, there could be no sexier and more intriguing place than Havana, what with the meeting of shady politics and stranded refugees, people-smuggling rings and handfuls of diamonds discreetly changing hands, the constant threat of German submarines, the exuberant nightlife camouflaging improvisation and despair. Yet no equivalent of *Casablanca* came out of it. Why no Bogey and Bacall in Havana, where, on top of it all, Hemingway was already living and could provide the script? Why then were all Havana productions so second-class, so "B"?

I can think of a few reasons. Many American movie stars used Havana for their real life escapades, and cared little to see them even more publicized. Maybe the mob sent its own extortionists to the sets, coming after Batista's men doing the same. But there is another argument that convinces me more.

Like the rest of the United States, Hollywood never understood Havana's complex character and the constant mix of spontaneous beauty and contrived elegance, corruption, playfulness, tragedy, sex, and despair. The tendency was to reduce the city to a set of "south of the border" commonplaces that completely missed the mark. Just as the Soviet propaganda in

Soy Cuba turned the city into moronic political formulas, so Hollywood, too, applied its own flat vision.

Actress Hedy Lamarr was a real life scientific genius, but she, too, let herself be cast in a Havana B movie – after turning down the part in Casablanca that became Ingrid Bergman's. *Woman without a Passport* could have become Lamarr's and Havana's *Casablanca* equivalent, but failed miserably. The refugee intrigue falls flat. Of the obligatory Havana stereotypes, admittedly the street-rumba dance number is excellent and convincingly real.

A bit more can be said for the film made after Graham Greene's *Our Man in Havana*, if only because it shows quite a bit of the city before the Revolution and thus has documentary value for judging today's decay.

But the least bad of Hollywood's Havana features is to my taste, and in spite of its terrible title, Errol Flynn's *The Big Boodle*.

Flynn roams Havana as a casino dealer with a mysterious past, a predictable but also very workable premise. Two *habanera* femmes fatales come into play, conveniently two sisters, and even more convieniently a brunette and a blonde. They drag him into a vast financial intrigue. Flynn spends most of his screentime being beaten up by various enforcers, till he manages to take things in hand. His wanderings show the very elegant 1950s neighborhoods, but also the decay that had already begun under Batista and much earlier. As a bonus, for the final shootout, we get a full tour of the Cabaña fort, including the execution chamber with the sinister *garrote vil* of Spanish times, a horrible implement of execution that gradually broke the neck with a screwing mechanism. For the somewhat absurdly contrived ending, deadly sharks deal with the principal bad guy in the harbor waters.

But that wasn't the end of Flynn's own Havana intrigues.

His widow Patricia Weymour, whom we knew well in Jamaica in the 1980s, always described him without any rancor as "a most loving rascal." However much the real life Flynn must have enjoyed the louche Havana nights of Batista's last years, the eternal rebel in him later became an ardent admirer of the Revolution. Hollywood gossip would argue this was because he fell for the girls in tight-fitting uniforms. But he spent time in the Sierra with Fidel and Raúl in 1958, and even published articles on this meeting in the United States. Later, of course, this was very much held against him, as were his last film efforts, semi-documentaries about the Revolution now dismissed as his pathetic swan songs.

But I always had great sympathy for this real Flynn. While living in Port Antonio, Jamaica, he had all the trappings of a lord of the manor: a spectacular house, a vast plantation, with his yacht the *Zacca* moored at his private island. But deep down he was still a naughty boy, soon on the run from creditors and ending his life in a hotel room in Canada. Nowhere but Havana had appealed to the real Flynn, thumbing his nose at Hollywood for his stage exit.

71. PIRATES OF ALL KINDS

As Flynn's fame was due in great part to his swashbuckling movies, we move to pirate stories next. Havana, as the shipping hub and the warehouse of all the riches of the Spanish colonies, was always a main target for buccaneers and privateers, pirates licensed by hostile European governments to attack enemy shipping in the Caribbean and on the Atlantic trade routes.

Sometimes they directly attacked the city. In Havana, the oldest part of the fortifications, the Castillo de la Fuerza Real, was built to ward off invasions by French privateers. At the opposite end of the *cantos de ida y vuelta*, it was the British lying in wait. They attacked and even sacked Cádiz twice.

The seventeenth- and eighteenth-century Caribbean piracy rightly became part of universal lore, not just thanks to Robert Louis Stevenson's *Treasure Island*, but also because it was part of the political land- and seascape. Some of the best-known pirates were libertarian philosophers, setting up democracies-at-sea, and dreaming of egalitarian republics to be established somewhere in the Bahamas. Spain, solidly anchored in Cuba, was the most conservative and most jealous power in the region, and the one with the richest ships and convoys. The Dutch corsair or privateer Piet Hein attacked and conquered the Spanish silver fleet in Matanzas Bay in 1628, and was immortalized in a children's song still current when I was young:

Piet Hein, Piet Hein,	Piet Hein, Peit Hein,
Piet Hein zijn naam is klein	Piet Hein's name is short
Zijn daden benne groot	but great are his deeds
Hij heeft gewonnen de zilvervloot.	He won the silver fleet.

As the Colombian historian Germán Arciniegas put it, the Caribbean was the "sea of the New World," where European powers fought their fiercest battles for naval supremacy. Not coincidentally is the Caribbean part English, part Spanish, part French, and part Dutch. It's a faithful reminder of what the major powers of the planet were up to a few centuries ago. They left behind an inextricable mix of drama, misery, beauty, and unfinished history.

With its thousands of miles of sheer uncontrollable coastline and its many outlying keys, and rich cargo constantly coming in and going out, Cuba was a favorite haunt of pirates. In traditional pirate lore, and not less in today's piracy-inspired TV series and video games, Havana and Matanzas became prime locations.

Piracy around Cuba also survived well into the nineteenth century, in part because Spain stayed away from the Vienna Congress in 1815, when the European and world order was redefined after the Napoleonic era. The British had by then consolidated their mastery on the high seas, and part of their self-ascribed mission as the policemen of the oceans became to intercept Cuba-bound slavers. Abolition would follow in the British territories in the 1830s, but not in Cuba (and Brazil) until more than half a century later. As far as Havana was concerned, the now internationally outlawed transatlantic slave trade lived on with the surviving piracy, in a weird symbiosis of illegality, anarchy, and officially embraced contraband.

It took the roughest and the most unscrupulous of *negreros* out of Havana and Matanzas to maintain the slave-runs from West Africa. The British navy now considered and treated the clandestine slave traders as pirates, and for that very reason in Havana they became symbols of resistance against the British Empire, and were popular heroes of sorts. The most famous of them, Pedro Blanco, even established his own small kingdom in West Africa, and taunted the British for twenty years before dying, insane, in Barcelona in 1854. There was a famous female *negrera*, the Portugese María Cruz Gómez, operating her ship the *María Pequeña* out of Matanzas.

The clandestine trade by these new pirates even extended to the United States, most notably to New Orleans.

Piracy around the Crescent City also subsisted long after the transatlantic ban, as illustrated by the epic stories surrounding the Lafitte Brothers. A frequent trick to ship new slaves from Havana or Matanzas to New Orleans was to reg-ister them as crewmembers, who were then declared to have deserted upon arrival. Even or especially after the U.S. take-over of Louisiana, authorities willingly looked the other way.

Piet Hein received a statue in Matanzas in the 1990s, af-ter some diplomatic wrangling between The Netherlands and Cuba. A "great deed" in a Dutch shanty had also been a deep humiliation for the Cuban authorities – but in the end revo-lutionary Cuba relented and let the Dutch have their statue; undermining Spanish colonial rule was, after all, an act of subversion that could be explained in political terms.

As for the real motives behind the British actions, no less a figure than the German poet Goethe immediately saw through them. He told his confidant Eckerman in 1829: "The British claim to be such great humanitarians but we know well that they never do anything without a very practical mo-tive. They employ the Africans in their own colonies, and so their "export" is simply against their own commercial inter-ests. When at the Vienna Congress, the British made a big fuss about their philanthropy, the Portuguese delegate asked dryly if this congress had been convened to define morality . . ."

Immediately after the Vienna Congress, in a document of October 1816, the *negrero* lobby in Havana won all the official support they needed to sustain the new piracy. The captain general and the royal treasurer subscribed to the lobby's resis-tance against the *perfidia inglesa* "aiming simply at the disman-tling of all Spanish colonial wealth." From then on, the late flourishing of the slave imports in Cuba, with all the conse-quences seen earlier, went into overdrive.

The ongoing slave trade/piracy gave rise to dramatic epi-sodes, as the British navy sometimes chased the *negrero* ships to within sight of Havana and Matanzas, and in such instances the ruthless captains preferred to sink their ships rather than to surrender. This happened twice on record, in 1825 and 1826, with the loss of hundreds of souls, since the Africans remained chained in the hold.

The twentieth century, of course, brought no end to traditional piracy in the Caribbean. Luxury yachts are sometimes taken, and rival gangs and cartels often attack each other's cocaine transports. Even before the December 17 announcement, Cuba and the U.S. Coast Guard and the DEA worked together closely in trying to control and secure the shipping lanes around the island. It's fair to say that much of the discreet confidence building between the two sides that was necessary to advance to the December 2014 announcements was done in the areas of maritime cooperation.

And then there were the *balseros*, the successive waves of boat people. The largest one, in Cuba's annus horribilis 1994, is still remembered in Havana's whispered urban legends, not just for the many lives lost at sea to the currents and the sharks, but, worst of all, to new pirates attacking helpless rafters to steal body organs for sale in Guatemala and Brazil, or so the stories have it. The socially conscious rap group Orishas sings about a friend from the university, seventeen years old, disappeared at sea and victim of organ theft.

The lore surrounding this new piracy had nothing to do with colorful epic. It was sad and sordid.

72. ELIÁN

I heard some of those stories first hand. The one that impressed me most was the tale of a raft with two brothers setting off from Caibarién, one of the discreet fishing ports to the east of Havana from which many *balseros* tried their luck.

The raft had made it to Florida – with one of the brothers holding the lifeless torso of the other after sharks had ripped off his legs. I heard this in a letter from Miami read aloud by tearful relatives in a small room in Vedado, full of old family portraits and plastic flowers.

The most famous *balsero* of all is Elián González, the little boy whose mother was lost at sea, who was adrift for days and finally rescued, brought to relatives in Miami. The boy was six years old, a frail looking child with an angelic smile.

It was November 1999. The dramatic *balsero* crisis of 1994 was still fresh in *habaneros'* minds. In spite of the horror stories, people were still taking their chances. Elián and his mother, together with a group of other *balseros*, had set off from Matanzas. The engine of their small metal boat had failed mid-crossing. Such tragic mishaps were frequent, at least in part due to the sale of watered-down contraband gasoline to the *balseros* by black marketeers, a truly despicable practice. Next the boat had sunk, the mother and the other passengers drowned, and Elián, the sole survivor, floated around in the inner tube of a truck tire for several days before being spotted and picked up by fishermen north of Miami.

As soon as this story became known in Havana, it was appropriated by a wide diversity of people for their own purposes. To the *santeros*, Elián's angelic countenance and his otherworldly smile could only mean that, during his episode adrift at sea and surrounded by sharks, he had been protected by the *orishas* – motherly Yemaya keeping the dark spirit of the deep, Olokún, at bay. A somewhat more practical but still poetic version was that he had been protected by dolphins.

The case turned into a cause célèbre on both sides of the Florida Straits. The father of the boy, back in Cuba, had been ignorant of the mother's plans of escape, set up by her boyfriend, who was already living in Miami. But Elián had siblings in Cuba, the father was a loving parent, and in Miami, in D.C., and in Havana, voices of reason argued that the boy belonged with his surviving parent, not with elderly relatives in Florida. The opposite side argued that Elián fell under the automatic admission as a refugee due to the "wet foot, dry foot" policy, the practical translation of the Cuban Normalization Act giving Cuban refugees an exceptional advantage over other illegal immigrants, but also blamed as the main culprit for the unsafe and often deadly crossings. Moreover, the relatives and old guard Cubans in Calle Ocho in Miami argued that it would be a crime to send a little angel back to communist hell. Common sense and simple humanity got lost in political agendas, but Janet Reno, then the U.S. attorney general, oversaw the case with great dignity and respect while it made its way through the courts.

Meanwhile in Havana, Fidel never trusted the outcome. The case was a welcome opportunity to assemble the people around a new common cause. Mass meetings were organized on the Malecón to demand the return of the boy. The yearly *zafra* (sugar cane harvest) was in full swing, but the work was interrupted to bus people by the thousands to the capital, each marcher provided with a T-shirt with a picture of the smiling Elián. Fidel marched in front, wearing his Nike sneakers for comfort as he himself half jokingly pointed out. This million-man march became the last political event of its kind in Havana, proving that the authorities could still pull this off, with all the necessary logistics and mobilization of men and means, in spite of the still difficult economic situation. Not only that.

Facing the U.S. interest section building on the Malecón (now the U.S. Embassy) almost overnight they built the Tri-

buna Anti-imperialista, a large event and concert space looking like a military bulwark and crowned at the far end with a
statue of the national hero José Martí holding a child against
his breast, and pointing an accusing arm to the imperialist
child stealers.

But Fidel's distrust of the U.S. courts proved to be wrong.
Finally, on April 19, 2000, the Circuit Court in Atlanta decided to return the boy to his father. In a military blitz operation, Elián was taken from his relatives' home in Miami,
against the hysterical protests of family and neighbors. The
boy himself now lost his composure for the first time and pan-
icked and cried like the child that he was, tossed to and fro by
incomprehensible forces – a fact that was sometimes forgotten
in the whole drama.

That same night from Matanzas, Fidel came out on the
radio and commented that this was a wise and welcome decision "*y un día de tregua*" ("a day of truce") in the confrontation
with the United States. Then he left a long moment of one
of his eloquent silences, and went on, in a voice raspy with a
mixture of fatigue and determination: "*Y mañana sigue la lu-
cha!*" ("Tomorrow the fight goes on!").

In Calle Ocho in Miami, the old guard now speculated
that Elián's father would stay behind himself when he came
to pick up his son, but they were wrong once again. Father
and child were reunited with great dignity and returned to a
heroes' welcome in Havana. In spite of all his traumatic experiences Elián grew up to be a well-spoken and thoughtful
young man.

Even many of those Cubans who had their own private
opinions about the Comandante and his system were glued to
the radio and were carried away with tearful emotion upon
listening to his Matanzas speech on the day of the decision.

They just couldn't help themselves. I witnessed the situation firsthand. A tearful friend wiped her face and said: "Even after all those years, and knowing what we know – this is still what the man does to me."

During his very last days in the White House, on January 12, 2017, President Obama revoked the wet foot, dry foot policy. Will one official signature mean the end of the many dramatic chapters in the Florida Straits?

73. NEW YORK CONNECTIONS

At the time of the Elián case, the hysterical flag waving in Miami stood in sharp contrast with the behavior of the other large Cuban exile community in the United States, the one in New Jersey. Just across the Hudson, they maintain strong ties between Havana and New York City.

In Manhattan, traces of old Cuban neighborhoods survived into the twenty-first century along Eighth Avenue just north of 14th Street. This was long a working-class immigrant neighborhood till the expansion of trendy Chelsea swallowed it, Cuban greasy spoons and all. Even on the affluent Upper West side, a few traces of Cuban presence remain. Old Cuban restaurants can still be manned by sturdy characters still not speaking one proper sentence of English after two generations in exile. They also held out against successive waves of gentrification, grudgingly producing some of the least healthy but most delicious deep-fried food on the planet. It was those restaurants advertising *comidas chinas y criollas* that made me wonder about the *Asia de Cuba* connections when I roamed Manhattan's streets in the rough 1980s.

But by and large, the Cubans in the New York area settled in New Jersey, where they continue to struggle and to thrive.

In Union City, a park is named after Celia Cruz, the feistiest of Cuban singers who defected after the Revolution. She was a child of the glitter of the Tropicana nights set on fire by the Mulatas del Fuego, and could not reconcile her spirit and her music with the new era of seriousness and sacrifice. She kept up her feisty persona till her passing in 2003, with Tito Puente's club in The Bronx as her headquarters. In private she seems to have been a rather subdued person, but on stage she always stayed true to her musical fireworks, maintaining till the end *"que la vida es un carnival y las penas se van cantando"* ("that life is a carnival, and sorrows disappear with singing"). Like all her compatriots in exile, she remained deeply Cuban. Forbidden to return to her homeland where even her music was banned, she literally proved her attachment to her native soil when she could briefly visit U.S.-held Guantanamo and there collected a handful of sand to be buried with her. It followed her to her grave in The Bronx.

There also rests La Lupe, the most dramatic Cuban voice of the 1960s and '70s. She was the theatrical troubadour of unanswered love and female revenge. Reflecting her personality, her first album was called *Con el Diablo en el Cuerpo*. She died more or less forgotten in 1992, after giving up her lifelong Santería rites for born-again Christianity. But in her younger years she had relished her persona of "La Mala" during performances often seen as excessively sexy and emotional, to the delight of early admirers such as Marlon Brando.

74. MUSIC HAS NO ENEMIES?

When Celia Cruz and La Lupe left Cuba, an Iron Curtain of sorts also came down to separate what had been a very interactive music scene between the island and the United States.

In the 1940s and '50s, all major U.S. musicians had performed regularly in Havana. The best Cuban performers were also houschold names in New York. The percussion genius Chano Pozo teamed up with Dizzy Gillespie as the co-founder of Latin Jazz. Pozo was murdered in Harlem before the Revolution, in 1948, and it's typical that he was buried in the Cementerio Colón in Havana, while even in death Celia Cruz and La Lupe were unwelcome there, and their music was censored on Cuban radio stations. There were occasional cracks in the Cold War wall separating music and musicians. My friend Dr. Meg Crahan of Columbia University fondly recalls that she went to Cuba in 1977 with Dizzy, Earl Fatha Hines, and Stan Getz to help them track down some of the musicians they had played with. It resulted in an impromptu jam session at the Teatro Nacional.

As late as 1990, the brilliant trumpet player Arturo Sandoval defected in turn, after becoming the greatest Afro-Cuban jazz performer. His flight was portrayed in the movie with Andy García acting his part. It was a Cuban family affair: García himself was born in Havana in 1956 but had left with his parents in 1961.

While such movies always had obvious political angles, even before the December 17 reconciliation the musical iron curtain had become somewhat porous. As of the year 2000, more exiled Cuban musicians returned for performances in Havana, especially at the time of the yearly jazz festival in December. And at the same time in Miami, the old guard gradually let go of the bad habit of calling in with bomb threats or organizing picketing when a Cuban from Cuba came to perform in the city. Some Miami *salseros* such as Willy Chirino used their music to critize the situation in Havana, but by and large music was ahead of politics. Still, U.S. visa requirements for Cuban musicians or bands were often used arbitrarily, sometimes even preventing Cuban nominees from attending Grammy or Latin Grammy events.

The interactive music scene received a tremendous boost after December 17. Comings and goings of musicians in both directions are now almost routine, giving talents such as Descemer Bueno, the new *conguero* master Pedrito Martínez, Alexander Abreu, and so many others the benefit of renewed roots of the Cuban traditions mingling with the vibrant Latin music scene in Miami and, not to forget, New York. Star Latin music producer Andrés Levin is moving back and forth constantly.

In contrast with Miami, New York had never swallowed the musical apartheid practiced in Florida and had always booked Cuban performers, especially the legendary Elaine Gordon at the even more legendary Village Vanguard. Gordon regularly vented her deep scorn for all politics, especially when a performer like Chucho Valdés, booked months in advance, saw himself yet again denied a U.S. visa. But the salsa music scene in New York also benefitted from the large Puerto Rican presence. The blend of Cuban and *boricua* salsa was illustrated not just by the alliance of Celia Cruz and Tito Puente in the Bronx, but also by a performer like La India, who kept Santería themes alive in New York salsa even when, in the 1990s, married to Latin superDJ and producer Louie Vega, she was part of the avant-garde New York club scene.

The greatest Cuban voice of her generation, Xiomara Laugart, also became a New York–based U.S. citizen, however much she remained completely Cuban, much like the late Celia Cruz whom she portrayed on Broadway. Her son Axel is one of the best all-round pianists of his generation, and an eccentric character just as original as Thelonious Monk in his day. Mother and son routinely perform together for memorable mixtures of Xiomara's rich voice, her playful and spontaneous stage presence, and Axel's strict musical discipline from behind the piano, in spite of the extraterrestrial appearance of his enormous yellow afro and his pharaonic beard.

Producer Andrés Levin is married to Cuban singer and actress Cucu Diamantes, as feisty a performer as her 1950s retro-kitsch alias and persona announce. But together they are also promoting an ever more vital bicoastal arts scene. Andrés runs a foundation called Music Has No Enemies. This slogan is, sadly, not true everywhere in our complicated world – but between Cuba and the United States it is becoming more and more of a reality, and a very talented, loud, and cheerful one.

By some magical coincidence, New York salsa diva La India was our neighbor in the East Village in 1992–1995, just before my first move to Havana. As the kitchens of our apartments on East 12th Street were contiguous, we often heard her sing to Yemaya and Ochún while she was cooking or doing the dishes.

The Havana–New York music scene was joined by an explosion of contacts in the visual arts as of the 2015 Havana Biennale, when almost overnight many Cuban painters became celebrities in Chelsea, as we'll see later. Some Cuban visual artists such as the avant-garde group of sculptors *Los Carpinteros* had gained fame earlier in the United States, but now there was a more general breakthrough and recognition.

75. *EL PAQUETE*

Not only for musicians and painters is the border gradually melting. To counter the mostly predictable programming of

Cuban national TV, some five years ago computer hard drives with the best and the worst of U.S. television began to be discreetly imported to Havana in the enormous bundles of luggage passing through Terminal II of the José Martí airport. It became known as *el paquete*. In spite of much official warning about "cultural pollution," the phenomenon soon became island-wide and unstoppable. It has now expanded into a vast network of professional piracy, even providing subtitles adapted to Cuban Spanish, and homemade local commercials. This was one example of how a society spontaneously claims freedoms that are not on offer, and politics and social controls have to let go when the phenomenon becomes irreversible.

While visual artists, filmmakers, and musicians do their utmost to save Cuba's own creativity under complicated circumstances, popular demand for cheaper entertainment created a vast foreign presence in a typical Cuban *por la izquierda* (under-the-table) kind of way.

To some extent, the *paquete* made up for the extremely limited internet and cable access. The *paquete* kept the people at home, watching, and maybe the authorities relented because there was some fringe benefit in terms of appeasement. Cuban tastes took to the World Wrestling Federation with the same or more gusto than to the serious content of the History Channel, to mindless action movies as well as the better Hollywood and independent productions, to all HBO series and to late night comedy shows. When the *Fast & Furious* franchise filmed scenes for the next installment on the Malecon in 2016, many *habaneros* had seen all the previous ones and mobbed the stars appearing in the flesh. The Discovery Channel became a favorite with many. The news of the rest of the world, which had always been carefully filtered through official interpretations in the Cuban media, was especially eye-opening.

The *paquete* soon had a growing impact on conversations and on the routines of stand-up comedians, about the latest events in the outside world, about the next season of *Game of Thrones*, and about Kim Kardashian's latest skimpy outfit. Most of all, what the *paquete* and its success revealed was an immense hunger for connectivity. Cuba is an educated society, but intelligence needs to be fed input to sustain itself.

The new takes on foreign affairs did a lot to soften black-and-white interpretations of current events, to add the nuances and gray areas needed to judge and to gauge what's going on in our complicated, divided, and fascinating world, where so few situations can still be explained in the simplistic terms of pre-ordained truth. On official TV, frequent *mesas redondas*, round-table discussions, try hard to maintain those truths. Too hard, sometimes. I'm often amused at the content, especially when the experts explain to me from their home-based perspective what is really going on in my own backyard in Europe. They know everything so well and with such finality . . . I take it in stride, as an almost endearing phenomenon. But occasionally a less tolerant colleague, irritated by this or the other far-fetched statement, asks for a right of reply. The deadpan answers received from Cuban officials in those instances are almost as interesting as the *mesas redondas* themselves: "we as diplomats should be the first to know that one cannot control the press . . ." In fairness, the younger generation of *Granma* journalists has been far more responsive to dialogue with the outside world, and has gradually begun to practice some more even-handed reporting. The pendulum has swung yet again in the other direction; Fidel Castro's passing in late 2016 made the official press more conservative again, as the old guard circled the wagons before the unavoidable changes that loom ahead, underscored by the Comandante's physical disappearance.

The *paquete* soon found its way into private projection rooms with 3D TVs. These had been tolerated under licenses to organize children's birthday parties or *quinceañera* celebrations (the coming-out party thrown when a girl turns fifteen, a strong Latin American tradition on which much money is spent). At this point, as mental pollution of young souls by trashy non-culture loomed, a line was drawn, and the 3D theaters were closed down amid much official disgust and popular disappointment. As in other such circumstances, the surviving 3D sets moved to a backroom, and business went on.

76. HEMINGWAY

When restoration works in Old Havana got under steam in the mid-1990s, to attract tourism as the new national industry, one of the very first buildings to be refurbished on the Plaza de Armas was the Hotel Ambos Mundos. Apart from the colonial governors' palace, the Palacio de los Capitanes Generales, most of this square – the very heart of Spanish Havana – was badly neglected. Ambos Mundos became a priority because of its most famous onetime resident: Ernest Hemingway.

Hemingway stayed at the hotel during his first years in Cuba in the 1930s. He's said to have written *For Whom the Bell Tolls* in room 511. Legend has it that he bought his home outside the city, the Finca La Vigía in San Francisco de Paula, with the royalties.

His ghost still resides there, amid memorabilia and trophies of all kinds, including his uniform as a war correspondent. There are scribblings on the bathroom wall above his scale:

he worried about his weight. First, his growing alcoholism had made him too fat, and then he started to lose weight too fast and was feared to have cancer. His well-advertised drinking habits in some expatriate bars in Havana in the 1940s and '50s not only ruined his health, they also created some of the worst tourist-traps in town, La Bodeguita del Medio and El Floridita.

His fishing boat, the Pilar, was anchored in the eastern suburb of Cojimar, still a quiet fishermen's community in those days. We've been there already, but let's pay another visit. Here Hemingway met Gregorio Fuentes, who became the skipper of the Pilar, steadying the boat for her often drunk captain on marlin fishing trips. Fuentes and other Cojimar fishermen knew the surrounding seas well, as they had been very active rumrunners to Florida during Prohibition. In a

Papa Hemingway's shrunken ghost, bored to death
in Cojimar.

confused episode, Hemingway used his private yacht to help spot Nazi submarines around Cuba during World War II, or at the very least to assign himself a new heroic part while he was slowly sinking.

The Pilar is not there anymore: it was moved to the tennis court of the house in San Francisco de Paula after Hemingway's death.

The unavoidable combo of old men dressed in *guayaberas* and smoking soggy cigars is sitting on the steps of the monument, waiting for the busloads of Hemingway-theme tourists to sing and play their squeaky "Guantanamera" under the cynical eye of the writer's bronze bust. Next to the weathered Spanish fort, its coral stone slowly becoming reef again, dirty jetsam and flotsam collects along the pier. When the bus is gone after its fifteen-minute stop, leaving the community at the same time disappointed and relieved, the square becomes timeless again, and the Cojimar waterfront returns once more to its listless peace of mind.

It was probably in and out of Cojimar that the writer had his best times. According to his Cuban house staff, he never understood much about the country, apart from cockfights and struggling swordfish. He once confided his regrets at never having fallen in love with a Cuban. Maybe it was to make up for this failure that he donated his Nobel Prize insignia to the most Cuban seductress of them all: to Ochún in her sanctuary at El Cobre. By then he was a wreck, plagued by writer's block and jealously guarded by his then-wife, Miss Mary, whose motherly attentions he needed but could not stand. Maybe worse than cancer, he had to confess to fabricated episodes of heroism during the liberation of France in 1944.

The large marina to the west of the capital is named after him. Long cherished (by me, at any rate) for its semi-abandoned peace and quiet, it is now seeing a growing influx of foreign yachts and marlin-fishing vessels.

In the clubhouse or captaincy of the marina, the com modore of the club will show you the original pictures of white-bearded Papa H. meeting black-bearded Fidel in 1960. This was potentially a highly macho encounter, yet each looks surprisingly benign. The picture doesn't let on that Hemingway's stay in Cuba was fast becoming problematic. In the 1930s his anti-fascist stand during the Spanish Civil War had been popular in the United States, too. But that was no longer the case with the Cold War in full swing, and with the systematic confrontations with the United States Fidel was now seeking daily.

It was a three-sided historical meeting that day.

The same wall holds the pictures of a long-haired Che Guevara, very much the rock star, sitting bare-chested in the breeze in the back of a boat, relaxed and happy while fishing for marlin with a rod religiously preserved as a relic on the wall of remembrance. This was a short time before he became an apocalyptic prophet in his cave, and somewhat longer before his emaciated corpse was viciously mutilated by pathetic Cold War minions, after a failed revolution deep in Bolivia's backwaters. Papa H. had shot himself long before that. But weren't both of them suicidal, in their vastly different ways? Were they conscious of entering legend, in their last moments?

Gregorio Fuentes, the captain of Hemingway's boat, is said to have been the inspiration for *The Old Man and the Sea*. He celebrated his one-hundredth birthday back in 1997 at the Ferminia restaurant in Siboney. I unexpectedly met some minor European royals among the guests. Gregorio smoked his cigars and didn't say a word. He looked ancient and weathered for sure. Nobody had cared to check his birth certificate –

which wasn't to be traced in Cuba anyhow, as he was reportedly born on Lanzarote in the Canary Islands. Was he the original old man from the sea? It doesn't matter. Never check legends too closely.

The Hemingway of the last episodes in Havana was a shadow of himself. Drinking escapades from his *finca* to the city became increasingly difficult and rare due to Miss Mary's vigilance. Havana, always the jealous mistress, hit him where it hurt most: his self-esteem. The predictable ending is well known. Now the dead writer, set in life-size bronze at the counter of El Floridita, can pose endlessly with tourists who will remain just as ignorant of the real Havana as he was in his lifetime.

A witty and cynical bar owner in Old Havana recently put up a sign at the door of his establishment: "Hemingway never entered here."

77. FUSTER

Leaving the Marina Hemingway and turning left, just to the west of Siboney, where the grand, royal palm lined Quinta Avenida finally peters out from its ten-kilometer trajectory, we reach the quiet village of Jaimanitas. It's a fishermen's place, next to a naval base. Here lives and works José Fuster, Cuba's foremost ceramic artist.

Fuster's family is of Catalan origin, and he claims inspiration from Gaudí for his living masterpiece: a spontaneous and playful palace entirely built of mosaics and shards of chinaware artfully assembled into his own colorful universe, surrounding his gallery and workshop. But he's a social artist. Not limiting himself to his private environment, his work is now transforming the entire village, as he has been decorating

Cubanía creativity at its feisty best:
Fuster's dreamland in Jaimanitas

bus stops, the local clinic, and other public buildings, and has provided murals all over the village. The entire work is an ode to Cuban creativity, its stubborn resolve to stand out even when the struggle with materials and circumstances would seem overwhelming. It's also a loud cry of *cubanía*, of proclaiming the national soul with all its ingredients and contradictions, from mermaids to Hugo Chávez. Nothing could be further from officially sanctioned art in a communist system, and yet here it is, totally itself.

Fuster himself is a modest and rather shy man, at times ill at ease with the groups of tourists visiting his yard of marvels. His son now mostly oversees the flow of visitors. But even as a TV crew from Barcelona, mindful of the separatist politicians they are responding to, tries to convince him to declare on camera that he is Catalan at heart, he proudly maintains that he is Cuban first and foremost.

78. THE LAST *CIMARRÓN*

Leaving Fuster's dream palace, we head back east towards the city on Quinta Avenida. Passing Siboney, we cross the Río Quibú. It seems like nothing but an unremarkable urbanized river now, at times no more than a sordid urban sewer. But it has a remarkable history of its own.

Because slavery survived so long in Cuba – till 1886 – living memory of it died out much later than even in the U.S. South. Also, whereas most slaves in the United States were probably born in the Americas as of, say, the 1820s, the transatlantic slave trade with Cuba went on till the very end. Sometimes slaves out of Cuba were smuggled into the United States, using various legal tricks. As we have seen earlier, one of these was to register Africans as crewmembers on merchant ships plying the trade between Havana and New Orleans, and then to declare them deserters when they were sold up the Mississippi. The late influx of African-born slaves into Cuba guarantees to this day the survival of ancestral traditions.

But resistance also survived till the end. Although the Spanish *code noir* was more liberal than the British and the French slavery laws, allowing Africans to have an income of their own, to save money, and to buy their freedom after seven years of servitude, many still resisted or fled. Runaways, maroons, or *cimarrones* in Spanish, established free settlements in Cuba as elsewhere.

Those were sometimes surprisingly near the cities.

During slavery, the Río Quibú was a frontier sheltering runaways from the packs of well-organized slave hunters or *rancheadores*. As we have seen, when the Indians fled Havana in the very early days of the city, they ran to the west. Two rivers gave them protection: first and nearest to the city, the Almendares (known as La Chorrera in runaway times). A few miles farther to the west, for good measure, the Río Quibú. After crossing the second river, the *cimarrones* felt safe enough to establish a settlement, called a *palenque*.

By today's standards, they were still close to the colonial downtown. It's about a twenty-minute drive from Prado, the walled city's limit till 1863, to the Quibú. The coastal badlands beyond the Almendares only became Miramar, now Havana's fanciest suburb, in the 1920s. In the eighteenth century, when even Vedado, just outside the city walls, was considered a dangerous no-go area after dark, the Río Quibú and its valley were in deep country and offered shelter to those slaves too rebellious to take advantage of the Havana underworld, or to save from their masters' gambling money for their manumission.

The Río Quibú settlement today is still remembered by a restaurant called Palenque in the same area.

Again because of late abolition, runaways survived to tell their personal stories in the second half of the twentieth century after the Revolution, when their resistance to the slavery system became a welcome political issue. Miguel Barnet, the present chair of the Cuban Writers' Union, personally recorded the oral history of the last Cuban maroon, Esteban Montejo, which was published in 1966. The fiftieth anniversary of the publication was celebrated during the Havana Book Fair in February 2016. The book is a true Cuban classic, and the increased official recognition of Afro-Cuban themes in national culture, thanks to the Fundación Fernando Ortiz among others, is lending it lasting relevance.

The survival of the Cuban cimarrones in the wilds – *en el monte* – also linked them with the early stages of the revolutionary campaign in the Sierra Maestra, and thus became a precursor story to the carefully maintained revolutionary epic. It's been the Revolution's constant theme that the rebels in Oriente in the 1950s were the spiritual heirs both of the *mambises* of the war of independence against Spain from the 1860s to the 1890s, and of the much older rebellious slave tradition. For that very reason, you'll see both the terms *mambi* and *cimarrón* in use as current vocabulary, not as remote historical references. It's part of the intriguing beauty of Havana that history is still so alive where you least expect it, as if the city is unwilling to forget or to forgo any part of what she ever was or witnessed.

The survival of the *cimarrón* doesn't even end there. In a way, the one immortalized by Miguel Barnet was far from the last of his kind. Here's why.

When crossing the Quibú on Quinta Avenida, the river gives no hint of what goes on farther upstream. Along its banks, bordering the suburb of Marianao to the east, are the roughest squatter areas of Havana. They are much more discreet than shantytowns elsewhere in Latin America and the Caribbean. They came into being as of the 1930s, when Havana attracted more and more migration from poorer Oriente, the still ongoing movement of *palestinos* we observed earlier. In many ways, the *palestinos* were the new *cimarrones*, only in reverse: fleeing *toward* Havana. Quite a few of the Río Quibú camps are now too deeply rooted to be wiped out. They are officially designated "*focos insalubres*" ("public health hazards"). The older and well established ones, labyrinths of wood, concrete and corrugated sheets, are named El Hueco, La Escalera, and, apparently in a reference to the oldest Indian runaways, Indaya. Of the newer ones, still threatened by the bulldozer, the snappily named Llega y Pon (Arrive and Settle Down) is the best known, or at any rate, the most quoted.

Deep in those neighborhoods, the African culture of the *solar* is more alive than anywhere else. Here even the elegant ruins of cosmopolitan Havana are far away: this is the Caribbean ghetto life as it was lived by the young Bob Marley in Jamaica. In the hidden yards, under spare light bulbs fed with improvised wiring connected to a remote power line, people cook in locally made cast-iron pots on charcoal fires, children run and roll, and loud games of dominoes are in progress at any time of day or night. At dusk, amid the loud crowing of roosters and the rhythms of a *tambor* in progress, street corner youths with a gold chain and a gold tooth leave their hideouts and roam the banks of the river, painting Havana's very first gangland graffiti on a wall next to the muddy water: "Los Animales Malos del Barrio."

Maybe this writing on the wall is where Havana's remote past is meeting her uncertain future.

79. FABELO

We make our way towards the city. In Miramar, in a quiet cross street between Tercera and Quinta Avenidas, Cuba's foremost living artist, Roberto Fabelo, has his studio.

On the superbly restored Plaza Vieja in the old town – a near formless heap of rubble well into the 1990s – a provocative sculpture of a nude, bald girl riding an enormous rooster welcomes and sometimes scares visitors. It's Havana-in-your-face, perfectly serving the purpose to make especially elderly tourists from more puritanical backgrounds uncomfortable. This is Fabelo's most recognized public work. Although he's known first and foremost as a painter and printmaker, he's a sculptor of genius, a master of lost-wax bronze modeling and casting, which he practices on both epic and almost microscopic scales.

His best-known works are prints of naked girls in profile, crowned with improbable headgear showing enormous seashells, crouching animals or humans. Nudes with a variety of baroque headgear were already printed by earlier Cuban artists, but Fabelo turned them into a signature motif. All of them, to me, are portraits of Havana in her many incarnations and with her contradictions and her experience weighing on her head. These prints certainly show Fabelo's sensitivity to the curves and secrets of female seduction; but at times he deviates into cultivated ugliness, with exaggerated and distorted anatomies that scare me, because I get the message all too well: that under all our superficial beauty, there lurks unspeakable ugliness, too. There is much physical beauty in Havana, and maybe for that very reason Fabelo sometimes chooses to explore the exact opposite – extreme anatomies, man as meat or even as a pig – rubbing in our face the realities we'd rather ignore. Fabelo's ugliest bodies also contain hidden themes of hunger. He has clearly seen hard times.

His spacious and luminous workshop offers insights into the workings of his hyperactive brain. Everywhere in the studio, spontaneous agglomerations of found objects – from vast collections of animal bones to the packagings of exotic luxury goods – are becoming altars to a private religion, and discreet odes to his unfathomable inspirations. His wife, a cheerful Cuban-Japanese woman, accompanies even his most disturbing visions with good-humored camaraderie.

In a Caribbean region where art is often reduced to either spontaneous or commercially upheld primitivism, Fabelo illustrates best what Cuban creativity stands for: complex inspiration, and a struggle with demons.

80. KCHO / STAINLESS / CUTY

The Havana Arts Biennale of 2015 brought us the street kid with dictatorial ambitions, among many other works, sights, and performances. The entire city got involved – there was even a car-free Malecón on weekends – all the way to the faraway Romerillo neighborhood, and across the bay to the Cabaña fortress and beyond as far as Casablanca.

Many of the works/installations in the Cabaña were edgy, focusing on themes of exodus and exile, and other sensitive issues. The fort was declared an artistic *zona franca*, a "free zone." The name was unabashedly cynical. The works on display opened up people's minds and mouths much more than activity is freed in the real *zonas francas*. Cuban art was shown once more as being way ahead of national politics and the economy.

One of the most telling installations was a collection of thousands of snorkeling mouthpieces and tubes hung from a high ceiling, open to many interpretations but to me signifying a need for air to prevent suffocation, and a call from the deep, including from those drowned in the Florida Straits.

The Romerillo street show was concentrated around the workshop of the painter and sculptor known as Kcho. Born Alexis Leiva Machado in 1970, Kcho was Fidel Castro's favorite artist because he is heavily involved in the political establishment, very socially conscious, famous in Latin America and well-known in Europe, but has been repeatedly denied a visa to show his work in the United States. That very detail endeared him to the Comandante, whose last known foray into the city was for the opening of a Kcho exhibition – his very last outing was to the Communist Party Congress in April 2016.

Kcho's Romerillo neighborhood to the southwest of Quinta Avenida is somewhat more urban-marginal than Fuster's in Jaimanitas. It's essentially a rough-and-ready crossroads for the improvised but quite efficient fixed-route collective *almendrón* taxis. The idea to set up street art and installations here definitely brought the Biennale out of its art-reservation comfort zones, and connected even the humble citizen in a shabby car to exuberant creativity. Wired youths like to hang out around the Kcho studio, because it was one of the first free wifi-zones in the entire city, with *abajoelbloqueo* – "downwiththeembargo" – as its password.

At opposite political ends stands a group of much younger artists calling themselves Stainless, among whom is Roberto Fabelo's son. The Stainless like to provoke in extremely unsubtle ways by perverting establishment symbols. They did a large painting showing the forest of Cuban patriotic flag-masts forming part of the Tribuna Anti-imperialista in front of the U.S. Embassy being used by stripping pole dancers, leaving absolutely nothing to the imagination. Another work shows a large cake of the kind the CDRs still hand out at birthday parties, inscribed with *palabras* ("words"), and crowned with a large, licking tongue: sugary words, sticky appeasement, real hunger.

The painter Cuty made a name for himself in the Havana underground over many years with paintings of attractive chicks sitting on toilets. He now also produces politically provocative work. A large recent painting shows a nude model holding the separated hammer and sickle of communist imagery in either hand, with a profile of Lenin against a backdrop of menacing gray artillery. When I complimented him on the work, a little sarcastically, Cuty answered in a deadpan tone that it was his interpretation of *Freedom Leading the People* by Delacroix.

All in all, the Biennale, just like the more permanent arts scene at La Fábrica, shows that censorship in the arts – relative even in days of harsher communist rhetoric – is definitely on its way out. No arts police appeared to put stars on nipples and vaginas, a stoic Lenin stared past the freedom of the people, and the allegorical use of flags and other national and communist symbols, however playful or disrespectful, did not close down any galleries. I even wonder if similar desecrations of national symbols would have been tolerated in the United States.

Cuty and several other Cuban artists prominently featured at the Biennale expressed both appreciation for the presence of curators, collectors and gallery owners from the United States, and a certain apprehension that the Biennale would become another art market. The events allowed for existing and newly established links with New York to flourish: the Robert Miller Gallery in Chelsea soon brought a group show of all the great Cuban names from the Biennale, and the Bronx Museum strengthened cooperation with *Bellas Artes* in Havana. Cuban artists have to sell their work like any creative person anywhere. The ones over forty have known personal hardship in their lives and difficult access to materials for their creations. But still, they walk a fine line between soul and success, and their continued inspiration and relevance could be smothered by too much cash. From all the country's experiences and its complicated past and present, Cuban art remains grounded in content and meaning, not in the vain aesthetics or shameless self-promotion of more commercialized arts scenes.

81. CASA VERDE

Still approaching Havana from the west, right before we enter the tunnel between Quinta Avenida and the Malecón, we pass the Casa de Tejas Verdes standing by a small park on the left side of the avenue. The Green Tiled House, or simply the Casa Verde, was for many years a famous symbol of resistance against the nationalizations. The elderly lady living in the house by herself, accompanied only by her parrot, retreated from room to room while the ceilings under her glazed tiles caved in one by one, and eventually large holes appeared in the green roof itself. She stubbornly held on to her belief that she would live to see the end of the Revolution and the return of better times for her social class.

The fact that she was living by herself in the once grand villa illustrated a frequent fact from the times of the *reforma urbana*. Families were allowed to keep a house in private property as long as it was lived in. There are countless stories – or legends – in Havana about an elderly parent or a bewildered teenager left to occupy a property to save it from confiscation when the rest of the family fled to Miami. More than half a century later, when real estate sales between Cubans were finally authorized again, even stranger stories emerged. Some families now tried to sell the house with the left-behind occupant still in it, the onetime forgotten adolescent grown old with the revolution.

All of this leads to the question: what will happen to all the buildings of Havana? There is no simple answer, but we can give it a try.

Most people in Havana hold the property title to their home. In theory, a Cuban citizen may even own two properties: a townhouse or apartment, a seaside home or a *finca* in the country. Much of the Cuban legal system is based on norms very different from U.S. or European law, but the careful registration and administration of property titles and their transfers is operating very professionally. At the moment of the nationalizations, many people who were living in rented homes, or even squatting, were given property titles. Thus many a grand abandoned mansion became subdivided and turned into a multifamily dwelling, like those we see today. The titles could not be sold, but as of the *Período Especial*, and especially when the cash flow from Miami increased, there grew a system of officially tolerated property swaps or *permutas*. It was nigh impossible to control the respective values of the houses in such exchanges, and so the *permuta* system gradually became a true real estate market under the guise of the swaps. As long as the legal requirement that two properties changed hands between parties was fulfilled, absurdly uneven exchanges could be set up – one room in El Cerro for a villa in Miramar – and a price for the transaction was paid under the table. This system flourished, and was soon overseen by clandestine but very eager brokers, or *corredores*.

When this system could no longer be scaled back, the law followed suit, and in 2014 simple sales of properties among Cuban citizens were finally allowed. This is one more instance of leaders following citizens to grant freedoms already taken.

Properties that were part of the *permuta* system, or are now being bought and sold, soon benefited from much needed repairs. The real estate market indicated where a good chunk of the Miami money went. There is a chronic shortage of building materials of all kinds in Havana, but by somehow finding arrangements to find supplies – *resolver* is a key verb for life in Havana – the owners of recently acquired properties in all *bar-*

rios are now busy repairing and rebuilding. Anywhere you go in Havana's neighborhoods today, there is a growing contrast between crumbling buildings and freshly repaired ones. The tolerated loose interpretation of *cuentapropista* licenses, with an independent worker registered as a mere stonemason gradually becoming a full-fledged building contractor, helps too. This discreetly growing private initiative may yet save neighborhoods from the bulldozer.

But even while the phenomenon is growing, so far it remains a small corrective to the overall neglect of many parts of town. At best, it prevents wholesale demolition and may result in a later urban landscape where the textures are made up of patterns of old and new buildings side by side. Havana's many urban charms may thus not be erased completely, as Leonardo Padura fears in the quote at the beginning of this book. The Oficina del Historiador is working on this, too, compiling an inventory of buildings and city blocks in all neighborhoods to be saved from demolition.

The historic city will further benefit from restorations such as the ones achieved since 1995. That's a priority both for national pride and for tourism, and tourism was the main generator of cash to start and to sustain the restorations in the first place. The Oficina del Historiador de la Ciudad (the City Historian's Office), led by Eusebio Leal, was for more than twenty years a privileged island within the Cuban administration and the economy, in the sense that the steadily growing proceeds in hard currency from activities in the restored buildings and streets – hotels, restaurants, shops, horse-driven carriages, etc. – could be directly reinvested in further recuperations of historic edifices and sites. That autonomous system of multiplication was an enormous concession in an economy constantly starved of hard cash, with financial authorities often having to look for dollars anywhere they could find them to fulfill their social obligations. Thus the systematic expansion of restored Habana Vieja, block by block, will continue, hopefully preserving the tireless inspiration and vision of Dr. Leal into the next generation.

But between the discreet private repairs and the ongoing rebirth of the colonial city, large parts of Havana still present enormous challenges for the future. I remain deeply convinced that Havana is all about people, much more than about buildings — but still, what will happen to the physical city where it hurts most? It's a complicated question we may wish to avoid, but between Cuba and the U.S. walls may crumble, and yet many of the crumbling walls of Havana herself are still in bitter dispute. For my part, I may be fascinated by the buildings-gone-organic of much of the real Havana, but that's a purely poetic vision, and harsher realities are to be faced. There are billions of dollars' worth of U.S.-based claims on countless buildings in Havana that were nationalized during the *reforma urbana*. Real estate aspects are also part of the U.S. embargo legislation. For the old guard of anti-Castro Cubans in Miami, the properties lost to the Revolution are not just capital, they are tangible tools of hatred. Finding solutions cannot wait forever. Collapses of buildings are on the increase and many more are fast becoming safety hazards. After a hurricane or after heavy rains, the porous walls absorb enormous quantities of water, and next, when the sun comes out again, the humidity expands the entire structure, and it simply caves in — sometimes spectacularly, sometimes fatally. It's good to go and see those neighborhoods as they still are, as they are living on borrowed time, between melancholy and the wrecking ball.

It's clear, however, that most of those properties can't be

saved by being returned to their original pre-revolution owners. Present owners and occupants will have to remain where
they are, as one cannot evict or dislodge hundreds of thousands of inhabitants of the capital. Can old and new owners
coexist? It's not unheard of. In Manhattan, in older apartment
buildings being refurbished, dynamic young buyers sometimes live next door to elderly occupants sitting out their time
under rent control while the building becomes a condo. In
Havana, even by international standards, the present owners
are entitled to protection as bona fide occupants. But that's
not even the question. The real point is that it's impossible to
evict so many people from the housing they or their family
have occupied for half a century.

In a comprehensive deal with the United States, some
form of compensation other than physical restitution for the
previous owners may be the way to go. In post-communist
eastern and central Europe, a number of similar solutions may
inspire the one applicable to Cuba.

The number of formerly palatial homes in Havana is astonishing. Their post-1960s use and occupancy became very
diverse. As a consequence, the discussion about their future is
full of gray areas, not the black and white situation the former
owners would wish.

A good percentage of the mansions ended up as Party and
government offices, as health clinics, schools, nurseries, and,
not to forget, as embassies or diplomatic residences. Those are
the buildings most exposed to hatred from Miami and, from
a legal point of view – according to how politics will evolve –
may become clear-cut cases for restitution. But most cases are
far more complicated than that.

Back at the Casa Verde the authorities, partly out of their
desire to save the property, and partly out of concern for the

lady's wellbeing, tirelessly tried to convince her to move to a better location they offered in exchange. But she held out stubbornly, committed to her family's oath to outlive the Revolution.

She didn't, and after her passing, the house was eventually taken over and restored. It's standing there again in its former glory, even provided with a sculpture garden in the back. Mostly it's vacant, and only very occasionally put to use for an exhibition or some other *actividad cultural*. It's too easy to say that the spirit of a stubborn old witch keeps life away. But as the story goes, her parrot survived her. It's well known that parrots religiously preserve the voice of their dead owners, and so, somewhere in Havana, the bird may still be cursing the Revolution under its breath.

82. RÍO ALMENDARES

After passing Casa Verde, crossing the tunnel under the Almendares River is now simply a question of traffic flow, no longer the crossing of a border between worlds as it was in the days of slavery. The Almendares reaches the sea just next to the tunnel exit on the city side, in a deep cove watched over by the Chorrera fort – the western counterpart of the Cojimar outpost – and the romantic pavilions on the *diente de perro* – dog's teeth – reefs behind the 1830 bar and concert hall, "El Milocho" in neighbourhood slang. It was on this spot that the British admiral Albermarle positioned his flagship for the invasion of Havana in 1762. The river may have supplied fresh water to the fleet, but it didn't to the city under siege.

In spite of its short run from the hills to the southwest of the city to the sea, the Almendares is still a kind of pocket Amazon. Upstream, it shelters the true urban jungle of the

Jardines de la Tropical and, under the bridge on Calle Vein-
titrés in Vedado, the somewhat more park-like Bosque de La
Habana – a hangout for lovers, a discreet location for the occasional rare *habanero* graffiti tagger, and, not to forget, a place
where Santería initiates can fulfill the obligations to throw
offerings or discarded clothes from ceremonies in flowing water, a frequent ritual requirement.

A Cuban diplomat who was recalled home after ambassa-
dorships in Brazil, India, and Egypt, was cynically welcomed
home by a colleague having spent the same years in a career
dead end, stuck at headquarters: "*Compadre*, you'll have lived
on the banks of all the great rivers of this planet: the Ganges,
the Nile, the Amazon – and now even the Almendares!"

83. HAVANA AND THE CHOCOLATE FACTORY

Cuba is not a major cacao producer, but in the far east of the
island, around Baracoa where the Spanish conquest began,
some of the bean is grown. Part of the harvest goes to export,
but there is also a small local chocolate factory. It was inaugu-
rated by no less a person than Che Guevara on April 1, 1963.
In the sequence of political functions that could never satisfy
him, he was at that time Minister of Industry. In Baracoa
there is even a local Santería variant with the *santos* fond of
the bean.

But Havana's best chocolate-related story is that of the
Hershey train. The Pennsylvania chocolate king Milton Hershey owned a factory near Matanzas. In order to move his
staff back and forth in comfort, in 1917 he built his own electric train. It was the only electric line of Cuba's vast railway
network, and the Hershey train is still running daily to and
from the small terminal in Casablanca, just past the Cristo

de La Habana across from the port channel. If you're lucky, you may travel in the bright red repainted car marked "Trans Hershey" parked before departure under the exuberant poincianas facing the station. The surrounding neighborhood is sleepily provincial and, if you pause to wonder, time stands still even more than in the city across the bay. It's a miracle that this train is still running at all, considering the state of neglect you'll find other railroad memorabilia in around town, from the grand central station on the edge of the port, via the Cristina terminal in Cuatro Caminos – where the oldest locomotives stand frozen in time and rust, having forever ended a mysterious last run here – to the railroad crossings between Nuevo Vedado and El Cerro, where along the tracks the ancient signal posts and cinematically picturesque wild west stations suggest even more ghost rides. At certain tourist

Where journeys ended once and for all: ancient
trains rusting away in Cristina Station

spots, restored locomotives are now parked just for decoration, but hopefully more trains will soon follow the brave Hershey cars and get moving again.

I also wonder in passing about the care Mr. Hershey had for his workers, as the clever and apparently caring capitalist that he was. That kind of sweetness was lost, too.

Cuban chocolate is, in all frankness, far from a superior quality product to a connoisseur. The most popular local candy bar is a small cookie called Africana, once more with typical Cuban carelessness about being politically correct. The cookie is dipped in dark chocolate but is snow-white within: another unconscious metaphor? It joins the Kid Chocolate boxing gym and Los Van Van unrepentantly singing to a black *novia* as "*mi chocolate.*" Don't try this at home.

But *Cuba and the Chocolate Train* could be a fascinating

Legacy of the U.S. chocolate empire:
the Hershey train in Casablanca

children's book by the late Roald Dahl. Let's forget for a moment about the legal complications of U.S. industrial property in Cuba. The Hershey train runs sweetly and, once it's on the downward slope, smooth as chocolate. History is not always bitter.

84. TALLAPIEDRA (HAVANA HIGH LINE)

Just as Mr. Hershey was building his railway line at Casablanca, across the bay the Tallapiedra power station was going up in 1915. It stands where the Avenida del Puerto runs past the Castillo de Atares – the only part of the Havana's historic fortifications still in a state of neglect. Looking grand even in its menacing abandon, the Tallapiedra building towers over the poor Barrio Jesús María behind it.

As part of the 2015 Arts Biennale, the building was used for one night for a happening combining live Santería-based percussion performances with a light show. Santería's most prominent intellectual, Natalia Bolívar, now in her eighties, gleefully pushed buttons on the computer, setting and changing the rhythms and bringing color-coded groups of *batá* drummers into action by varying the lights on a high light pole inspired by traditional carnival *linternas*. She was visibly delighted with this new avatar of her beliefs and rites. The vast abandoned spaces of the building resonated among the mysterious artifacts of its industrial archeology. On the terraced roof just outside the main hall, during the after-party, the crowd saw a rusty freight train slowly passing on the elevated line, while the sun was setting over the inner port in the background.

The surrounding industrial landscape, scarred and neglected, became magical. Some New Yorkers in the crowd, myself

Grandiose
industrial
archeology: the
elevated railway
and the 1915
Tallapiedra power
plant loom over the
Barrio Jesús-María

included, remembered the state of the High Line in the 1980s, when the old West Side elevated bridges were just as abandoned and spooky – a delight for fearless urban archeologists, but in the long term supposedly condemned to demolition and oblivion. The memories were especially vivid to me personally: in the 1980s, I lived just next to the roughly adventurous High Line, on the last block before reaching the Hudson on West 12th street. I feared its imminent destruction by collapse or by real estate development. But no: the New York High Line was reborn, to everyone's delight. Why not also these parts of Havana?

All the commercial shipping activities will gradually be moved from Havana's inner bay to the new port of Mariel to the west of the city. Endless dreams are possible as to what to do with old warehouses, hangars, wharfs, cranes, and all kinds of installations located between the fringes of Havana Vieja and the municipality of Regla. Parks, expensive lofts, bars, art galleries, and – successful – artists' workshops, fancy boutique hotels . . . Will the old port be given over to gigantic cruise ships disgorging thousands of passengers,so that the predictable tourist traps grow up in the *barrio*?

Here are all the risks and the challenges of gentrification. The people most forgotten by communism may now simply be chased out by a mix of overnight visitors and fashionable new residents. On the West Side in Manhattan, it took years of patient civic activism to save the High Line from greedy developers. In the absence of independent forces in a society, who can and will take up such challenges here? Will inspired city planning be able to stay ahead of wild capitalist real estate speculation? The Jesús María barrio behind Tallapiedra would benefit mostly if the power station simply provided reliable power again. How this will play out is one of the many questions about Havana's future that fascinate and haunt me.

85. RADIO RELOJ & RADIO BEMBA

I often lie awake at night thinking about Havana's future. To the sleepless all over the city, Radio Reloj may be the soundtrack to their insomnia.

Radio Reloj, Clock Radio, continuously broadcasts news episodes peppered with characteristic time-announcing beeps every minute. The news is mostly of a rather dry kind, of

statistics and achievements, sometimes allowing for an edifying anecdote or two in between.

Sleepless in Havana, you either love or hate Radio Reloj.
It's company of a kind if you're lonely, but the insistent mark-
ing of time passing also feels like a warning of mortality, as in
the old Latin proverb set on sundials: *Vulnerant omnes, ultima
necat* – every hour injures, the last one kills.

One is tempted to think that this somewhat absurd medium is an invention of the Revolution, as an ideal instrument for the ceaseless drop-by-drop feeding of propaganda.
But no. It existed and was popular well before that. To what
extent is shown by the fact that the occupation of Radio Reloj was an important target when a group of revolutionaries attacked Batista's presidential palace on March 13th, 1957.
This group was not really coordinating with Fidel, who was
already fighting in the Sierra. It consisted of a mixture of
activists from Havana University, Spanish republicans having found refuge in Havana, and more shady characters of
the political *gangsterismo* that had existed in Havana since the
Machado years. The attackers of Radio Reloj succeeded, and
one of them, José Antonio Echeverría, announced over the
airwaves: "Citizens of Havana! The Revolution is in progress! The palace has been occupied and the dictator has been
killed in his lair!" This was, unfortunately, untrue. Batista's
guard fought back vigorously on the steps of the palace, and
indoors on the stairs leading to the private apartments. The
assailants were either killed on the spot or later summarily
executed. Echevarría was killed in the street. The Revolution
later declared him one of her precursor saints. Radio Reloj
broadcast the news of the failed coup as one more random
event in its ceaseless flow.

That still ongoing and just as relentless flow with its present contents is not only irritating at times. It becomes something deeper and more disturbing.

To me it often feels as if Radio Reloj has been made responsible for maintaining the dynamics of the flow of time, to deny the immobility and the stagnation. Even though the news it brings is of the carefully sanctioned kind, and is meant to illustrate that things will be as they are forever, the speakers are pushing time forward, in their bored or dramatic voices. There is no remedy, and all things must pass. Radio Reloj thus becomes a hopeless incantation against time itself. Meant to be reassuring, it becomes disturbing for those clinging to unchangeable truths. Late at night, it feels like the child singing to herself in the dark to calm her own fears.

At opposite ends, Radio Bemba or "lip radio" is slang for the grapevine – the popular whispers that become a main source of information, either true or fictional, when your daily newspaper's heroic headlines are stuck in the 1960s, if not the 1890s.

Long before the *paquete* arrived with verifiable news of the outside world, Radio Bemba transmitted it in a flow as constant as that of Radio Reloj, but now exaggerated with the vivid imagination of the sidewalk, and colored with the inventions of swift intelligence operating in a vacuum.

After the December 17 reconciliation, it was Radio Bemba that spread the rumor on the street that now the wet foot, dry foot policy favoring illegal Cuban refugees in the United States would soon come to an end. As a result, at least twenty thousand Cubans entered the United States illegally in 2015 either via Ecuador and Central America, or in smaller but somewhat growing numbers as *balseros*. Radio Bemba easily gets more credibility than Radio Reloj. As we've seen, *wet foot, dry foot* survived another two years.

While I've been writing this chapter, twenty minutes of mortal time have ticked away on Radio Reloj. I can stand it no longer and go out to roam the streets for a while. On a rough corner on Calle Monte, among the waiting *bicitaxis*, I hear that the winning number of the day of *la bolita*, or the clandestine street lottery, is *ocho, La muerte*. There is no escape.

86. *LA MUERTE*

Colón is a very grand cemetery, but death to the average *habanero* is anything but that. For the normal citizen, the final departure from the city and this life passes through the municipal *funeraria*, where death is thoroughly banal and desacralized. You have to be a member of the revolutionary *nomenklatura* to get more elaborate funerary honors. Dead dignitaries also offer the added advantage of silence – their opinions cannot change anymore and are forever safe. Without the slightest trace of irony, this or that deceased intellectual is sometimes made a posthumous member for eternity of an academy or establishment, setting lifelong good behavior as an example even for the hereafter. It took all of Alejo Carpentier's deep talents to circumvent this final honor.

Those not enjoying it will be seen off in *funeraria* like chaotic and grimy marketplaces, where any attention for grieving family members is in short supply, where drivers of improvised hearses are on the outlook for customers, and where you have to elbow your way through the crowd for a quick greeting of your friend or relative's coffin. Abundant flowers add some dignity to the dirty walls, and the occasional thoughtful family member may have provided a thermos of coffee to console the mourners. But mostly the rooms and corridors breathe a tired resignation at the lack of privacy that applies to the dead and the living alike. As a way of handling the deceased it feels not even bureaucratic, but almost industrial. Price lists of funerary services are advertised bluntly on the sticky walls. A standard cremation costs 340 pesos. You may still die in *moneda nacional.*

In this unforgiving climate, the dead are evacuated swiftly. Granny has died at three a.m. and by three p.m. she's at her final resting place in the Colón. If she's lucky, there is still a well-preserved family tomb there. When the slab is moved to lower the coffin, the indifferent workers may reveal traces of much older burials vandalized for valuables or voodoo. Mostly even this last part goes unremarked, and in an almost brutal matter-of-fact way. Even when the deceased was neither family nor a close acquaintance, one feels strangely lost when walking back to the city out of the monumental gate on Zapata, expecting something more meaningful to surround death.

87. APOTHEOSIS

But Havana also rises above death daily, whenever she dances for her favorite spirit Ochún, pleased and celebrated with gold and honey and sunflowers. The national patron saint La Virgen de la Caridad, hijacked by the *santeros*, has become Havana's most loved universal sister. One has to know her well to understand how close and intimate that relationship is. Or even if it's not for Ochún, Havana dancing for the simple pleasure of her own supple waist somehow keeps the world turning, much as the Shiva of Indian mythology dancingly preserves a cosmic balance. Havana whirls against all sadness, finding solace in moments of bodily ecstasy. At those moments her sure feet truly define a chakra of the planet, a focal point where the vanished Taínos and Siboneys converse with the Africans fleeing slavery, with the patient Chinese, with the *gallego* and the *andaluz* and the *asturiano*, with the Jewish refugees, and even with the hopelessly misplaced Russians. She has danced with Rome and Paris and Madrid and Buenos Aires and Toronto, and will dance again with Miami and New York. She is such a wonderful place, always inspired and inspiring with her unique features and encounters. And so is Cuba as a whole, and hopefully it will forever remain, saving her unconquered soul. Never underestimate her, she's always much more than she lets on.

And these are just some fragments of the world under Havana's whirling feet:

Nights on the Malecón wall. The mysterious side streets of Centro Habana at three a.m. The lazy sexiness of bare arms and bellies resting against rough concrete. Mothers and daughters of different skin and size proudly wearing each other's clothes. Stubborn old revolutionaries with holes in their shoes selling *Granma* and *Juventud rebelde* for a symbolic coin. The forlorn Canadian tourist overwhelmed by his one-night stand. Old Guard Communist Party leaders standing rod-straight at official functions, harsh and dogmatic white men stubbornly denying the outside world, and willfully ignorant of the dancing and irrepressible life all around them. Fidel's pale, freckled, manicured hands perorating to sleepy visitors during an endless dinner. The salsa and *timba* soundtrack of the nights, and the bodies young and old answering its mating calls. The musty antiques of the Museo Napoleónico. Ghosts from Cementerio Colón quietly walking around in the city, nagging my conscience. A girl in a trance dancing for Ochún, hugging the bare earth. Alicia Alonzo, the world's most elegant mummy, holding court backstage at the Teatro Nacional. The leafy campus of Havana University, and the bright young people sitting on the steps of grand buildings, waiting for a future. Little schoolchildren in red and white *pionero* uniforms paying homage to ubiquitous and mournful plaster José Martí statues every morning. The endless ruins of once grand mansions along *Calzada del Cerro*, still teeming with life. The acrid taste of *chispetrén* rum drunk from a plastic cola bottle. Dealers with lizard eyes in doorways in Los Sitios, procuring highs on the ruins of slavery fortunes. Nineteenth-century ghost trains in the Cristina station. All the Santería implements for sale at Cuatro Caminos. Thirty-foot waves crashing over the Malecón wall under bright moonlight. Meyer Lansky's sour specter still apparent in the deserted lobby of the Hotel Riviera. The Cuban version of Frank Lloyd Wright's visionary architecture in Las Ruinas in Parque Lenin. In the same park, the stillness around the colossal sculpture of Lenin's head, history gone dumb. The all-female Camerata Romeu playing Guido Lopez Gavilán's *Guaguancó*, and the darkest one shaking colorful braids, dancing a provocative *rumba* with the cellos, while her colleagues keep rhythm using the classical instruments for percussion. Girls running barefoot in pouring rain under exuberant yellow blossoming trees on Quinta Avenida in Miramar, high-heeled shoes in hand, laughing like wild children. The church of the Loma del Angel, haunted by the tragic character of Cecilia Valdés, the most gorgeous *mulata* of Cuba's nineteenth-century literature, in love with her no-good aristocratic half-brother (and one more book murdered by a totally inadequate movie). The city as seen from the Morro castle, on a luminous day of strong breezes, welcoming ships and sailors, and as Carlos Varela sings shamelessly, opening her legs for them – "*Cuando al Morro llegó, La Habana le abrió sus piernas.*" The entire city as seen from the top of the FOSCA building, once the hideout of the U.S. mafiosi: the amazing urbanism, the chaotic roofs, the view reaching all the way to Mariel on a clear day. The Chinese eyes and African lips of my beautiful best friend, Y. The rowdy crowd at live concerts at La Tropical. Late night discussions with young Cubans in semi-legal bars, the youngsters as serious and committed to meaningful life as their peers in Paris's existentialist cellars in St. Germain in the late 1940s. The casually met boy in Buena Vista, friend of a friend of a friend, who out of sheer boredom was creating a very convincing life-size papier maché lion. The late Cesar Portillo de la Luz singing 1950s *"filin"* ("feeling") ballads at four a.m. at the Gato Tuerto club, capturing all the melancholy of the late hour, with Gabriel García Márquez hiding from history in a dark corner. Haley's Comet dragging an enormous, gold-red tail over the deserted rocky coastline west of the city – a portent of what future? The *palero* ritual in the most secret backroom of the Hijos de San Lázaro in Guanabacoa, next to an impressive *Sarabanda* altar sticky with remnants of old sacrifices. The long perspective of Calle San Lázaro all the way from Prado to the University, looking first like a bombed-out zone and next like a tropical part of Paris...

Those images, with all their anarchy and their complexity and their exuberance spell the real *Soy Cuba* – an ideal movie in the head of an onlooker, an actor in his own documentary, desperately in love with a place so special that it could hardly exist.

But it does.

Havana – New York – Havana
2013–2017

POSTSCRIPT

ELEGGUA OF THE CROSSROADS

In Santería, one of the most popular spirits is Eleggua, the lord of the crossroads. Eleggua is the Master of Destinies, the one who opens and closes roads to the future and in the personal development of the worshipper.

Eleggua is always the first to be invoked in Santería ceremonies.

But he is seen as a playful and sometimes naughty child – as destiny is always fickle. The tired metaphor of a country at a crossroads is always applicable in and to Cuba, since the island is a crossroads by definition – through her history, her geographical location (the key to the Caribbean and the Americas, as shown in the national coat of arms), and the people who came and were brought together on all the trade winds of the planet to fill her streets and her fields. And within Cuba, Havana is the crossroads of all crossroads.

But the Eleggua at the present economic and political crossroads seems even more unpredictable and fickle. Where to, Havana? What is the next turn?

In Siboney, Fidel Castro celebrated his ninetieth birthday

in August 2016. As we have seen, he received his last foreign visitor, the president of Vietnam, on November 15 in the morning. After that he vanished from the media. He had last been seen in public in April, when he spoke about his own mortality at a Communist Party Congress.

He died at 10:29 p.m. on Friday, November 25.

We heard the news in the company of visiting family members, around midnight, on our way back from downtown to Siboney. I was up the whole night, working with colleagues in Europe to find the right words to remember him by. It turned out to be a politically sensitive exercise to show respect and to acknowledge a figure of historical importance without subscribing to all he stood for. In the end, as he had it himself already as a young man, history will judge. As if to underscore the point, Fidel's grand departure coincided with the date on which his boat, the *Granma*, had sailed from Mexico in 1956 to overthrow Batista – an almost surreal undertaking in retrospect.

President Obama, who visited Cuba in March 2016, was not among El Comandante's foreign visitors during the last months of his life. The visit was undoubtedly a landmark in Mr. Obama's very personal brand of diplomacy. His speech at the Gran Teatro was a subtle mixture of respect and well-argued criticism. Most Cubans were deeply impressed by his skills as a communicator, and maybe even more by his – very Cuba-like– post-racial grace and presence. But the old guard reacted harshly: even in its new and seductive wrapping, U.S. policy is still out for *regime change*.

Fidel himself, rather than joining the reconciliation engineered by his brother Raúl, haughtily rejected the intentions of the visit in a letter to the Communist Party newspaper *Granma*: "we need nothing from the Empire."

It was typical of the way in which his absence from the political scene was still a presence. His passing left Raúl standing alone as the last of the three Castro brothers, after the earlier death of the oldest, Ramón.

Was it now five to midnight for Cuba's politics – and for the people – as well?

We know the ingredients of the future, but not the outcome, and it often seems now, in a place so sure of itself, if only through half a century of slogans having worked themselves like mantras into the collective consciousness, that there is no clear horizon any more.

And we sit on the wall along the Malecón, and watch the ocean and the clouds, waiting for the future to arrive like a ship from another world, but uncertain as to the color of its sails.

Like when the conquistadors arrived, new gods will disembark once again, and will clash with local idols. Will gold and greed become the only true religion, here as elsewhere? How will the soul of the city survive, where will it find refuge?

In March 2017, the military checkpoints on the block where Celia Sanchez had lived off Calle 12 in Vedado were discreetly removed. A few months after Fidel's death, the ghost of the woman who had been his guardian angel was finally set free.

A Eleggua y Ochún
Dedico mi tambor

HP

ACKNOWLEDGMENTS

This book would not have been published without the help of the persons listed below, with whom I came into contact and could develop a professional relationship thanks to typical New York chance encounters and serendipity.

First of all, thanks to Liliane Wilcox for her introductions.

To Anne Ekstrom for her tireless support, her good advice, her insightful editing, and for sharing her own network of literary contacts.

To Marianne Strong and the Marianne Strong Literary Agency for their enthusiasm for my writings in general.

Most of all, to Ruth Greenstein for assisting and advising me first as an editor and consultant, and eventually as my publisher.

Thanks also to the dapper Mr. Jonathan Rabinowitz, founder of Turtle Point Press, for his appreciation of the text and for his suggestions.

I'm forever grateful to Professor Margaret Crahan of the Institute of Latin American Studies at Columbia University for her tireless work to improve the text both as to form and as to content. Her long and profound experience in and with Cuba forced me to reassess opinions and to correct facts, all to the benefit of a more balanced and nuanced book.

NOTES AND REFERENCES

This book is first and foremost meant to inform and entertain. I didn't want to burden it with systematic referencing. Nevertheless, the interested reader may find some additional information and background here. Much of the material may only be available in Spanish.

CHAPTER 5: HAVANA IN BLACK AND WHITE

Fernando Ortiz, *Los negros curros*, Edición póstuma, La Habana, 1986. The book began as a series of conference notes as early as 1909, but Ortiz reworked it till the end of his life, never completing a final version. He died in 1969. The introduction to the posthumous edition, by Diana Iznaga (1981), contains much additional research on the themes of slavery and race relations in Havana in the seventeenth and eighteenth centuries.

CHAPTER 6: *RUMBA*

Fernando Ortiz's excursions to the black neighborhoods of Havana: Conference in December 1942 in the *Club Atenas*: "In those days I had the bad idea to become a politician, and every time I was about in Marianao, Regla, Guanabacoa, and the black neighborhoods in Havana, I heard various comments. One liberal said: this fine intellectual is just going after the black vote. A conservative (himself a wise mulatto) argued: what a mistake to bring back those things from the days of slavery! A matronly lady suggested that I

257

was more attracted by the daughters of the Virgen de Regla, than by the Mother of the Waters" (Yemaya, the Santería equivalent of the Virgen de Regla).

See Araceli García-Carranza et al., *Cronología Fernando Ortiz*, Fundación Fernando Ortiz, La Habana, 1996.

CHAPTER 8: SANTERÍA AND THE RACIAL DIVIDE

On the recent political interpretations of Santería, see Heriberto Feraudy Espino, *De la Africanía en Cuba*, Editorial de Ciencias Sociales, La Habana, 2005.

CHAPTER 9: COMMUNIST *ORISHAS?*

Heriberto Feraudy (see previous note), while expanding on Santería as a form of solace against a universal crisis of values and as a remedy against capitalism, also ascribes the popularity of the rites in the Cuban diaspora to the growing racial diversity in Miami after the Mariel and *balsero* waves of migration (1980 and 1994). The original exodus to Miami was by and large of the white middle class. Feraudy (rightly) pokes fun at the *"Orisha* Tours" organized out of Miami as the initiations become more and more commercialized. At the same time, he has to admit that the active repression of the rites in Cuba, practiced in the 1970s and '80s by the Communist Party, failed completely.

CHAPTER 22: *EL CAÑONAZO*

For the description of the outfits of the *negros curros* and *negras curras*, see Ortiz, *Los negros curros*, Chapter 3.

The supposed repression of vice: A 1747 report by Governor Francisco Cagigal to the Consejo de Indias in Sevilla enumerates all the ingredients of the *"mala vida"* in Havana: "indecent" interracial dancing, gambling, prostitution and rampant venereal disease, rackets and blackmail, etc., but in fact the corruption of the colonial governors made them accomplices of all those situations. This had become worse as of 1740 when the royal Havana trading house (Real Compañía de Comerio de La Habana) was given a monopoly to control all foreign trade, but was bypassed by its very agents to import and sell cheap contraband of all kinds from the English and French islands. This was done so openly that the local government lost practically all credibility.

Unflattering parallels with state monopolies under communism, and their black market sequels, have sometimes been detected.

The **"most exciting music":** Ortiz, *La clave xilofónica de la música cubana*, Estudios Afrocubanos, La Habana, 1945–46.

CHAPTER 24: 1762: BRITISH OCCUPATION AND A DEFINING MOMENT

For a detailed description of the British occupation and its consequences, see *La toma de la Habana por los ingleses*, Biblioteca Nacional de Cuba José Martí, 2012.

Comments on the captain general Juan de Prado Portocarrero: Much of the blame for the fall of Havana rested on the shoulders of the captain general, whose military career in Spain left him "sin historia americana y desconocedor de la guerra irregular y de las características caribeñas." Eduardo Torres-Cuevas, *La Habana 1752: ingleses, españoles y criollos* in *op. cit.*

Not only was he unprepared, he accumulated tactical mistakes from the moment he saw the sails appearing on the horizon and took them for a merchant fleet (as he noted in his own diary on June 6). The bishop Morel, with whom Portocarrero refused to cooperate, would have instigated the earliest anti-colonial *guerrilla* in Cuba.

CHAPTER 29: GHOSTS OF REVOLUTIONS PAST

The full inscription on the tomb of Alejo Carpentier reads: "Hombre de mi tiempo soy y mi tiempo trascendente es el de la Revolución Cubana. Alejo Carpentier 1904–1980" (see photograph).

Quote from Alejo Carpentier, *El siglo de las luces*, Letras Cubanas, La Habana, 2001.

CHAPTER 30: MUCH LOUDER GHOSTS

The latest research on the Maine explosion concluded that it was an accident, caused by the buildup of gases in the hold. Information provided by Professor Margaret Crahan of Columbia University.

CHAPTER 31: NAPOLEON IN CUBA

Napoleon as the "vile Corsican": José Marti, "En torno al marmol rojo," *Versos Libres*, Centro de Estudios Martianos/Ediciones Boloña, La Habana, 2013. Free partial translation:

Around the red marble where sleeps
That vile Corsican, infamous Napoleon,
I saw like accusing hands
The blood-soaked flags
Of many mutilated peoples.
My soul stood like a flag there too,
On a pole straight like a pine,
None more torn
Among those decorating the dark crypt
Where rests the infamous Napoleon.

CHAPTER 33: THE CAVE AT THE END OF THE WORLD

The exact quote from the *Verde Olive* article "Táctica y estrategia de la Revolución Latinoamericana" reads: "*Tenemos que caminar por el sendero de la liberación aunque esto cueste milliones de víctimas atómicas . . . El pueblo sin miedo tratando de avanzar hacia la hecatombe que significará la redención definitiva.*"

Richard Gott's doubts about the identity of the corpse: Richard Gott, *The last journey of Che Guevara*, Vallegrande, Bolivia, October 10, 1967. Article in *The Guardian*, reprinted in *The Mammoth Book of How It Happened*, Jon E. Lewis, ed., Robinson, London, 2006.

CHAPTER 34: CONVERSATION IN CAFÉ DEL ORIENTE

Conversation with Dr. González: The meeting took place in January 2016.

CHAPTER 45: NEXT YEAR IN HAVANA / JERUSALEM

On the Jewish presence in Havana and its history, see Ruth Behar, *An Island Called Home: Returning to Jewish Cuba*, Rutgers University Press, 2007.

CHAPTER 47: *MULATAS DE RUMBA & PUELLAE GADITANAE*

The gypsy girl dancing "the Vito Sevillano," see *Doré's Spain*, Dover Publications, 2014, p. 103. The original illustrations were published between 1862 and 1874, precisely at the time when the first steamships made the crossings between Cádiz and Havana much faster, and music and dance styles were blending more and more.

Havana not seen by Gustave Doré: Cirilo Villaverde, in *Cecilia Valdés o la loma del angel*, the best nineteenth-century novel documenting colonial Havana (published in exile in New York, 1879–1882), warns readers that his rendering of the city and its characters may seem too somber and shady, "as if I used for mere effect the darkest colors and overburdened the painting with shadows like a Rembrandt or a Gustave Doré." It's striking that this great novelist saw Havana through Doré's eyes. The book is still a very readable classic, and many of the situations it describes in the poorer parts of the city remain practically unchanged. See the introduction in *Cecilia Valdés o la loma del angel*, Letras Cubanas, La Habana, 2001.

CHAPTER 48: ALMA MATER

The architecture of Havana University: The signature style of classicism mixed with art deco elements is best illustrated by the library building by Joaquin Weiss (1894–1968), who studied at Cornell University but became dean of the faculty of architecture in Havana after his return to Cuba.

CHAPTER 52: BLOGGERS' BREAKFAST

Churchill on communism: The full quote reads: "But in the main human society will grow in many forms not comprehended by a party machine." Epilogue of the abridged version of the *Memoirs of the Second World War*, Houghton Mifflin Company, Boston, 1957, p. 1016.

CHAPTER 54: THE PEN & THE SWORD

Edmundo Desnoes's book is sometimes still referred to as *Inconsolable Memories*, an earlier working title also retained for an English translation.

Padura "writing the silence": *El Hombre que amaba a los perros*, Ediciones Unión (UNEAC), La Habana, 2012.

The quote freely translated reads: ". . . all those writers who produced the empty and complacent literature of the 1970s and '80s, those lamentable books, practically the only ones possible under the omnipresent cloak of suspicion, intolerance, and national uniformity. Like Rimbaud in his days in Harrar, I would have preferred to forget the existence of literature. Like Isaac Babel, I preferred to *write the silence*. At least with my mouth closed I could feel at peace with myself."

Note that the book was published by the Cuban National Artists' and Writers Union (UNEAC), the very organism to blame for the "lamentable books" of the 1970s and '80s. But the accusation is hidden on page 380 of a 550 page novel.

CHAPTER 57: HATUEY & HURACÁN

The founding of Havana: In fact, the city was founded somewhat by trial and error, looking for a location on the west side of the island in the early days of the conquest of Mexico. The future city needed a strategic location, natural defenses, and access to food and water. No location was found to be ideal, and the city was moved three or four times before settling at the inner end of the deep natural harbor where it is now located, with good protection from enemies and hurricanes, but with little access to drinking water. See Fernando Ortiz, *Historia de una pelea cubana contra los demonios*, Editorial de Ciencias Sociales, La Habana, 1975.

The story of Hatuey and Havana's first runaways: Bartolomé de las Casas, *Brevísima relacion de la destrucción de las Indias*, Editorial Fontamara, Barcelona, 1981, chapter "*De la ysla de Cuba*": "*Comencaron unos a huyr a los montes, otros a ahorcarse de deseperados; y ahorcavanse maridos e mugeres e consigo ahorcavan los hijos . . .*" (quoted in the original archaic spelling); "Some started fleeing to the mountains, others hung themselves out of despair, and husbands and wives hung themselves together with their children."

CHAPTER 58: *TODO EL MUNDO CANTA*

Havana as the capital of all vices: "*La Habana fue durante siglos la Sevilla de América y como esta, pudo merecer el dictado de Babilonia de la* *picardía . . .*" Fernando Ortiz, *Estudios afrocubanos*, La Habana, 1945–1956 ("For centuries, Havana was the Sevilla of America and as such could deserve the title of the Babylon of Rascals").

The Catholic Church and the "mala vida": a conference of Cuban bishops in 1684 published a report illustrating all the sins, and the tolerance they enjoyed from civilian authorities. The same sins were practiced by the clergy, who even escaped the jurisdiction of the colonial court system. The fact that the sailors of the colonial fleet and all soldiers were also immune from the governor's judiciary, further encouraged Havana's wildness. The convergence of vices in the city was also a result of its being the hub of the fleets between the colonies and Spain. Ruffians escaping or deported from Peru, Mexico, etc., ended up in the city, while at the same time the underworld connections between Sevilla, Cádiz, and Havana never ceased.

The code of conduct for churchgoers was also published by the same bishops' conference in 1684. See details in Diana Iznaga's introduction to Fernando Ortiz's *Los negros curros*, supra. The repeated ordinances of the Church insisting on celibacy of the clergy illustrate that they were never obeyed. The bishop who first tried to reform the vices of the clergy, Juan Montiel, was poisoned in 1683. The early *toquesantos* or Santería sessions by slaves and freed Africans were supposed to be held at the doors of the churches and "without dancing, betting or other indecent entertainments ("bayles, danzas, juegos y otros entretenimientos indecentes"). As usual, the pleasures forbidden give an exact picture of what was really going on.

Mambises: The term "mambi" as a generic description of a creole freedom fighter against Spanish colonialism seems to have originated in Santo Domingo from the name of a black Spanish officer who joined the rebellion in 1846. His name was Juan Mamby. Some of the Dominicans, most notably Antonio Maceo, later joined the Cuban independence wars. Maceo, "the Bronze Titan," is still much revered in Cuba as the greatest general of the independence struggle, and an illustration of its multiracial character.

CHAPTER 71: PIRATES OF ALL KINDS

The slave trade after 1815 as piracy: See Francisco Mota, *Piratas y corsarios en las costas de Cuba*, Editorial Gente Nueva, La Habana, 1997.

Goethe on the British slave trade ban: See José Luciano Franco, *Comercio clandestino de esclavos*, Editorial de Ciencias Sociales, La Habana, 1996.

CHAPTER 78: THE LAST *CIMARRÓN*

The last cimarrón: Miguel Barnet, *Biografía de un Cimarrón*, Letras Cubanas, La Habana, 1966–2001. Esteban Montejo was said to be 104 years old when he told his story to Miguel Barnet in a veterans' home in 1963. He had been a slave and a runaway in the wilds of Las Villas province, including during the years of the independence wars. The author is very careful to present him as an early example of revolutionary attitudes, even though Montejo is at times very critical of some of the leaders and fighters of the independence war.

CHAPTER 87: APOTHEOSIS

The film *Cecilia Valdés*: Directed by Humberto Solas, 1982. Cecilia, a lively – almost feral – urban child in the novel, is played unconvincingly by Daisy Granados, who was not only in her late thirties but also failed to convey Cecilia's racial mix. It seems that, under the revolutionary ethic, Cecilia had to be a tragic character, a victim of colonial race relations, and could never be the fun-loving *mulata* she is at the opening of the book.

INDEX

Page numbers in italics represent photographs.

Abreu, Alexander, 212

Acosta, Carlos, 162

Afro-Cubans, 12–27; African traditions, 13, 16–23, 25–26; black gangs (*los negros curros*) and Spanish underworld customs, 16–17, 56–57, 128; *cabildos*, 13–14, 16, 19; and the Cuban Revolution, 23–25; culture of the *solar*, 17, 225; Día de Reyes carnival, 14, 16–17, 20; jazz and the Havana–New York music scene, 211; Ortiz on cultural divide between black and white Cuba, 16–17, 21, 26; population of Oriente, 119–20, 224–25; port area neighborhoods, 57; religious freedom and revival of African cultural identity, 25–26; transatlantic slave trade and introduction of African-born slaves, 166, 222. *See also* Santería;

slavery in Cuba

air travel and airports, 51, 114, 115–18; exit visa (*tarjeta blanca*), 117; historic restricted travel laws, 116–17; Miami Cubans and charter flights to Havana, 51, 114; and new international freedom of movement, 117; plastic-wrapped bundles of luggage and goods (*pacotilla*), 51, 114, 116, 117–18; Terminal II of José Martí Airport, 115–18, 214; U.S.-Cuba charter flights/commercial flights, 51, 114, 115–18; visa requirements for Cuban musicians, 211–12

Alberti, Rafael, 132

Algeria, 79

Allende, Salvador, 92

almendrones ("big almonds"), 4–5, 102, 228

Alonso, Alicia, 160–62

Angola, 18, 26

Antommarchi, Francisco, 82
architecture: Art Nouveau, 106, 107–8; art-deco style, 108–9; socialist realism, 107, 159. *See also* buildings, Havana's
Arciniegas, Germán, 202
Argentina: Che Guevara's remains, 91–92; delegation at Havana's May Day parade, 150, 152
Armed Forces, Cuban, 45, 49, 53, 95–96
Art Nouveau movement, 106, 107–8
art-deco style, *108*, 108–9; Freemasons' headquarters, *25*, 109, 120, *121*, 179; Miami's South Beach, 108; restorations, 109, *111*
arts and culture: ceramic artist José Fuster, 220–22, *221*; classical ballet, 159–62; classical music, 184–86; Fabelo's sculpture studio in Miramar, 225–27; the Fábrica de Arte Cubano, 141–42; the Havana Arts Biennale (2015), 186–88, *187*, 213, 227–29, 239; interactive Havana–New York music scene, 210–13; young creative Cubans and the art scene, 141–42, 158. *See also* films, Cuban; writers, Cuban
Asociación Yoruba de Cuba, *148*

Babalú Aye, xiii, 20
Bacardí family, 110–11
Ballet Nacional, 159–62
balseros (boatpeople) crisis of 1994,

36–37, 40, 65, 205–9; Caribbean piracy and attacks on (organ theft rumors), 205; Elián González story and Miami Cubans, 205–9; Fidel Castro and, 207–9; and the Malecón wall, 36–37, 40, 207–8; "wet foot, dry foot" policy and refugees, 207, 209, 243
Barnet, Miguel, 17, 223, 224
Barrio Chino, *29*, 29–33, 179
baseball (*la pelota*), 64, 188–93; baseball politics and U.S.-Cuba relations, 64, 188–90, 193; and Caribbean sports culture, 188–93; the Estadio Latinoamericano in El Cerro (the "baseball cathedral"), 190, 192–93; players' defections to U.S., 189–90; and soccer, 190–91; team names, 188
Batista, Fulgencio, 95, 102, 129, 136–37; Cuban Revolution and the attack on Batista's palace, 242; Cuban Revolution and the Moncada attack, 137; flight from Havana, 83, 194–96; gambling culture and U.S. mob, 193, 194–96
Benedict XVI, Pope, 181
Bernhard, Sarah, 81
Beth Shalom Jewish community, xiv, 122–27, 177
Betto, Frei, 181–82
bicitaxis, 50, *126*, 244
Big Boodle, The (film), 70, 200–201
Blanco, Pedro, 203
B'nai B'rith, 53
Bobadilla, Inés de, 132

Bolívar Aróstegui, Natalia, 83–85, 239

Bolivia: Che Guevara's death in, 89–94, 219; history of slavery, 167

Bonaparte, Pauline, 80–81

Bosque de La Habana, 236

botellón tradition, 36–38

boxing, 191–92

Brazil-Cuba relations, 63–64; Brazilian delegation at Havana's May Day parade, 151; and Brazil's economic downturn, 63–64, 151; and Lula, 63–64; soccer world cup (2014), 191

Brevísima relación de la destrucción de las Indias (Las Casas), 164

British Empire: occupation of Havana (1762–1763), 7, 14–15, 60–63, 235; piracy and transatlantic slave trade, 203–4; slave system, 14–15, 19, 62, 203–4; and sugar industry, 14–15

Bronx Museum (New York), 229

Bueno, Descemer, 212

buildings, Havana's, 230–35; Centro Habana's urban neglect, 7–8, 33, 71, 96; formerly palatial homes, 8, 71–72, 234; future of, 233–34; the Oficina del Historiador de la Ciudad, 232; ownership of property titles, 230–31; permuta system during the Período Especial, 231; real estate market and private property ownership, 230–35; repairing and rebuilding older buildings, 231–34; restoration of the historic city, 3, 177, 216, 232–34; safety hazards, 233; simple sales of properties, 231; social housing apartment complexes, 103; and U.S. embargo legislation, 233; U.S.-based claims on, 233

Bush, George H. W., 64

Bush, George W., 64, 113

Cabaña fortress, 55, 93, 200, 227

Cabrera Infante, Guillermo, 153, 154

cacao production, 236

Cádiz, Spain, 127–32

Calle Aramburu neighborhood, 17–18

Calzada del Cerro, 7, 9, 247

Camerata Romeu (all-female musical group), 185, 247

Canada-Cuba relations, 44, 64, 116, 181

Capitolio (at the city center), 4, 7, 11, 29, 95, 162, 191

Caribbean-Cuba relations, 67–68, 167; and Caribbean piracy, 59–60, 201–5; sports culture, 188–93

Caritas (Catholic charity), 53, 174

Carpentier, Alejo, 16, 74–78, 153, 157, 159, 244; as Cuban ambassador to France, 75–77; and the Cuban Revolution, 74–78; life and background, 75–76; tomb at Cementerio Colón, 74–78, 75, 259

Los Carpinteros (avant-garde group of sculptors), 213

cars and car culture, 4–5

Carter, Jimmy, 64

Casa de las Américas on Calle G (Avenida de los Presidentes), 109

Casa de los Arabes cultural center, 179

Casa de Tejas Verdes (Green Tiled House), 230, 234–35

Casa Orestes Ferrara: and the Museo Napoleónico, 82–83, 85; secret underground tunnels, 84–85

Casablanca railway line, 236–39

Castillo de la Fuerza, 132, 201–2

Castro, Fidel, 7, 10, 102, 155, 249–51; and artist Kcho, 227–28; and baseball, 190; and the Catholic Church, 169–72, 181–82; and the Coubre explosion in Havana harbor, 79–80; creation of the CDRs, 139–40; and Cuban Communist Party, 95–96; death, 119, 181, 215–16, 249–51; economic reforms, 44–45, 48; Elián González story and U.S.-Cuban relations, 207–9; and Gorbachev's Havana visit, 39; and Hemingway, 219; military tunnels and Cold War doctrine of national defense, 85–86; and Napoleon's tomb, 81; and the Oriente, 119; proclamation of socialism (April 16, 1961), 72; retirement in Siboney neighborhood, 1, 249–50; as student activist leader at Havana University, 136–37

Castro, Mariela, 34–36, 184

Castro, Raúl, 32, 250–51; and Catholic Cardinal Ortega, 176–77; and the Cuban Armed Forces, 95–96; economic issues, 38, 45; and Gutiérrez Alea's film *Guantanamera*, 155; and the U.S.-Cuba reconciliation, 177, 250; and women's liberation, 34

Catholic Church, Cuban, 25, 167–77, 180–84; Cardinal Ortega, 171, 174–77; colonial Spanish Catholic clergy and vice-ridden Havana, 167–69, 263; and the Cuban Revolution, 169–71; and dissident Catholic groups, 175–76, 182–84; early republic, 170; Fidel Castro and, 169–72, 181–82; liberation theology, 181; new archbishop García, 176; papal visit of Benedict XVI (2012), 181; papal visit of Francis (2015), 175, 182–84; papal visit of John Paul II (1998), 125, 171–74, 177; and post-1992 religious freedoms, 24, 125; Raúl Castro and, 176–77; and Santería, xiii, 19–20, 171, 263; social conservatism, 176, 183–84; social role of, 174, 176, 180; Spanish church's opposition to Cuban independence, 169; and U.S.-Cuba diplomatic normalization, 175, 182; and women's rights, 33–34, 176

14ymedio, 145

Cecilia Valdés o la loma del angel (Villaverde), 247, 261, 264

Cejas, Paul, 113

Cementerio Colón, 72, 74–78, 129, 211, 244; Carpentier's tomb, 74–78, *75*, 259; Masonic tombs, 121, 179; monument to victims of the USS *Maine*, 78–79; Oya, mistress of the graveyard, 74; Pantheon of the Armed Forces, 74

CENESEX (national center for sexual education), 35–36

Central de Trabajadores de Cuba, 143

Centro Habana, 3, 7–12, *8*, 33, 56; Masonic headquarters on the corner of Salvador Allende and Calle Belascoaín, *25*, 109, 120, *121*, 179; Teatro de las Américas on Calle Galeano, 27; urban neglect, 7–8, 33, 71, 96; the wall around Habana Vieja, 55–57. *See also* Habana Vieja (Old Havana)

ceramic art, 220–22, *221*

Céspedes, Carlos Manuel de, 15–16

chabacano (street slang), 62

Changó, 20, 28, 163

Charles III, King (Carlos Tercero), 169

Chávez, Hugo, 44–46, 63, 65

Chernobyl disaster, children of, 105

China model of economic reforms, 48–50

Chinese traditions in Havana, 29–33, 48–50; Barrio Chino, *29*, 29–33, 179; Chinese cemetery in Nuevo Vedado, 32–33; Chinese immigrants, 31–32; colonial trade, 30; *pacotilla china* (Chinese merchandise), 30, 48; restaurants, 29, 31, 33

Chirino, Willy, 211

chivatos (informers), 135

chocolate, Cuban: the Africana cookie, 238; cacao production in Baracoa, 236; the Hershey train, 236–39, *238*

Churchill, Winston, 149, 197, 261

Cienfuegos, Camilo, 150

cigars, Cuban, 110, 112

cimarrones (runaway slaves), 169–70, 222–25; and the Cuban Revolution, 223–24; and *mambises* of the war for independence, 169, 224, 263; and *palestinos* of Oriente, 224–25; Río Quibú settlements, 222–25

Cinco Prisoneros del Imperio, xiv

classical ballet, 159–62

classical music culture, 184–86

Clinton, Bill, 64

Cohiba cigars, 112

Cojimar (seaside suburb), 102–3, *217*, 217–20

Cold War: Castro's doctrine of national defense against U.S. invasion, 85–86; Cuban missile crisis, 87–89; end of Soviet communism, 7, 38–39, 66; Havana–New York music scene, 210–11; Havana's underground shelters, 84–86; Malecón wall, 5; nuclear weapons race, 87–89; U.S.-Cuba relations, xiv, 77, 85–86, 87, 219

college students and career decisions, 133–36

Colombia: Cuba's mediating role in peace negotiations with FARC, 97–99; ELN (Ejército de Liberacón Nacional), 98; FARC and the Cuban Revolution, 98

Comités de Defensa de la Revolución (CDRs), 139–41; the grinning crocodile logo, *139*, 140–41; and John Paul II's visit, 172; triangular all-seeing-eye logo, 138–41

Communist Party, Cuban: church licensing and Office for Religious Affairs, 178; and dissident community, 146–49; and the Federation of University Students (FEU), 136; Fidel Castro and, 95–96; Fidel's final speech to the Communist Party Congress, 228, 250; *Granma* (newspaper), 142–43, 159, 170, 181, 188, 215, 250; May Day parade, *146*, 146, 149–52; Palacio de la Revolución offices, 94–96; and Santería, 23–25

Community of Latin American and Caribbean States, 167

Conducta (film), 157

consumer goods, American, 51–52, 114–15, 213–16; consumption and the changes coming with normalized relations, 114–15; plastic-wrapped bundles of luggage and goods (*pacotilla*), 51, 114, 116, 117–18; television, media, and news from the outside world (*el paquete*), 213–16, 243

Cortés, José Luis "El Tosco," 28

costumbrista ("traditionalist") artists, 56–57

La Coubre explosion in Havana harbor (1960), 79–80

Council of Churches, 178

Crahan, Meg, 211

Cruz, Celia, 132, 210, 212

Cruz, Raúl Ernesto, 97

Cruz Gómez, María, 203

Cuatro Caminos (train station), 9, 237

Cuba Posible (Catholic think tank), 184

Cuban constitution, 145; religious freedom amendment (1992), 24, 125; and socialism, 145

Cuban exceptionalism, 6, 149

Cuban missile crisis, 87–89

Cuban Normalization Act ("wet foot, dry foot" policy), 207, 209, 243

Cuban Revolution: arms/weapons, 79–80; attack on Batista's palace, 242; Batista's flight from Havana, 83, 194–96; Carpentier and, 74–78; and the Catholic Church, 169–71; the CDRs and logos, *139*, 139–41; Che Guevara's hideout in the Sierra Candelaria mountains, 86–89; and Chinese immigrants, 31; and *cimarrones* (runaway slaves), 223–24; La Coubre explosion in Havana harbor (1960), 79–80; and the FARC in Colombia, 98; and Freemasons, 120; gambling and mob culture,

195–96; and Havana University, 136–38, 242; July 26 movement, 119; and labor unions, 150; Moncada attack (1956), 137; and the Oriente, 119, 224; and the Plaza de la Revolución, 94–95, 150; and Radio Reloj, 242; and Santería, 23–25; and sexual attitudes, 33–35; vandalism and theft of Havana's art treasures, 83; writers and, 153

Cuban Writers' Union, 223

Curaçao, 122

Cuty (painter), 228–29

Damas de Blanco (Ladies in White), 175

Daranas, Ernesto, 157

death penalty moratorium, 59–60, 97

Desnoes, Edmundo, 154

Día de Reyes carnival, 14, 16–17, 20

Diamantes, Cucu, 213

Díaz, Manny, 113

Diez de Octubre (suburb), 3, 5, 15, 196

Dirty Havana Trilogy (Gutiérrez), 155

dissident community, 144–49; blogger Sánchez and 14ymedio, 145; Catholic groups, 175–76, 182–84; digital literacy campaign, 147; and Obama's 2016 visit, 145–46; public shaming (*actos de repudio*) in front of activists' homes, 140

Dominican Republic, 188, 195

Doré, Gustave, 131, 261

drug trade (cocaine), 144, 205

Dutch Antilles, 188

Echeverría, José Antonio, 242

economics: Arab states' financing of public works, 178; black market and *el sector no estatal* (non-state sector), 37, 38–41, 54; China model of economic reform, 48–51; the convertible peso (*peso convertible*), 43–44, 52–55; CUC-denominated commerce, 43–44; double money standard (*moneda nacional* and the U.S. dollar), 43–44, 52–55; and the east-west division of Cuba, 119–20; economic reforms, 44–51, 68; EU Member States and economic partnerships with Cuba, 66–67; industrial development and manufacturing, 49–50; and Miami Cubans, 43, 48, 49, 50, 51–52, 119–20; network of *mulas* from Miami, 51–52; *El Período Especial*, 7, 34, 36, 38–55, 62, 68, 153–54; poverty of the Oriente, 119–20; prostitution economy, 42–43; rationing booklets (*las libretas*) and subsidized neighborhood *bodegas*, 43–44, 54–55; remittances, 43, 48, 51–52, 119–20; salaries and growing social inequality, 44, 53–55; U.S. dollar economy, 41–45, 52–55; and U.S. embargo/embargo legislation, 49, 64,

economics (*cont.*)
　173, 233; Venezuela's Chávez
　and economic support, 44–45,
　63; Vietnam model of economic
　reforms, 48–49
Ecuador, 167, 243
Edificio Bacardí (on Avenida de
　Bélgica), 109, *111*
Eleggua (male *orisha*), 19, 249
ELN (Ejército de Liberacón
　Nacional) (Colombia), 98
Espacio Laical (Catholic Church
　magazine), 184
Espín, Vilma, 34–35
Estadio Latinoamericano in El
　Cerro (the "baseball cathedral"),
　190, 192–93
European Union, 66–69; EU-Cuba
　relations and 2016 comprehensive
　agreement, 69; EU-Cuba
　relations and the 1996 Common
　Position, 66–67, 69; European
　social model and "neoliberal
　authoritarianism," 68; and
　FARC-Colombian government
　peace process, 98; post-2008
　"collapse" and budget austerity
　measures, 68–69; refugee crisis,
　68
evangelical Christians, 125, 177–78
Evtushenko, Evgeniy, 69

Fabelo, Roberto, 225–27, 228
Fábrica de Arte Cubano, 141–42
FARC (Fuerzas Armadas
　Revolucionarias de Colombia),
　97–99

Fast & Furious movie franchise, 214
Fátima o El Parque de la Fraternidad
　(film), 29, 157
Federación de Mujeres Cubanas
　(Cuban Women's Federation), 34
Federación Estudiantil Universitaria
　(Federation of University
　Students) (FEU), 133–34, 136
Félix Varela Catholic cultural
　center, 183
Fernández, Leonel, 195
Fernández, Roberto, 195
Ferrara, Orestes, 82–85
films, Cuban, 69–71, 153–55,
　199–201; censorship and controls
　on, 153–55, 157; Cuban-Soviet
　production *Soy Cuba*, 8–9,
　69–71, 154, 200; Flynn's *The
　Big Boodle*, 70, 200–201; *Fresa y
　chocolate*, 8, 35, 154; *Guantanamera*,
　154–55; and Gutiérrez Alea,
　71, 141, 153–55; Havana film
　festival (2014), 157; Hollywood
　productions in pre-revolutionary
　Havana, 199–201; *Memorias del
　subdesarrollo*, 71, 141, 154; Padura's
　script for *Return to Ithaca*, 157;
　productions of Padura's Mario
　Conde detective novels, 157–58
flamenco, 128, 130–32, 179
flights between U.S. and Cuba. *See*
　air travel and airports
Flynn, Errol, 70, 200–201
food production and distribution,
　43–44, 54–55; cacao production,
　236; food shortages during the
　Período Especial, 39–40, 41;

malnourishment, 53; rationing booklets (*las libretas*) and neighborhood *bodega* culture, 43–44, 54–55; sugar cane, 14–15, 39–40, 62, 110

Formell, Juan, 27–28

France: Carpentier as Cuban ambassador to, 75–77; Communist party, 77; La Coubre explosion in Havana harbor (1960), 79; Cuban rum and, 111–12; French Revolution, 76, 176–77; Haitian independence wars, 120; Napoleon and the Caribbean, 80–82

Francis, Pope: and Catholic dissident groups, 182–83; meeting with Russian Orthodox patriarch Kirill, 180; papal visit to Cuba (2015), 175, 182–84; and U.S.-Cuba diplomatic normalization, 175, 182

Franco, Francisco, 63, 67, 129–30

Freemasons, 25, 120–21, 179–80; and the Catholic Church, 169; and the Cuban Revolution, 120; headquarters (the art-deco Gran Logia on the corner of Salvador Allende and Calle Belascoaín), 25, 109, 120, 121, 179; Masonic tombs at Cementerio Colón, 121, 179; and the Oriente, 120; and Santería, 24, 120–21, 179–80

French Revolution, 76, 176–77

Fresa y chocolate (film), 8, 35, 154

Fuentes, Gregorio, 217, 219–20

Fundación Fernando Ortiz, 223

funeraria (municipal funeral customs), 244–45

Fuster, José, 220–22, 221

Gades, Antonio, 132

gambling, 58, 193; card game *monte*, 58, 168; early Catholic clergy and culture of, 168; lottery, 58; slaves' use of winnings to buy freedom, 58. *See also* mob, Cuban

gangs and gangland culture, 103; Habana Vieja's historic gangland neighborhoods, 56–57; *los negros curros* and Spanish underworld customs, 16–17, 56–57, 128; and social housing complexes, 103

García, Andy, 211

García, Archbishop Juan de la Caridad, 176

García Márquez, Gabriel, 77–78

Germany: Berlin Wall, 112, 113; Nazi occupation of Belgium and persecution of Jews, 122; reunification, 115

Getz, Stan, 211

Gillespie, Dizzy, 211

Godfather, The (film), 194, 199

Goethe, Johann Wolfgang von, 204

González, Elián, 205–9

González, Jorge, 90–94

Gorbachev, Mikael, 38–39

Gordon, Elaine, 212

Gott, Richard, 89–90

Gran Teatro Alicia Alonso, 159–60, 162

grandparents, 34

Granma (Communist Party newspaper), 142–43, 159, 170, 181, 188, 215, 250

Greek Orthodox Church, 177

Greene, Graham, 200

Gross, Alan, xiv, 64, 127

Guantanamera (film), 154–55

guaracha, 28, 131

Guevara, Alfredo, 153, 155

Guevara, Ernesto "Che," 86–94, 150, 170, 219, 236; on the Cuban missile crisis and nuclear war, 88–89; Cueva de los Portales hideout in the Sierra Candelaria mountains, 86–89; death in Bolivia and conspiracy theories around, 89–94, 219; ghost in Havana locations, 93; Korda's iconic portrait taken at Coubre memorial service, 80, 86; as president of the National Bank, 82, 86, 93

Gutiérrez, Pedro Juan, 155–56, 159

Gutiérrez Alea, Tomás, 71, 141, 153–55

Habana Club rum, 111–12

Habana Libre hotel, 197

Habana Vieja (Old Havana), 7–12; Ballet Nacional school on Prado, 161–62; Barrio Jesús María, xiii, 57, 178, 239–41; Capitolio (in the city center), 4, 7, 11, 29, 95, 162, 191; classical concerts and music culture, 184–86; the daily *cañonazo*, 55, 57, 59–60; gardens devoted to Mother Theresa and Princess Diana, 179; gentrification's risks and challenges, 241; historic gangland neighborhoods, 56–57; historic Havana-by-night (lawlessness), 57–58; historic restoration projects, 3, 177, 216, 232–33; Hotel Ambos Mundos, 216–17; Muslim community and mosque, 178–79; orthodox churches, 177; Plaza de Armas, 11, 42, 216; Plaza San Francisco, 90, 184–86; Plaza Vieja, 11, 225; port area and neighborhoods, 56–59, 241; railway station, 56; tourism, 3, 10–11, 23, 216, 232–33; wall around, 55–57

"Habáname" (song), 3

Haiti, 14–15, 80–81, 120

Hatuey (Indian cacique), 164–65

Havana Arts Biennale (2015), 186–88, *187*, 213, 227–29, 239; the artistic *zona franca* at Cabaña fortress, 227; and New York art scene, 229; political work, 227–29; Romerillo street show and Kcho's workshop, 227–28; Santería-based percussion performances, 239

Havana Book Fair (2016), 223

Havana Cathedral, 185–86

Havana Hilton, 197

Havana University, 132–38; *Alma Mater* statue, 132–33, 137–38; college students' career decisions, 133–36; and the Communist Party, 136–37; and the Cuban

Revolution, 136–38, 242; Fidel
Castro and, 136–37
Hearst, William Randolph, 78
Hein, Piet, 202, 204
Hemingway, Ernest, 102–3,
199, 216–20; and Cojimar
community, 102–3, 217, 217–20;
and Fidel Castro, 219; fishing
boat (the Pilar), 102–3, 217–18;
the Marina Hemingway, 218–20;
tourism inspired by, 217–20; and
Virgen de la Caridad del Cobre,
118, 218
Hermanos Amejeiras Hospital, 84
Hershey, Milton, 236
Hershey train, 236–39, *238*
High Line (elevated railway), 239–
41, *240*
Hines, Earl Fatha, 211
La Historia me Absolverá (History
Will Absolve Me) (Castro), 137
hitchhiking (*pedir botella*), 103
El Hombre que Amaba a los Perros
(Padura), 156, 157, 158, 262
homophobia and anti-gay prejudice,
34–36
Hotel Ambos Mundos, 216–17
Hotel Atlántico, 104
Hotel Capri, 83, 195, 199
Hotel Nacional, 37, 78, 162, 197–98
Hugo, Victor, 81

Iglesias, Aracelio, 57, 150
Indians: Hatuey (cacique), 164–65;
the *Leyendra Negra* (the Black
Legend of Spanish atrocities),
166, 167; Spanish colonial slavery

and genocide, 163–67; statue next
to the Parque de la Fraternidad
(La Fuente de la India), 166–67;
Taíno and Siboney populations,
162–63, 164–66; today, 166
Indio Hatuey (weather station),
164–65
Instituto Cubano de Arte y Industria
Cinematográfica (ICAIC), 153,
155
Instituto Cubano del Libro, 158
intellectuals, Cuban, 74–78;
Carpentier, 74–78; and García
Márquez, 77–78
internet access, 147, 183, 214. See
also *el paquete*
Islam, 178–79; Casa de los Arabes
cultural center, 179; Cuba's ties
with the Islamic world, 126–27
Israel-Cuba relations, 124–26

Jaimanitas village and Fuster's
ceramic art, 220–22, *221*
Jamaica, 122, 165, 201, 225
Jardín Diana de Gales, 179
Jardines de la Tropical (amusement
park), 105–7, 236
Jesús María barrio, xiii, 57, 178,
239–41
Jewish community of Havana,
xiv, 122–27; and Alan Gross's
imprisonment, xiv, 127;
Ashkenazi Jews, 122; diamond
cutters, 124; and Israel-Cuba
relations, 124–26; Jewish
cemeteries in Guanabacoa, 33,
122, *123*; reopened synagogue and

Jewish community of Havana (*cont.*)
new state doctrine of religious
freedom, 125, 177; Sephardic
synagogue in Old Havana,
122; Vedado's Beth Shalom
congregation, xiv, 122–27, 177;
wartime refugees from Antwerp,
122–24, *123*; worship prohibitions
in communist atheist Cuba, 124
John Paul II, Pope: papal mass in the
Plaza de la Revolución, 172–73,
183; papal visit (1998), 125,
171–74, 177
John XXIII, Pope, 170
José Martí Airport, 115–18, 214. *See
also* air travel and airports
Juan de los Muertos (film), 8–9
July 26 movement, 119
Juventud Rebelde (newspaper), 143

Kalatozov, Mikhael, 69
Kcho (artist), 227–28
Kid Chocolate boxing gym, 135,
191–92, *192*, 238
Korbel, Mario, 137
Korda, Alberto, 80, 86

La India (salsa diva), 28, 212, 213
La Lupe (singer), 210
La Tropical brewery, 106
labor unions, 70, 143, 150–51; and
May Day parade, 150–51; pre-
revolutionary longshoremen's
union, 150; and the Revolution,
150; *Trabajadores* (newspaper), 143
Lam, Wilfredo, 71
Lamarr, Hedy, 200

Landaluze, Patrizio, 56
Lansky, Meyer, 193–97
Las Casas, Bartolomé de, 164–66
Las Ruinas restaurant in Parque
Lenin, *99*, 100
Laugart, Xiomara, 212–13
Leal, Eusebio, 3, 177, 232–33
Lenin, Vladimir, 100–101, *101*
Leninism, 39, 136, 158
Leopold III, King of the Belgians,
197–98
Levin, Andrés, 212, 213
LGBT rights movement, 34–36;
and the Cuban Catholic Church,
176, 183–84; Mariela Castro and
CENESEX, 35–36
literature, Cuban. *See* writers,
Cuban
Lobo, Julio, 81–82, 85
Lonja del Comercio, 184
López, Rigoberto, 155
López Gavilán, Guido, 185
Los Sitios (neighborhood), 57, 168
Los Van Van (salsa orchestra),
27–28, 238
lottery, 58
L'Ouverture, Toussaint, 80
Lucía, Paco de, 131
Lula da Silva, Luiz Inácio, 63–64

Maceo ("El Titán de Bronce"), 15
Machado, Gerardo, 11, 83–84
mafia. *See* mob, Cuban
Magriña, Ramón, 106
Malecón wall, 5, 36–38, 112–15;
and *balseros* crisis, 36–37, 40,
207–8; Havana Arts Biennale

(2015), 186–88, *187*; as metaphor
of Miami-Cuba relations, 112–15;
monument to victims of the
USS *Maine*, 78–79; and secret
underground tunnels, 84; street
vendors, 37; Tribuna Anti-
Imperialista event, 207–8, 228;
U.S. embassy, 112–13, 207–8; the
weekly *botellón*, 36–38

mambises, 169, 224, 263. See also
cimarrones (runaway slaves)

Maradona, Diego, 150

Marina Hemingway, 218–20

Martí, José, 16, 81–82, 133, 170;
monument at the Plaza de la
Revolución, 93–94, 149; and
Napoleon, 81–82. *See also* José
Martí Airport

Martínez, Pedrito, 212

Marxism, 10–12, 77, 133, 136, 189

Masons. *See* Freemasons

May Day parade, 146, *146*, 149–52

Memorias del subdesarrollo (film), 71,
141, 154

Mialhe, Federico, 56

Miami Cubans, 112–15; *balseros* crisis
of 1994, 36–37, 40, 65, 205–9;
Calle Ocho neighborhood and
old guard Cubans, 207, 208;
charter flights to Havana, 51, 114;
and Elián González story, 205–9;
entrepreneurial success, 49, 115;
labor markets, 50; Malecón wall
as metaphor of Miami-Cuba
relations, 112–15; *mulas* bringing
U.S. goods to Cuba, 51–52;
remittances, 43, 48, 51–52, 119–

20; Santería traditions, 22, 258;
South Beach's tropical art-deco
style, 108

middle class, pre-revolutionary:
exodus of, 59, 141, 154; Soviet
propaganda about, 69–71;
Vedado neighborhood, 71

MININT (Ministry of the Interior)
building, 95–96, 150

Miramar suburb, 85, 132, 189, 223,
225–27

Miranda, Francisco de, 130

mob, Cuban, 193–97; Batista and,
193, 194–96; and the Cuban
Revolution, 195–96; Lansky
and the Riviera Hotel, 193–97,
194; U.S. mafia culture and pre-
revolution Cuba, 193–97

Moncada attack (1956), 137

money standard, double, 43–44,
52–55; the convertible peso (*peso
convertible*), 43–44, 52–55; CUC-
denominated commerce, 43–44;
the U.S. dollar and the *moneda
nacional*, 43–44, 52–55. *See also*
economics

monte (card game), 58, 168

Montejo, Esteban, 223, 264

Morel, bishop of Santiago, 62

Mozart festival (October 2015),
185–86

Mulatas del Fuego, 131–32, 210

Museo de Bellas Artes, 56

Museo Napoleónico, 82–83, 85

music: Afro-Cuban jazz, 211;
classical, 184–86; interactive
Havana–New York music scene,

music (*cont.*)
  210–13; *jineteras* and the Havana
  music scene, 42–43; New York
  Cuban singers in exile (Celia
  Cruz and La Lupe), 210; *rumba*,
  17–18, 128, 130–31; salsa, 25,
  27–28, 212; Santería themes, 25,
  27–28
Music Has No Enemies
  (foundation), 213

Napoleon Bonaparte, 80–82, 130;
  Havana museum of, 82–83, 85
National Conference of Catholic
  Bishops, 174
los negros curros (the black gangs),
  16–17, 56–57, 128
Netherlands, 202, 204
New York exile community, 209–
  13; Cuban musicians and singers
  as defectors, 210, 211; interactive
  Havana–New York music scene,
  210–13; New Jersey, 209–10;
  old Cuban neighborhoods and
  restaurants of Manhattan and
  Upper West Side, 209
NG La Banda, 28
North Korea, 79–80
Nube Roja (rock band), 35

Obama, Barack, 64, 99, 167; and
  the Cuban dissident community,
  145–46; March 2016 visit,
  145–46, 193, 250; revocation
  of "wet foot, dry foot policy,"
  209; U.S.-Cuba reconciliation,
  65, 177

Ochún (female *orisha*), *xv*, 19, 24,
  28, 118, 171, 183, 218, 245
Oficina del Historiador de la
  Ciudad, 232
Old Havana. *See* Habana Vieja (Old
  Havana)
Organization of American States,
  167
Oriente (eastern Cuba), 118–21,
  224; Afro-Cuban population,
  119–20, 224–25; and the Cuban
  Revolution, 119, 224; the east-
  west division of Cuba, 118–21;
  Freemasons, 120; and *palestinos*
  (internal refugees), 120, 121,
  224–25; poverty, 119–20;
  Santiago as first colonial capital,
  118
orishas, 19–23, 28, 206. *See also*
  Eleggua (male *orisha*); Ochún
  (female *orisha*)
Orishas (rap group), 205
Ortega, Cardinal Jaime, 171, 174–77
Ortiz, Fernando, 16–17, 58, 257;
  on cultural divide between black
  and white Cuba, 16–17, 21, 26,
  257; on early Catholic priests in
  Havana, 168; on early Cuban
  music, 28; on *los negros curros* (the
  black gangs) of Old Havana, 16–
  17, 56–57, 128; and *rumbas*, 18
Our Man in Havana (film), 200
OXFAM, 53
Oya (mistress of the graveyard), 74

pacotilla: Chinese merchandise
  (*pacotilla china*), 30, 48; plastic-

wrapped bundles of luggage and goods, 51, 114, 116, 117–18

Padura, Leonardo, 155–58; detective character, Mario Conde, 156–58; script for *Return to Ithaca*, 157

Paez, Amelia, 100

Paisaje de Otoño (Padura), 157

Palacio de la Revolución, xiv, 94–96

palestinos: and *cimarrones* tradition, 224–25; internal refugees of Oriente as, 120, 121, 224

Palmer, Amanda, 106

Panama, 188

Panamerican Games, 102

el paquete, 214–16, 243

Parajón, Saturnino, 109

Le Parisien cabaret at the Hotel Nacional, 162–63

Parque Central, 99, 159–60

Parque de la Fraternidad, 5, 29, 40, 166–67

Parque Lenin, 74, 99–101; Frank Lloyd Wright–like architecture, *99*, 100; Las Ruinas restaurant, *99*, 100; Lenin monument, 100–101, *101*

Patenaude, Bertrand, 158

Peña, Lázaro, 150

Peña Literaria, 100

Pérez, Alain, 131

El Período Especial, 7, 34, 36, 38–55, 62, 68, 153–54; end of Soviet communism and economic support, 7, 38–40; food and energy shortages, 39–40, 41; property swaps (*permuta*

system), 231; tourism following, 41–42

Perrugoria, Jorge "Pichi," 35–36, 158

Petit, Andrés Facundo Cristo de Dolores, 21–22

piracy, Caribbean, 59–60, 201–5; and *balsero* crisis of 1994, 205; British navy, 203–5; death penalty for three hijackers (2003), 59–60, 97; Lafitte Brothers and New Orleans, 203–4; seventeenth- and eighteenth-century, 201–2; Spanish colonial rule, 203–4; and transatlantic slave trade, 203–5; U.S.-Cuba relations and maritime cooperation to secure shipping lanes, 205

Platt Amendment, 78

Playas del Este, 102–5; and Cuban missile crisis, 87; gated villa complex of Tarara, 105; Guanabo, 104–5; hotels, 104–5; Puente de Madera, 105; Santa María del Mar, 104; the seaside suburb of Cojimar, 102–3; the trip from Havana to, 102–4

Plaza de Armas, 11, 42, 216

Plaza de la Revolución, 71–72, 94–96, 138; Martí monument, 93–94, 149; May Day parade, 146, *146*, 149–52; MININT building, 95–96, 150; Pope Francis's mass, 182–83; Pope John Paul II's mass, 172–73, 183

Plaza San Francisco, 90, 184–86

Plaza Vieja, 11, 225

port of Mariel expansion project, 48, 63, 241

Portocarrero, Juan de Prado, 62, 259

Portocarrero, René, 70–71, 95, 100

Posada Carriles, Luis, 97

Pozo, Chano, 211

Prensa Latina (government press agency), 158

press, government-controlled: and Castro's death, 215–16; *Granma* (newspaper), 142–43, 159, 170, 181, 188, 215; news and "Radio Bemba," 243–44; news and Radio Reloj, 241–44; *el paquete* and news foreign affairs and the outside world, 213–16, 243; Prensa Latina, 158

property: ownership of property titles, 230–31; property swaps (*permuta* system) during the *Período Especial*, 231; real estate market and private property ownership, 230–35; simple sales (allowed in 2014), 231

prostitution, 42–43, 155

Protestant Christianity, 178, 184; evangelical Christians, 125, 177–78

Puente, Tito, 210, 212

Puerto Rico: baseball, 188; Habana Club rum produced in, 111–12; salsa music scene in New York, 212; slaves of, 165

racial attitudes: and Afro-Cubans, 12–15, 16–17, 21, 26, 120;

Chinese immigrants and racial mixing (*achinado*), 31–32; and the Cuban Revolution, 23–25; and Cuba's independence, 15–17; mixed-race population, 31–32, 33; Oriente and east-west division of Cuba, 120; Ortiz on cultural divide between black and white Cuba, 16–17, 21, 26, 257; Santería and, 21–23. *See also* slavery in Cuba

"Radio Bemba," 243–44

Radio Reloj, 241–44

Raft, George, 83, 195–96, 199

railways: Cristina station at Cuatro Caminos, 9, 237, *237*; the electric Hershey train and Casablanca terminal, 236–39, *238*; Habana Vieja station, 56; neglect and disrepair, 237–38; Tallapiedra power station and High Line, 239–41, *240*

Reconquista, 163–64

recreational escapes: Jardines de la Tropical, 105–7; Parque Lenin, 99–101; Playas del Este, 102–5

religious freedom, 24–25, 125, 177; Afro-Cubans and revival of African cultural identity, 25–26; constitutional amendment of 1992 and change from atheist to agnostic state, 24, 125; evangelical churches and missionaries, 125, 177–78; Islam, 178–79; Jewish community of Havana, 124, 125, 177; and pre-revolution religious observance,

170; and social role of churches, 174, 176, 180

remittances, 43, 48, 51–52, 119–20

Reno, Janet, 207

Río Almendares, 106, 165, 223, 235–36

Río Quibú, 165, 222–25

Riviera Hotel, 193–97, *194*

Robert Miller Gallery in Chelsea (New York City), 229

Romerillo neighborhood, 227–28

Roosevelt, Theodore, 78

Rousseff, Dilma, 151

rum, Cuban, 109–12; Habana Club brand, 111–12; pre-revolutionary Cuba and the Bacardí family and, 110–11; U.S.-Cuba rum wars, 109–12

rumba, 17–18, 128, 130–31; Calle Aramburu neighborhood, 17–18; Cuban roots of contemporary Andalusian music, 130–31

Russian Orthodox Church, 177, 180

Sala Avellana of the National Theatre, 159–60

salsa: diva La India, 28, 212, 213; Los Van Van (orchestra), 27–28, 238; New York scene and Puerto Ricans/Cubans, 212; Santería roots, 25, 27–28

San Egidio Community, 174

Sánchez, Celia, 73–74, 251

Sánchez, Yoani, 145

Sandoval, Arturo, 211

Santa Bárbara (saint), 28

Santa Ifigenia cemetery (Santiago), 119

Santería, xiii–xv, *xv*, 18–27, 21, 170, 249; and the Catholic Church, xiii, 19–20, 171, 263; and the Cuban Revolution, 23–25; and Elián González's survival, 206; and Freemasons, 24, 120–21, 179–80; the Havana Arts Biennale and Santería-based percussion performances, 239; headquarters at Asociación Yoruba de Cuba, *148*; initiates (*iyabos*), 22, 22–23, 27, 74, 83, 121, 236; Miami Cubans, 22, 258; music and tourism, 25; Night of San Lázaro celebrations at sanctuary of El Rincón, xiii–xv; *orishas*, 19–23, 28, 206; and the racial divide, 21–23; religious freedom and revival of, 25–26; and Spanish colonial empire, 128–29; *tambor* or *toquesanto*, 18, 263

Santos Suárez (suburb), 3, 5

Sardiñas Montalvo, Eligio, 191

Saudi Arabia, 178

secret underground. *See* underground tunnels and shelters

Seven Years War (1756–1763), 60–62

sexual attitudes, 33–36, 86, 167–68, 183–84

Siboney native population, 162–63, 162–66

Siboney neighborhood of Havana, 1, 1 5, 249–50

Sierra Candelaria mountains, 86–89, 165

Sierra Maestra mountain range, 73, 119, 224

El siglo de las luces (Carpentier), 76, 77

Síntesis (rock group), 142

slavery in Cuba, 6, 12–15, 18–19, 222–25; British Empire, 14–15, 19, 62, 203–4; and Caribbean piracy, 203–5; and Chinese presence, 30; *cimarrones* (runaway slaves), 169–70, 222–25; and contemporary Afro-Cubans, 12–15, 18–19; and the Cuban Revolution, 223–24; free African *cabildos*, 13–14, 16, 19; Indian slavery and Spanish colonial system, 163–67; late abolition of, 13, 203, 223; October tenth holiday, 15; and Le Parisien cabaret at the Hotel Nacional, 162–63; post-colonial legacies of transatlantic Spain-Cuba slave trade, 127–32; reparations issue, 167; Spanish colonial system, 6, 13–15, 18–19, 62, 127–28, 163–67, 203–4, 222; and sugar industry, 14–15, 62; Vienna Congress's decree ending the transatlantic slave trade, 13, 203, 204

Sloppy Joe's bar (Old Havana), 70

soccer (*fútbol*), 190–91

social housing complexes, 103

solares culture of poor neighborhoods, 17, 225

Soviet Union-Cuba relations: Cuban missile crisis, 87; end of communism, 7, 38–39, 66; end of economic support to Cuba, 7, 38–40; Gorbachev visit, 38–39; post-1960 Soviet agenda and interests in Cuba, 63; propaganda about pre-revolution Cuban social classes, 69–71

Soy Cuba (film), 69–71, 154, 200

Soy Cuba poster (Portocarrero), 70–71

Spain: the *cantos de ida y vuelta* between Cádiz and Havana, 127–32; Catalan architects and Art Nouveau movement, 107; Cuban roots of contemporary Andalusian music, 130–32; and the EU Common Position, 67; Franco regime, 63, 67, 129–30; post-colonial legacies of transatlantic trade and colonialism, 127–32; Reconquista of Arab Andalucía and fall of Granada, 163–64; soccer teams, 190; Spanish Civil War and Spanish Cubans, 129–30, 219. *See also* Spanish colonial system in Cuba

Spanglish, 62

Spanish Civil War, 129–30, 219

Spanish colonial system in Cuba, 127–32; and the British occupation, 60–63; and the Catholic Church, 167–69; and Chinese presence in Cuba, 30; Cuban war of independence against, 15–16, 55–56, 78, 169–

70; Indian slavery and genocide, 163–67; the *Leyendra Negra*, 166, 167; piracy and the Spanish navy, 202, 203; post-colonial legacies of, 127–32; resistance by the Taínos and Siboneys, 162–65; Santiago as colonial capital, 118; Seville administration, 127; slavery, 6, 13–15, 18–19, 62, 127–28, 163–67, 203–4, 222

Spanish Inquisition, 122, 128, 159, 164

Spanish-American War, 63, 78–79

sports culture, Caribbean: baseball (*la pelota*), 64, 188–93; boxing, 191–92; soccer, 190–91

Stainless (artists' group), 228

Stalinism, 39, 156, 158

Stalin's Nemesis, The Exile and Murder of Leon Trotsky (Patenaude), 158

sugar cane cultivation and sugar industry, 14–15, 39–40, 62, 110

surveillance, 96, *139*, 139–41; the CDRs and logos, *139*, 139–41; CDRs and neighborhood network today, 140; censorship and controls on Cuban writers and films, 153–59; *chivatos* (informers), 135; public shaming (*actos de repudio*) in front of dissidents' homes, 140

Taíno native population, 162–63, 164–66

Tallapiedra power station and High Line, 239–41, *240*

Tarara villa complex, 105

Teatro de las Américas on Calle Galeano, 27–28

Teatro Karl Marx, 159–60

Teatro Nacional, 211

Terminal II of José Martí Airport, 115–18, 214

terrorism, 96–99; Cuba and the U.S. State Department's terror-sponsor list, 96–99; Cuba's mediating role between FARC and Colombia, 97–99; death penalty for three hijackers/pirates (2003), 59–60, 97; the explosion of La Coubre in Havana harbor (1960), 79; terrorist attacks suffered by Cuba, 97

Tosca, Axel, 212–13

tourism: and building restorations, 3, 216, 232–33; Cuban music, 25; following the *Período Especial* of the 1990s, 41–42; Habana Vieja, 3, 10–11, 23, 216, 232–33; Hemingway and Cojimar, 217–20; and hitchhikers, 103

Trabajadores (labor union newspaper), 143

trademark disputes: Cuban cigars, 110, 112; Cuban rum, 109–12

Treasure Island (Stevenson), 202

Tres Tristes Tigres (Cabrera Infante), 153

Tribuna Anti-Imperialista, 207–8, 228

Tropicana nightclub, 37, 131–32, 162, 210

Trotsky, Leon, 156, 158

Trudeau, Justin, 181

Trujillo, Rafael, 195

Túnel de la Bahía, 102

tunnels. *See* underground tunnels
and shelters

ultramarinos ("overseas" shops), 129

UN Security Council, 79–80

underground tunnels and shelters,
84–86; and the Casa Orestes
Ferrara, 84–85; the Peña Literaria
under the Parque Lenin, 100;
under the Plaza de la Revolución,
96; Túnel de la Bahía, 102

Unión Arabe de Cuba, 124–25

Union of Writers and Artists
(UNEAC), 153

Union of Young Communists, 143

unions. *See* labor unions

United Fruit, 140

U.S.-Cuba relations, xiv, 64–65,
112–15; Alan Gross spy case and
imprisonment, xiv, 64, 127;
American consumer goods,
51–52, 114–15, 213–16; American
television and media, 213–16,
243; *balseros* crisis of 1994,
36–37, 40, 65, 205–9; baseball
politics, 64, 188–90, 193; Cold
War, xiv, 77, 85–86, 87, 219;
Cuban attitudes toward the
U.S., 6, 64; and Cuban dissident
community, 144–46; December
17, 2014 announcement of
diplomatic normalization, xiv,
51, 65, 96–97, 113, 175, 177,
182, 250; defections, 189–90,

210, 211; evangelical churches
in Cuba, 178; flights and travel
between, 51, 114, 115–18, 211–12;
and the Havana Arts Biennale
(2015), 229; Hollywood film
productions, 199–201; interactive
Havana–New York music scene,
210–13; mafia culture and
gambling, 193–97; Malecón
wall as metaphor of Miami-
Cuba relations, 112–15; maritime
cooperation to secure shipping
lanes from piracy, 205; Obama
administration, 64, 65, 167, 177;
Obama's March 2016 visit, 145–
46, 193, 250; and racial attitudes,
15–16; refugees and "wet foot,
dry foot" policy, 207, 209,
243; remittances, 43, 48, 51–52,
119–20; rum wars and trademark
disputes, 109–12; Spanish-
American War, 78–79; the State
Department's terror-sponsor list,
96–99; U.S. dollar economy,
41–45, 52–55; U.S. embargo, 49,
64, 173, 233; U.S.-based claims
on Havana buildings, 233. *See also*
Miami Cubans; New York exile
community

USS *Maine*, 78–79

Valdés, Chucho, 212

Valley of San Gerónimo, 106

Varela, Carlos, 2–3, 113, 247

Varela, Felix, 169

Vasallo, Juan Luis, 132

Vedado neighborhood, 71–74; art-deco apartments, *108*, 109; Chinese cemetery in Nuevo Vedado, 32–33; Cuban Arts Factory and Havana art scene, 141–42; the ghost of Celia Sánchez, 73–74, 251; Jewish community (Beth Shalom congregation), xiv, 122–27, 177; main thoroughfares and side streets (Calle 12 and its traffic lights), 72–73; and pre-revolutionary middle class, 71. *See also* Cementerio Colón

Vega, Louie, 212

Venezuela-Cuba relations: baseball, 188; Chávez's support for Cuba, 44–46, 63; and the economic crisis, 45–46, 65; Havana's May Day parade delegation, 150; soccer, 190

Vía Monumental, 102

Vienna Congress (1815), 13, 203, 204

Vietnam model of economic reforms, 48–49

Virgen de la Candelaria, 74

Virgen de la Caridad del Cobre, 24, 118, 171, 218, 245

Virgen de Regla, 19, 128

"wet foot, dry foot" policy, 207, 209, 243

Weymour, Patricia, 201

Woman without a Passport (film), 200

women's rights, 33–35, 178–79; and the Cuban Catholic Church, 33–34, 176; and Muslim community in Cuba, 178–79

World Trade Organization, 111

World War II, 122, 218

writers, Cuban, 152–58; Carpentier, 74–78; censorship and controls on, 153–59; Gutiérrez (Pedro Juan), 155–56, 159; Padura's Mario Conde detective novels, 156–58; screenwriter Gutiérrez Alea, 153–55

X Alfonso, 142

Yemaya (ocean spirit), 19, 28, 36, 114, 128, 206

Yoruba, 18, 21, 28, 142